The FitzPatrick Tapes

The FitzPatrick Tapes

TOM LYONS *and*
BRIAN CAREY

PENGUIN
IRELAND

PENGUIN IRELAND

Published by the Penguin Group
Penguin Ireland, 25 St Stephen's Green, Dublin 2, Ireland (a division of Penguin Books Ltd)
Penguin Books Ltd, 80 Strand, London WC2R ORL, England
Penguin Group (USA) Inc., 375 Hudson Street, New York, New York 10014, USA
Penguin Group (Canada), 90 Eglinton Avenue East, Suite 700, Toronto, Ontario, Canada M4P 2Y3
(a division of Pearson Penguin Canada Inc.)
Penguin Group (Australia), 250 Camberwell Road,
Camberwell, Victoria 3124, Australia (a division of Pearson Australia Group Pty Ltd)
Penguin Books India Pvt Ltd, 11 Community Centre,
Panchsheel Park, New Delhi – 110 017, India
Penguin Group (NZ), 67 Apollo Drive, Rosedale, Auckland 0632, New Zealand
(a division of Pearson New Zealand Ltd)
Penguin Books (South Africa) (Pty) Ltd, 24 Sturdee Avenue,
Rosebank, Johannesburg 2196, South Africa

Penguin Books Ltd, Registered Offices: 80 Strand, London WC2R ORL, England

www.penguin.com

First published 2011
1

Typeset by Penguin Books Ltd
Printed in Great Britain by Clays Ltd, St Ives plc

A CIP catalogue record for this book is available from the British Library

ISBN: 978–1–844–88260–1

www.greenpenguin.co.uk

Penguin Books is committed to a sustainable
future for our business, our readers and our
planet. This book is made from paper certified
by the Forest Stewardship Council.

Contents

Authors' Note

ANGLO LENT CASH TO BUY ITS SHARES

by Tom Lyons, Sunday Times, 25 January 2009

Anglo Irish Bank assembled a 'golden circle' of investors to buy about €300 million of its shares last summer to prevent them being dumped on the market, driving down the price.

The operation to buy 10 per cent of the bank was largely funded by borrowings from Anglo Irish itself and organized by Sean FitzPatrick, its former chairman . . . The group of business people was assembled in the weeks leading up to 15 July, when the family of Sean Quinn, the insurance-to-cement tycoon, had to reveal that it owned a 15 per cent stake in Anglo Irish . . . Anglo Irish funded the Quinn family's conversion of the CFDs into shares in return for the right to take control of a significant percentage of the Quinn Group if the family defaulted on its loans.

When Quinn indicated that he was not prepared to convert his entire CFD holding into Anglo Irish shares, it raised the possibility that the 10 per cent balance of his holding would be sold on the open market. This would have decimated the price.

FitzPatrick then turned to a group of businessmen for help. The deal valued the 10 per cent stake at about €300 million, but no single buyer took more than 3 per cent, thereby keeping the share purchases below the disclosure levels required by the Stock Exchange. The identities of the businessmen have not been confirmed but are thought to include well-known names. Many are long-standing customers of Anglo Irish, which was nationalized last week.

At about 5 p.m. on Sunday, 25 January 2009, an unknown number flashed up on the mobile phone of Tom Lyons, who was at home in his apartment in Dublin's city centre. Lyons stepped out on to his small balcony, as the reception was better there.

The caller was the former chairman of Anglo Irish Bank, which had been nationalized only ten days before.

'Tom, it's Sean FitzPatrick. You got your story wrong today. I am not supposed to be talking to you, my lawyers would go mad if they knew, but I am just telling you, you got your story wrong today.'

'OK. So how was I wrong?' Lyons replied.

'I didn't organize it. I didn't put together the "golden circle",' Fitz-Patrick said.

'Now hold on, when I rang you up and put the story to you two weeks ago, you denied a "golden circle" even existed,' Lyons replied. 'Now you are admitting it actually did exist but you didn't do it. Why should I believe you now? You were Anglo Irish Bank; you must have put it together.'

'Lookit, you asked me did I put a "golden circle" together and I told you I didn't,' FitzPatrick replied.

'I also asked you did you know about a group of big businessmen buying shares in your bank. You told me they didn't, when they did. Why should I believe you now?'

'Look, I am not giving out to you or blaming you for writing the story. You have a job to do. I am just telling you as one guy to another I didn't do it.'

'Well, who did, then?'

'I can't say. I can't talk any more on this. All I'm saying is you were wrong today. I didn't put it together.'

Lyons put a series of further questions to FitzPatrick, hoping to find out more about the deal. FitzPatrick declined to answer the questions and just kept repeating one point: it wasn't him.

'Sean, this doesn't make sense,' Lyons said. 'You were Mr Anglo and yet you're saying you didn't put the deal together. Will you meet me for a coffee and tell me what is going on?'

'No. I won't. I have got to go. I can't say any more.'

In the months after that phone call, Lyons tried intermittently to convince FitzPatrick to meet. New scandals were breaking on a weekly basis about Anglo Irish Bank. FitzPatrick – who had been the bank's chief executive for eighteen years and then chairman for four years until he resigned in disgrace in December 2008 – had to be the key to finding out what had occurred.

In May 2009 FitzPatrick finally agreed to meet in the Holiday Inn, a less than salubrious three-star hotel on gritty Pearse Street in Dublin. Lyons had met FitzPatrick only once before, briefly, at the company's annual general meeting for shareholders in Dublin's Mansion House on 2 February 2007.

It was a different world. Ireland's property bubble had yet to burst, and the chairman of Anglo confidently described another spectacular year for his bank to its shareholders. 'During the period we achieved a number of significant milestones in this the bank's twenty-first year of successive profit growth,' FitzPatrick said. 'Total income increased by 35 per cent to €1.2 billion – the first time the group's revenues have broken the €1 billion mark. The bank's market capitalization is now approaching €12 billion . . .'

The tone of the shareholders' questions from the floor was accurately described afterwards by the *Irish Independent* as 'good-humoured and hugely complimentary [of Anglo]'. Concern was expressed about the escalating cost of land and the prices of houses, but FitzPatrick batted such worries away. 'We are aware of some areas of concern,' he said. 'It's down to risk management and we take that very seriously and we're happy with our exposure.' He added: 'The bank was built always on a conservative [lending] policy.'

The market liked what it heard, sending Anglo higher by 1 per cent to €16.20 by the close of the day's trading.

But over a ham and cheese sandwich in the Holiday Inn's unglamorous restaurant, FitzPatrick was a different man – no longer the confident, dynamic character Lyons had observed in the Mansion House only two years before.

The last thing FitzPatrick seemed to want to talk about was Anglo. Instead, he asked Lyons about himself: his family; his career; had he played rugby; what position; did he play golf; why did he not play golf; and so on. FitzPatrick's interests seemed to be very much the ordinary ones of any retired businessman. Unlike his peers, however, he was not anonymous. His fellow diners kept glancing at him in a way that suggested they recognized his face from the newspapers.

When, after about half an hour, FitzPatrick eventually began to talk about the bank, a lot of what he said seemed hard to credit.

He insisted, for instance, that he did not know the names of the 'golden circle'. Then he added he believed the deal had been approved by the state – but refused to elaborate on why he thought that.

It went on and on like that, as other scandals and issues were discussed. First FitzPatrick would say something really interesting; then he would draw back either by being vague – claiming not to know, claiming not to remember – or by refusing to comment.

The meeting ended with FitzPatrick agreeing to think about doing a formal interview, while stressing that everything he had said that day was not only strictly off the record but not even to be used as a source for any article. FitzPatrick was open to meeting again, but he was not committing to anything yet.

It took another seven months, and three more sandwich lunches, before FitzPatrick agreed to do a formal tape-recorded interview.

Initially the agreement between Lyons and FitzPatrick was that the interviews were not to be quoted or cited in the *Sunday Times* or in a book.

The first interview took place on 25 January 2010 – a year to the day after the publication of the 'golden circle' story that had prompted FitzPatrick's initial phone call – in an almost bare room in a small office FitzPatrick uses in Dublin's docklands. It was not clear, afterwards, if FitzPatrick would agree to a second interview, but three weeks later he and Lyons sat down again.

At this second interview FitzPatrick gave his explanation for agreeing to be interviewed: 'I decided to do an interview because you asked me to do an interview. I am very sort of – nervous is not the word – I am very not sure as whether to do this or not do this. I suppose for the past nine, ten months various things have gone out in the media and it all seems very one-sided to me from where I am looking . . . I see this as some sort of opportunity . . . of giving my side of the story.'

Lyons and FitzPatrick had already discussed the ground rules for the interviews. The banker had to tell his story warts and all or else

Lyons was not interested in continuing. FitzPatrick agreed to these conditions.

It would be another thirty-four days before the next interview, as FitzPatrick was outside the country pursuing his business affairs. Thereafter the interviews became more frequent, taking place about twice a month on average. The interviews frequently digressed into anecdotes and backtracked as FitzPatrick recalled more information as he went along.

The dates of key events in particular were a blind-spot: FitzPatrick's diary had been kept by his personal assistant in Anglo and he did not have access to it for most of the period during which the interviews took place. Even when he did obtain the diary, he realized that not every meeting had been recorded. Dates often had to be pieced together using other sources.

Another obstacle was that FitzPatrick had learned to use e-mail only after he left the bank. Thus there was no archive of e-mail conversations between him and other key players; those communications happened face to face or over the phone, and had to be reconstructed from memory. FitzPatrick's degree of recall and enthusiasm varied dramatically depending on the subject under discussion or what had been happening in his life at that time.

Lyons was naturally keen to make use of the material, but FitzPatrick still wasn't sure if he wished to allow it to be published, and asked to be given more time to decide. He was keen that the story be told in its entirety – something that would not be possible in a single piece or series of pieces in the *Sunday Times*. A book – in which Lyons could draw upon all of the material, without restriction – was the solution that was agreed.

Lyons began to plan a book that would look not only at the catastrophic demise of Anglo Irish Bank and of FitzPatrick's reputation, but also at their beginnings. Such a project would involve both a high degree of urgency and the careful sifting of documents and interview material to convey a highly complex story that had not yet been told. With these things in mind, Lyons asked Brian Carey, the *Sunday Times*'s Ireland Business Editor, to come on board as co-author. Carey brought to the project his considerable experience as a business journalist, his intimate knowledge of the Anglo story, and his own distinctive contacts and sources. In addition to the seventeen tape-recorded interviews Lyons conducted with FitzPatrick, Carey interviewed the former Anglo boss on a one-to-one basis himself in October 2010.

The transcripts of the FitzPatrick tapes – comprising 177,000 words – are the book's central source, but not its only source. They could not have been. The need to check the veracity of FitzPatrick's recollections was obvious, and wherever possible we used contemporary documentary evidence, public statements and other people's recollections for this purpose. Verbal recollections and documentary information used in this book was supplied by more than fifty people who were interviewed in the course of researching articles by both Lyons and Carey for the *Sunday Times* – none of whom knew they might also be contributing to a book about Sean FitzPatrick.

Much of what FitzPatrick said in the early interviews about the knowledge of regulators and politicians of key events in the bank's collapse seemed at first unbelievable. Time and again, though, the veracity of his recollections was backed up by documents and secondary sources. Where FitzPatrick's recollections do not match other sources, we point this out; and where we have only the FitzPatrick tapes to go on, we have left it to readers to make their own judgements.

The collapse of Anglo Irish Bank is the central drama in a series of events that has culminated in the Irish state requiring a bailout from the International Monetary Fund and the European Union – an extraordinarily dramatic downfall. This book is dedicated to the sources who took real risks to shine a light on Anglo, and on the regulatory system that, in the end, failed to protect Ireland.

Prologue

'You are telling me it is wrong. I accept that you are saying it is wrong.
Maybe it is wrong but I just don't know.'

18 March 2010

It was just after 6 a.m. when Sean FitzPatrick, the former chairman
of Anglo Irish Bank, was woken by the sound of the buzzer mounted
to the heavy security gate outside his home in the quiet suburb of
Greystones, Co. Wicklow.

He pulled his dressing gown over his pyjamas and spoke to his
visitors through the intercom. It was the gardaí. 'They told me they
wanted to come in immediately,' FitzPatrick recalls.

He hit the button to open the gates, which he had had installed only
a few months earlier after he started to receive anonymous death threats.

The commotion woke FitzPatrick's wife, Triona, and his daughter,
Sarah. They were beside him when he opened his front door. The
lead detective from the Garda Bureau of Fraud Investigation stood at
the door with about eight other gardaí. 'I asked, Are you going to
arrest me? They said they were.'

In the front hallway of his home FitzPatrick was told formally that
he was to be arrested and taken for questioning at Bray Garda station,
a few miles up the coast from Greystones.

The gardaí showed FitzPatrick a search warrant for the house and
for a nearby house he also owned that was unoccupied at the time.
The warrant gave the gardaí the right to remove the hard drives of
computers and any business files or papers on either premises.

One of them ushered the banker upstairs into his bedroom and told
him to get dressed. 'It was all very polite and professional,' FitzPatrick
says.

At his kitchen table, the other gardaí had a cup of tea with his wife and daughter while they waited for him to return.

'At about 6.20 a.m. they said, It's time to move. The media are outside. I said, This is ridiculous. They said, Don't blame us, the media are here, it is nothing to do with us. I said, Well, it is very strange they have heard already.'

With television cameras positioned outside his front gate, Fitz-Patrick asked the gardaí if he could leave via the back garden. They obliged by telling a patrol car to pull around into a lane that ran alongside the garden. FitzPatrick walked with the gardaí past the family's disused tennis court to a gap in his back hedge where the car was waiting. Two male policemen sat in the front of the car and a female officer sat beside FitzPatrick in the back seat. The car pulled away at speed, out of sight of the television cameras that were filming through the bars of the front gate.

FitzPatrick had known this day would come.

Since the government had taken the dramatic step of guaranteeing the liabilities of the Irish banks in September 2008 – a move whose most immediate purpose had been to keep Anglo in business – his life had become a maelstrom. He resigned as chairman of Anglo on 18 December 2008 after it emerged that his bank had for years conspired with another bank to hide Anglo's loans to him – personal borrowings that at the end of October 2008 amounted to €87 million. In January 2009, Anglo – which FitzPatrick had built up from modest beginnings into one of Europe's most profitable and admired financial institutions – was nationalized by the Irish state.

That same month it emerged that Anglo had assembled and financed ten of its clients to buy 10 per cent of its shares from Sean Quinn – Anglo's biggest borrower and, at the time, Ireland's wealthiest man – in an effort to stabilize the bank's share price. The following month the news broke that the bank had doctored its 2008 year-end accounts to the tune of €7.2 billion by entering into a wholly artificial transaction with another financial institution, Irish Life & Permanent.

Losses at the bank, largely due to bad debts on loans advanced to property developers, were already heading for €13 billion, and would eventually exceed twice that. FitzPatrick, who boasted a net worth of €150 million in 2005, was himself facing bankruptcy.

From the day in February 2009 when the state announced it was investigating Anglo Irish Bank – in what justice minister Dermot Ahern would later describe as the 'biggest and most complex' criminal probe in Ireland's history – its former chairman was expecting a knock on the door.

The Garda station in Bray was literally a block away from where FitzPatrick grew up, and just a short walk from the gates of his old school, Presentation College. Senior members of the local gardaí would socialize in the seafront pub owned by one of his closest friends, Jackie O'Driscoll.

'I hadn't been on the inside of Bray Garda station since I was a child,' FitzPatrick says. 'I will remember it for the rest of my life, being in the Garda station at 6.50 a.m. Meeting the member in charge. Taking off my tie and my watch. There was no shoelaces because I was wearing slip-ons. They put me into a cell and referred to me formally as "the prisoner".

'[There was] a peephole where they check you out. Then a place in the middle of the door where they put the food through . . . When you are in the cell, you hear people walking towards it. You hear a bunch of rattling keys. You hear the door unlocking. It was exactly as you would see it on TV. [The cell] was six feet wide. I know that because I walked it and measured it. It was eight feet deep. It was rectangular with an open toilet on the floor with aluminium on it, just a hole down. You couldn't sit anywhere. It was just a hole with sort of aluminium protection around it.

'[It was] very difficult to actually sit there and eat because of the smell and you couldn't balance a tray. There was no table. No clock. The light was on all the time.'

FitzPatrick telephoned Michael Staines, his lawyer, to tell him he had been arrested. Staines, a well-known criminal solicitor, said he would come immediately to the police station. After the phone call, FitzPatrick was put back in a cell. Staines arrived in about half an hour to talk to the banker before the interviews began, taking him through what he could expect.

FitzPatrick was allowed to call his wife and speak to his daughter on the phone in between interviews. 'She [Triona] was worried about me and my insulin,' says FitzPatrick, who is diabetic. 'The police were very good on that. During the course of every interview, the member in charge would come in and ask me was I OK? Would I like a cup of tea, biscuits or anything like that? The fraud squad were making sure that I injected when I should have injected. All that sort of stuff. All very, very considerate.'

FitzPatrick faced a number of detectives working in pairs. They interviewed him six times, going over and over the same ground. Five of the six sessions focused on what the banker knew about the extraordinary set of transactions in September 2008 when Irish Life & Permanent deposited €7.2 billion in Anglo and Anglo transferred the same sum to IL&P. Anglo described the €7.2 billion it had received as a customer deposit, and the €7.2 billion it had sent to IL&P as an inter-bank loan. In cash terms, the two banks were quits; but Anglo's balance sheet now showed an extra €7.2 billion in customer deposits. At a time when Anglo's ability to continue trading was under threat because of a run on deposits, and with Anglo's year-end accounts due to be prepared, this artificial deposit made the figures look a lot better.

FitzPatrick told the detectives that he knew nothing about the September 2008 transactions.

'I said, Listen, guys, someone from Anglo Irish Bank met someone from Irish Life and they came together and they structured the deal. I don't know (a) who from Irish Life or more importantly from Anglo Irish Bank did that; (b) I don't know whether it was wrong. You are telling me it is wrong. I accept that you are saying it is wrong. Maybe it is wrong but I just don't know. Until I actually saw the innards of the deal I would not know for definite, but based on the information you are giving me I will accept it is wrong if that is what you want me to say.'

FitzPatrick says he was 'absolutely a million miles away from any liability on that particular case. I just told them all I knew and that was it.'

According to FitzPatrick, 'They never asked me one little thing about my loans' – i.e. the loans from Anglo that he had taken care every twelve months to transfer temporarily to Irish Nationwide Building Society, so that Anglo would not have to legally disclose them to share-holders at the bank's financial year-end. 'Maybe they planned to come back to me about that at a future date,' FitzPatrick muses. 'And they only sparingly asked me about the ten people' – i.e. the ten who had bought Anglo shares from Sean Quinn using loans from Anglo itself.

After each interview session FitzPatrick was locked back inside a cell.

'The sergeant in charge was a very decent man. He might knock on the door. He might bring me out and bring me for a walk for maybe twenty-five minutes all around Bray Garda station and the grounds, or maybe open a door where we would look out, keep [me] away from the media, and take a breath of fresh air. We would chat away about different things . . .

'They were very decent to me. There was no cheapness. There was no smart-aleck remarks. They asked all the questions they wanted to ask and I gave them all the answers I could possibly give them.'

FitzPatrick's family had sent him an overnight bag the night before, so the prisoner was able to shave and change clothes. He had passed the time in his cell between interviews with a book of Sudoku puzzles. After his interviews stopped for the night, he slept. Questioning resumed the following morning.

The night-shift journalists were replaced by the day shift. Photographers and camera crews held their position on the low wall surrounding the station. A small crowd of locals also gathered. A copy of the *Evening Herald*, with its lead story 'Seanie's night in cold cell', was passed around.

Just before lunchtime Inspector Colm O'Malley came out to speak to the media. He assured them FitzPatrick would leave through the front entrance of the station, so that they'd be able to get video and photographs. 'He's a detained man, which in my language is a pris-oner,' O'Malley said. 'He is treated the same as everybody else; he came in this way – all our prisoners are brought in this way and come out the same way. That's the way it is.'

At lunchtime a blue 2001 Volkswagen Golf, driven by a young man in a baseball cap, entered the station's car park. 'It's a FitzPatrick car,' one reporter said. 'I saw it in the driveway when I was up there looking through the gates.'

The car belonged to FitzPatrick's son David, who had flown home the night before from New York, where he worked as an accountant, to support his father. Inside the station FitzPatrick prepared to walk out into the glare of the cameras. A number of gardaí went out first, taking up positions around the station to ensure he was not rushed by the media. FitzPatrick waited a few moments and then walked out of the station. He got into the Golf and kissed his son on the cheek; then David drove away past the photographers and television crews.

At the height of the boom Sean FitzPatrick had been credited with helping to create the risk-taking culture of what was known internationally as the Celtic Tiger. As the property bubble burst and a vicious recession took hold, he was being blamed for sending Ireland towards the brink of bankruptcy.

It was a hell of a fall for the country's top banker.

Hero to zero in less than two years: this is his story.

1. The Accidental Banker

'I had no idea I was going to make a career in banking.
I just wanted a loan.'

Sean FitzPatrick was born in Bray, Co. Wicklow, in June 1948. His father, Michael FitzPatrick, was a dairy farmer, and his mother, Johanna Maher, was a civil servant. The farm was in Shankill, but the family lived in Bray, three miles away, in a semi-detached house on a quiet road at the foot of Bray Head, a headland that juts into the Irish Sea, close to the town's Victorian seafront promenade.

He was the couple's second (and last) child; his sister, Joyce, was eighteen months his senior.

'It was a very small farm, made up of land that [my father] owned and then conacre,' FitzPatrick says. 'We would have had, I am not sure, maybe fifteen or twenty cows, something like that. My father delivered milk out of his dairy around Shankill and Bray.'

Sean helped out in the business, known as the Tillystown Dairy, putting milk in churns, bottling it and delivering it. As Shankill developed as a suburb of Dublin, more land was set aside for housing. As a result, the 'county farmers', as they were known, were getting less and less conacre, so Michael FitzPatrick gave up dairying and set up as a tillage contractor.

Johanna Maher grew up in Tipperary. 'My mother was a country woman. She was the immigrant, if you like. My father was the home-grown Dubliner, South Dublin, Shankill. He would have been a lot more sophisticated and more worldly-wise. My mother was going to be a nun for a while. She spent two years in a novitiate. Then she came up to Dublin and she worked two years in the civil service . . . She would have been secretarial or clerical. She met my father and that was it.'

In recollections for Ivor Kenny's book *Leaders*, FitzPatrick recalled how he would go home to his mother and tell her he had finished second in a race and she would invariably ask who came first. 'She had serious ambitions for us,' FitzPatrick says. FitzPatrick attended primary school for one year at Loreto Convent Bray before going to the nearby Presentation College – 'Pres' – in 1954.

'It was a very small school. There was less than twenty in my class, less than 200 in the secondary school . . . I developed a great interest in rugby. Our year, and the year or two before us and the year or two behind us, were good . . . I was a member of the swimming club. I used to swim a lot during the summer. I used to play a lot of tennis. I was a member of the golf club. Then in the winter, I used to play rugby, soccer not so much. Soccer was social. You played casual soccer down on the seafront and formal rugby in Pres. There was no tradition of Gaelic football.'

FitzPatrick was never academically minded. 'Exams were there to be got. They weren't the biggest thing in my life. They became the biggest thing in my life for a week or two or three weeks beforehand. They were there. They were just part of school. Sport was there to be enjoyed.

'I wasn't a bright kid. I wasn't thick either. I would have been middle of the road in the class, probably at the upper end of the second level.'

Coming first in French or maths, he recalls, 'wouldn't have been my ambition. However, it would have been my ambition to lead Pres against Blackrock and beat them. Or to win a sprint over a hundred metres or to win the long jump. The type of athlete I was, maybe this is a terrible reflection on me, but I would say I was about twenty-seven or twenty-eight when I realized I probably wouldn't play for Ireland. Most people would have been able to tell me that at a much earlier age.'

FitzPatrick and his sister Joyce were not close when they were growing up. Joyce was the apple of her father's eye, bright and hard-working as well as sporty. She was captain of the local Loreto Convent basketball team and hockey teams, and got seven honours in her Leaving Certificate; Sean would get one. She went to University College Dublin, where she studied social science and was auditor of the Social Science Society. She was 'a name in college', FitzPatrick remembers, and went on to study for a doctorate.

Though less academically accomplished than his sister, Sean was more streetwise. Joyce tells a story of how, as a teenager, he came home to his mother and father one evening and told them he was considering a vocation as a Presentation brother or Jesuit priest. His parents were horrified at the idea. Joyce believes that the supposed vocation was a ruse, a means of getting more latitude to stay out later.

When FitzPatrick was preparing for his Inter. Cert., in 1963, he arranged to travel to France under a programme known as Étudiants de Travail. Landing at Paris-Orly airport without a place to stay, he rang the Irish embassy. He ended up staying with a French priest in a monastery in the centre of Paris recommended by the embassy.

In 1966, after he completed his Leaving Cert., FitzPatrick went to London to search for work for the summer. 'I lived in NW10,' he says. 'It wasn't Kilburn but it was near Kilburn. Near Hammersmith, but it wasn't Hammersmith. I stayed in a big Irish boarding house. I never had eaten a fry in my life and suddenly it was the first thing I got at six o'clock in the morning before I went out to work.

'I went over with three other students who are still friends of mine today . . . I went down to the local church and said where could I get digs? They gave us the name of the local digs place and we went in there. We were paying a fiver a week and we got bed, breakfast and dinner.'

FitzPatrick got a job in a local factory working with other students and emigrants. The job did not impress his fellow lodgers at the boarding house. 'According to my fellow Irishmen, who had this sort of snob view, no real Irishman would work there,' he says. 'The fact that I had what most people would have thought was a semi-Dublin accent wouldn't have endeared me either. Although when I was able to confirm that I was non-Dublin, and that I was from Wicklow, a county that never did any damage to anyone in the rest of Ireland, I was accepted as a non-Dubliner. Not quite one of them, but different.'

He was encouraged to find work in construction. 'I remember sitting down with them and they said, Lookit, Sean, you have got to go to the guy and you have got to wear a white shirt, a bit dirty, and a jacket, none of those sweaters or any of that. You have to go to the guy and you call him John, you never call him Paddy, it's John, that's the name. And you say, John, any chance of a start?

'I said, What does that mean? Start. Start? The job. That is what you say . . . Any chance of a start? Next Monday morning, in I went with the guys. We were picked up at the corner, we were in a Ford Transit van, and we got off in the heart of Kilburn . . . They would have lorries drive up and they would have Paddy Lyons, and Tommy, and Fitzpatrick Construction, and Mickey and Jimmy, or whatever it was. Then you would go and see your man and say "Any chance of a start?" Your man said, Uh, go on there, hop on that lorry there or hop on that wagon.'

FitzPatrick was eighteen years of age. He was not typical among the Irish people working on building sites in London at the time, but he was fascinated by the culture he was exposed to there. 'I hadn't a clue when the All-Ireland finals were going to be on. They certainly didn't know rugby. They were all from the country.

'I didn't drink much but they drank. They used to go off and "sub up" to the boss. I never heard of that before. You would go to the boss on Monday and say could I have a sub. That would be getting your pay in advance. They would have big hands and would lower maybe four or five pints at lunch hour. I would be looking at them, drinking orange and [eating] a sandwich.'

After working on the construction sites by day, he did bar work at night. 'I went straight home, I couldn't have a shower because we didn't have showers. You would fill the bath and you would wash from your fingernails to the top of your armpit and from your neck upwards and that was it. Then I used to go down to the pub and work three nights a week.

'It was just fantastic, absolutely brilliant. Here I was living with Irish people who were over there for years . . . They lived a very limited life. They talked only about Ireland and only about their past, never the future. It was sad and beautiful. It was just brilliant.'

Those three months, FitzPatrick says, were 'like the university of life', mixing with the diaspora.

'The only thing they were thinking about was the following Saturday, they were getting on a bus to the local train station, to go all the way to Holyhead, to get the boat over to get to the All-Ireland with the Kilkenny Association or the Kerry Association . . . And no one, absolutely no one, was ever staying. They were always going home but they were never going home.'

FitzPatrick was, of course, going home, to a degree course at UCD. University life in the late 1960s was a relatively relaxed affair. 'It was quite simple to get into university at the time. You didn't have to have really any qualification other than your Leaving Cert. It was before the points issue came in. There was a big failure rate in UCD at the time, not because the academic level was high but because it was so soft to get in.'

Nor was it a financial strain. 'We wouldn't have had a huge amount of money but we weren't poor either. We would have had enough money to get to university . . . The fees were very small at the time. My parents worked hard and we worked hard. We had jobs during the summer. I used to go away and Joyce used to go away. We worked and saved money and that used to put us through.'

He chose to study commerce, and from the beginning he viewed it as a stepping stone to a profession. Socially, UCD was very much a continuation of school life. FitzPatrick made friends easily, mostly through rugby. 'I never made the firsts but I got an odd game with the seconds,' he remembers. (He would play the game, in the backs with Greystones and later Bective, until he was thirty-eight, and rugby would be an important source of contacts in his early business life.) He lived at the family home in Bray throughout college, pushed on by his mother and indulged slightly by his father.

FitzPatrick remembers getting wound up about his final-year examinations in college. His father gave him £20 and told him to enjoy himself and not to go back to the books until the day of the examination. 'They were an incredible generation, that generation. We were brought up just after the [Second World] war. When I look back at that generation and the mothers and fathers just literally gave their whole life for their children. It was an incredibly unself-ish generation. That would be my whole memory of my mother and father's generation: incredibly unselfish, doing everything for the development of their kids, and certainly our home was like that.'

FitzPatrick qualified with an honours degree, Bachelor of Commerce. 'I always knew that I was going to have to do accountancy. I was very worried about chartered accountancy because you heard so many times of the failures in chartered accountancy.

'I remember going for interviews in Craig Gardner ... The managing partner or the interview partner said to me: Now, listen, Sean, it is a big social issue – these people who commit so much of their time and their youth to becoming chartered accountants and they don't get through their exams. The problem is this, if you failed, you could only do it so many times.'

FitzPatrick did his articles, or apprenticeship, with Reynolds, McCarron & O'Connor, which would later form part of Ernst & Young. 'We were paid £6 per week starting off. That was £300 a year and they used to take £1 off you so they only gave you £5 and they used to give you a bonus at Christmas, that was the £1 which they had taken off you.'

FitzPatrick failed two modules of his articles at the first attempt, but passed the exams six months later. He got a job straight away with the Dublin office of Atkins Chirnside & Co., a Cork firm. Shortly thereafter the firm merged with Craig Gardner. At Craig Gardner, FitzPatrick would meet Charlie McCreevy, a future minister for finance. The two men had been contemporaries at University College Dublin, and studied in the same B.Comm. class, but did not know each other well.

'I met him doing an audit of J. B. Carr, Joe Carr, the famous golfer,' FitzPatrick recalls. 'He had a clothing firm and other interests ... I would have seen myself as senior to [McCreevy] for no reason [other] than I felt to myself I should be. I said, Charlie, listen, will you ever prepare the papers and I will do the consolidation. Charlie said, Oh, no, no, Sean, I will do that, boy. I said, Oh, no, no, I will do that. I am doing all the bigger companies ... That was how I ended up meeting Charlie. I liked Charlie then. He was a nice guy.'

FitzPatrick's career ambitions were clearly defined. 'I really did want to become a chartered accountant. Then I was in a profession, and that seemed to be the place to be. After that, I would like to become a partner.'

Necessity changed his focus.

FitzPatrick first met his wife, Catriona O'Toole, when he was still in school. Bray in the 1950s was a busy seaside resort, not the commuter town it is now. Before the advent of the package holiday, visitors came from Scotland, Northern Ireland and the north of England to the town for their two-week holiday by the sea, and many Dubliners also rented homes there. There were amusement arcades and ballrooms and bandstands. 'Triona's parents used to take a house out in Bray for the summer. I was working in the amusement arcade. I was running the bumpers. Triona has a brother, who is fourteen years younger than her. He was just a baby and she was wheeling him around. She came in to look at the bumpers one day and there was this fantastic-looking guy jumping like Tarzan from the back of one bumper to the other.'

It was a brief encounter. 'It was no big deal. She was too young at the time.'

They met again some years later when FitzPatrick was studying at UCD. 'She was in Loreto Stephen's Green in school, a boarder, and I used to get off the train in Westland Row and I used to walk all the way up to UCD, which was up in Earlsfort Terrace. I had to walk past [Loreto]. One day she was coming out of school getting her breakfast, or getting her papers, whatever she was doing and she recognized me. She said, "How are ya?", I said, "How are ya?" . . . I think I was in third year, and didn't I invite her to the graduation ball for the B.Comm. I was going out with a girl and then it was all off and so suddenly I needed someone to go, so I invited her and that was it.'

The couple got engaged in 1972 and started saving to buy a house. 'It was just very difficult to get a loan from a building society. You had to be with them for a hundred years and you had to have 80 per cent of the deposit. Ridiculous stuff.

'Triona was working as a secretary in a company involved in ceilings. She was earning a few bob and I was earning a few bob but not a lot, I was still in articles. We used to go to the Educational Building Society up in Rathfarnham where she lived and place some money on deposit every Friday or every second Friday. Maybe with one

Friday it was her money and one Friday it was my money. That was it. That was going as a deposit.'

The couple saw a house out in Greystones that they hoped to buy for about £6,700, but it was not clear where the money would come from. FitzPatrick noticed an ad in the newspaper: the Irish Bank of Commerce was looking for a young chartered accountant. 'I said great, ticked that box. Good personality? Grand. Bright? Grand. There was preferential loans [available to employees]. I said, Jesus, that is very good.'

At the time, FitzPatrick recalls, he 'had no idea what banking was. I had no idea I was going to make a career in banking. I just wanted a loan. Really.'

The Irish Bank of Commerce was a merchant bank, but that designation owed more to its lineage in the tea-importing business than to its actual business in the early 1970s. By the 1960s, as trade freed up, the original tea-importing owners had moved into general business banking, a field where they had little expertise and that was changing rapidly. A number of smaller banks were merging, and from this emerged the two monoliths of Irish banking: Allied Irish Bank and Bank of Ireland.

By the time FitzPatrick joined Irish Bank of Commerce, it was under a new management team headed by Michael Sheehan and Gerry Watson.

The bank was based in a Georgian house of about 3,500 square feet on Merrion Square. The young FitzPatrick was impressed. Sheehan drove a Jaguar and Watson drove a top-of-the-range Citroën. FitzPatrick started work on 1 April 1974. He was led into his office, which had a deep pile carpet and a large desk upon which sat copies of that day's *Irish Times* and *Irish Independent*. The first thing FitzPatrick did was phone his mother.

He also got a loan for £7,200, which covered the cost of his new house in Greystones, and a separate £400 that his new bosses said he could use to play the gilt market. 'I didn't know what the gilt market was,' he told Ivor Kenny.

In September 1974, less than six months after FitzPatrick stepped into his new office, and weeks before his impending marriage, Irish

Bank of Commerce's largest shareholder, Jessel Securities, an insurance company, went bust. The Central Bank of Ireland rang up Gerry Murphy, chief executive of the City of Dublin Bank, and asked if he would consider taking over IBC.

City of Dublin was a leasing company, involved largely in car finance. It 'wouldn't have a banker within a million miles of it', says FitzPatrick. 'They were all sales guys.' By contrast, 'Irish Bank of Commerce were all, in British terms, Oxbridge educated. Gonzaga, the Jesuits. They were sophisticated merchant bankers and you had this crowd of shiny-suited chancers in charge. It wasn't a natural fit for the guys in Irish Bank of Commerce.'

The Irish banking industry in the late 1970s was populated by some colourful characters, and regulation was lax. Ken Bates, later to become owner of Chelsea Football Club, established the Irish Trust Bank by buying an off-the-shelf company called Kildare Banking Company and opening an office on Dublin's Dawson Street. The bank went bust in 1976, a victim of a falling property market. During the same decade Patrick Gallagher funded his own property empire with his own bank, Merchant Banking. It would collapse in the early 1980s.

IBC, with its clientele of largely trading companies, was by comparison a staid and steady outfit. FitzPatrick rose to become its financial controller. He credits his early education in banking to Gerry Watson, 'a man of the highest integrity'.

In 1980 Anglo Irish Bank — a cross between a finance house and a merchant bank — came on the market. It had failed, largely due to losses in its consumer hire-purchase business. IBC, now financially stable under the aegis of City of Dublin Bank, purchased Anglo Irish Bank.

FitzPatrick recalls that he was 'the bag carrier' on the acquisition, sitting in on the meetings but not directly involved in the negotiations. 'I literally carried the bags,' he says. Pat Casey, the chief executive of Anglo, left within a year of the deal to take up a new job in the insurance industry. FitzPatrick was told to go down to Hays MSL, the recruiters, and to ask them to find a new boss for Anglo Irish Bank.

'I said, What do we need? Gerry said, Well, a guy who is experienced in lending and can run a business. I asked, Will he be going on the board? No, he's not going on the board, we will make him general manager . . . What will we pay him? They said, Oh, we will pay him £10,000 a year. So here is me on six [thousand a year], I think.

'I said to myself, as I was driving down, Jesus, I would like that job. So I pulled the car in and I got out and I rang Gerry Watson from a phone booth. I said, Gerry, I would like that job. He said, Don't be so ridiculous, Sean, you have got a big, big future here. We are going to fly. I said, No, no, I want it. So it was cleared by Gerry Murphy and I got the job.'

At the age of thirty-two, the accidental banker FitzPatrick was the general manager of a financial institution, albeit a very small one. Its gross assets, or loans, were worth less than £500,000. Its offices were in St Stephen's Green, a short walk from IBC in Merrion Square.

Anglo occupied a sort of middle ground within the City of Dublin group. To avoid competing with the car-leasing business, Anglo would offer leasing on car fleets and machinery at higher loan values than its more mass-market parent. To avoid competing with IBC, it would offer smaller business loans, up to £150,000. As a result of this accommodation with its parent bank, Anglo became one of Ireland's first small-business banks.

In December 1981 Crédit Commercial de France decided to look at the Irish market, and sized up IBC. The interest was warmly welcomed within the walls of the merchant bank, particularly among those who felt uncomfortable about being owned by a car-finance company. FitzPatrick, too, was excited.

'We were like, thank God, we are getting out and away from that crowd of hucksters,' FitzPatrick recalls. 'We don't want those people, they wouldn't understand balance sheets or how to work calculators. We don't want that. The French don't want it. They want a merchant bank here in Ireland.'

CCF, the third-biggest private bank in France at the time, agreed to pay £1 million for a 40 per cent stake in IBC. The French showed no interest in Anglo Irish Bank and its smaller 'ticket' lending, however. CCF would end up with 80 per cent of Irish Bank of Commerce, with the remainder held by City of Dublin; Anglo was left to its own devices, still owned by the 'crowd of hucksters'.

Unperturbed, FitzPatrick went about building up the bank, carving out its niche as a small-business lender and finance house. There was, he says, 'lots of fun' with the French, as Anglo started angling for lending business from some of IBC's smaller clients.

In 1985 FitzPatrick hired Tiarnan O'Mahoney, a young treasury executive from IBC, a move that upset his erstwhile colleagues. It was an important job. Treasury was the engine room of the bank, responsible for controlling interest rates and raising capital to fund lending. By that stage Anglo Irish Bank was making more money than either IBC or City of Dublin Bank. In his year-end statement in 1984, Tom Kenny, City of Dublin Bank chairman, described Anglo as 'a jewel'.

With such a glowing commendation, FitzPatrick, the rising star, inveigled Gerry Watson to get Gerry Murphy to put him on the board of City of Dublin Bank. Then, in 1986, he went to Gerry Murphy with the idea of merging Anglo and City of Dublin to form a single bank.

'I said, Lookit, here we are, what are we doing here? You are down on Merrion Square, I am up on St Stephen's Green. You are fifty-four or fifty-five years of age. You need to retire now, Gerry, and I will look after you. You will become chairman and we will get rid of the chairman we have and I will become chief executive. You have got a premises and I have got a premises . . .

'I said, Right, what we will do is this: we'll put the two banks together and we will change the name of the bank from City of Dublin Bank to Anglo Irish Bank Corporation plc. Look at the ring about that! Beautiful ring. City of Dublin Bank was far too local. Because, do you know what? We are going to be huge in Ireland, huge in the UK, and we will probably have to change it to Anglo Irish Bank Europe later on because we will go out there too.'

2. The Rise

'They were very dismissive of us. We were seen as interlopers and
definitely outside the pale.'

In the reports of its launch in October 1986, Anglo Irish Bank
Corporation, formed through the merger of City of Dublin and
Anglo Irish Bank, was described as a 'reinvigorated bank'. FitzPatrick,
not yet forty years of age, was responsible for its creation and for
generating the momentum in its profits.

It was still a tiny bank. In the year to September 1987, FitzPatrick's
Anglo reported profits of £1.45 million, a big rise on the £800,000
profits reported the year before, but still minuscule. Economically
Ireland was at a low ebb. The country was racked by recession, high
unemployment and emigration. For the smaller banks, the collapse
of a single business client could wipe out a big chunk of a year's
profits.

'At that stage, 1986, a loan of £100,000 or £150,000 would have
been very significant [for Anglo],' FitzPatrick says. 'There wouldn't
have been very many of those.'

It was difficult for a small player to be both prudent and aggressive.
Three banks – AIB, Bank of Ireland and Ulster Bank – dominated
the market. 'They had the whole market to themselves,' FitzPatrick
says. 'They were very dismissive of us. We were seen as interlopers
and definitely outside the pale . . . We saw ourselves not as a primary
bank for any borrower . . . We saw ourselves as secondary with a
small "s", one of two banks that they dealt with. We would have been
focused on the business end of the relationship, not on the consumer
end, not on current accounts or chequebooks or anything like that.'

Anglo's main ambition was to widen the scope of its business lending. The 'biggest portion' of this expanding business, FitzPatrick
says, 'was individuals who did investment property'.

FitzPatrick convinced himself that investment property was a proxy for the entire economy. In FitzPatrick's view, the beauty of financing the purchase of an office 'was that it would give us an exposure to a wider market, through one person, who has got tenants in from different sectors. So we were lending to the cleaner, to the lawyer, the glass-repair man, all through you [the property investor], because you would have had them as tenants in a building. That was the whole idea. We were very well exposed right across the economy with income coming in and with property as security.'

One problem with this view was the last four words: 'with property as security'. FitzPatrick and his colleagues viewed property as a fundamentally stable asset class, overlooking the fact that if banks like Anglo pumped enough credit into the sector they would eventually create a bubble – and cause property to become deeply unstable. For a bank as heavily committed to property investment and development as Anglo, this was a recipe for catastrophe. By the time this had become clear to disinterested observers, Anglo had been thriving for more than two decades, and FitzPatrick's belief that the bank's risk was well diversified across the economy was a message he and his colleagues had repeated time and again to investors over that period. It was part of the Anglo gospel, and its wisdom was rarely challenged.

From the early days, FitzPatrick also believed that the bank stood out as being entrepreneurial. 'We had a very good name,' he says. 'Why? . . . We were charging more for money than other banks, but what we were doing was we were giving answers quickly. We were giving very good service. People didn't come in to Anglo and wander. We would turn around and say, Lookit, we are a niche bank. If you are looking for money to put wiring in yokes: no money. Buying a farm: no money. A home loan: no. Buy false teeth: no. If you are looking for money to go overseas: no.'

The climate for property development in Ireland in the late 1980s bore no relationship to the climate Anglo would help to create during the boom, and Anglo's lending policies in the early years reflected this. It was important that would-be borrowers were able to demonstrate that they had access to income from a source or sources other than the property venture in question. 'You could come in to us and say, Lookit, I have a fantastic property, a castle down in Leitrim worth £10 million. I don't really have a lot of income, I just want to borrow, say, £1 million. You can't lose. I will give you full security. We would say no. We would need to see cash flow.

'If you came in and said I just have cash flow, I am in the telecoms business and I have just got cash flow and I don't really have any security, we would say no thank you. We always wanted security *and* cash flow, borrowers needed to show the income coming through.'

FitzPatrick's efforts to grow the bank in his early years at the helm were not restricted to the realm of property. He jumped into a joint venture with Swithland Motors, a large car dealer in the English Midlands, in which the dealer would sell the cars and Anglo would provide the finance. Within two years, Anglo exited the joint venture: profit margins were too low and the risk of bad debts too high. It was something of a close shave for FitzPatrick: Swithland, which had had aspirations of a stock-market flotation, went into receivership in 1993, and two Swithland executives were convicted of fraud for a series of deals after the Anglo joint venture ended.

The fastest way to grow the bank was by acquisition, and Fitz-Patrick's purchases were driven more by gut instinct than by careful calculation. In 1989 Anglo purchased two stockbroking firms, Solo-man Abrahamson and Porter & Irvine. Stockbroking was far from the core of the business, and FitzPatrick later recounted that the move into stockbroking was driven by 'greed'. He could see that his professional clients were investing a lot of their money via stock-brokers rather than putting it on deposit at the bank, and he reckoned that he would go after that money. But when the stock market turned in late 1989 the brokers found it hard to make money, and in 1992 Anglo exited the businesses.

There were also opportunities on more familiar ground. In Ireland in the late 1980s there were plenty of small credit institutions, owned by foreign players, that were willing to bail out of a near-bankrupt economy. Anglo snapped up the Irish loan book of 3i, a venture-capital company, in 1987, paying £4.5 million.

Another overseas institution that ran into trouble in Ireland was

Crédit Commercial de France, the 80 per cent shareholder in Irish Bank of Commerce. IBC had taken losses on loans extended to a number of clients, including Enda Kelly of Dodder Properties, a Dublin-based property developer. CCF told FitzPatrick that IBC needed to be recapitalized to the tune of £5 million. The French bank wanted Anglo, as 20 per cent shareholder in IBC, to put up its share of the £5 million needed, or roughly £1 million. FitzPatrick refused.

Ernst & Young was called in as arbitrator, but without success, and the row continued. FitzPatrick did not have a high regard for his French ex-colleagues, and he took a stubborn line with them. 'I don't trust the people, I don't like them, I don't think they are any good. I think they are useless . . . haven't a clue about Ireland. I wouldn't dream of putting money in . . . I want to get out . . . And of course the more I wanted to get out, they then realized that they needed me to buy them out.'

CCF decided to pull out of Ireland. Anglo was the natural – and probably the only realistic – purchaser of IBC, but it did not have the money to buy out the French bank's 80 per cent share. FitzPatrick executed what is known in corporate finance as a vendor-finance deal: he borrowed the money from CCF by way of a loan note. The French also agreed to write off £3.3 million that Anglo owed IBC. FitzPatrick later raised money from his own shareholders to pay off the French bank. 'I stuffed them,' he says gleefully.

Buying loan books and acquiring customers was only part of the picture. The other key to growth was to access money that the bank could then lend. 'It was very simple,' says FitzPatrick. 'What was our restriction? Our restriction all the time was our funding. We had to make sure we had the funding . . . We were looking for a good solid deposit base to get money to lend.'

Unlike the big retail banks, Anglo did not have a large branch network to suck in deposits, so an alternative strategy was required. FitzPatrick says that the bank 'aimed at people's greed'. Whereas other banks profited from customer deposits by paying interest at less than the full money-market rate and pocketing the difference, Anglo decided to offer savers the full market rate for their money. 'We never made money on our deposit book,' FitzPatrick says. 'Ever. Why?

Because we had to pay market rates. Why? To widen our deposit base. Why? To get the money to lend.'

In the space of just four years, to the end of 1990, Anglo quadrupled the size of its deposit base to £400 million. This massive growth was helped by the decision, in 1987, to set up a deposit bank in the Isle of Man, a well-known tax haven. According to FitzPatrick, Anglo merely followed Bank of Ireland and AIB to the Isle of Man. 'The only way we were going to get it was to open over there,' FitzPatrick says, 'and we did and we got funds.'

Income-tax rates in 1980s Ireland were high, and any after-tax income placed on deposit was also liable to a substantial retention tax. A culture of widespread tax avoidance developed, and the Irish banks were wholly complicit. It spread from shopkeeper to stockbroker. The retail banks facilitated the establishment of entirely bogus 'non-resident' savings accounts for domestic customers, which did not incur deposit-interest retention tax.

The other option for those wishing to escape the taxman was to put money offshore. It was not illegal to open an offshore account – so long as the money was declared for tax before it was lodged. In the 1980s, undeclared income flooded out of Ireland into the tax-free offshore deposits.

The problem for businesses was getting access to the money locked away in the Isle of Man. To overcome this, companies would offer security over the deposit sitting in the Isle of Man account to the bank in Dublin. The customer would be able to keep his money offshore while at the same time putting it to use by raising funds from the Irish bank.

'The Isle of Man wouldn't have been clean in today's terms. It was clean enough then, but it wasn't clean,' FitzPatrick says. 'There was nothing illegal but it was on the tax edge.'

It took almost two decades for the Irish authorities to clamp down on offshore deposits and trusts, a trawl which began in 2002. By that stage the Irish banks' Isle of Man operations were so well established that they no longer needed hot Irish money. Lots of savers use offshore accounts for entirely legitimate reasons. With low overheads, offshore banks offered higher rates of interest, and tax-free interest.

They also offered investors, both corporate and individual, the ability to keep cash away from creditors and lawsuits.

Anglo built a strong franchise in the Isle of Man. At the time Anglo was nationalized, after a catastrophic loss of large corporate deposits in Dublin, the bank's deposit base in the Isle of Man was over €3 billion.

Alongside deposit growth, the bank also needed to raise capital. One of the first things that FitzPatrick had to do as chief executive at Anglo was to launch what is known as a rights issue: fundraising from existing shareholders. The extra funds were needed to shore up losses on leasing activities at City of Dublin Bank, but also to allow the bank to buy other banks and loan books.

Anglo's shareholders were a diverse group, but none were more colourful than the Clegg family – and the Cleggs would be central to Anglo's rights-issue strategy. Albert and John Clegg were identical twin brothers born in Sheffield in 1919, the sons of a bookmaker-turned-property-developer. After the Second World War, the brothers started buying up houses in the north of England.

At one point, the Clegg brothers had a portfolio of 600 houses. They went into the motor trade and insurance in the 1960s. Their South Yorkshire Motor Insurance went bust in 1967 and the brothers were bankrupted. By that stage, the two had developed a taste for punting on the stock market, but because of their bankrupt status a number of English brokers refused to deal with them.

In 1977 they started using a Dublin stockbroker, Porter & Irvine, to invest in the London stock market. They also, it later emerged, disguised their share-buying activities by investing in shares in the names of members of their extended family.

The Clegg family were 17 per cent shareholders in Anglo, by dint of an investment in the City of Dublin Bank. The stake in Anglo Irish Bank was held in the name of Jayne Riley, a daughter of John Clegg Sr. FitzPatrick says that he is not too sure how the Cleggs managed to build such a large stake in City of Dublin Bank. 'I don't know how they got to the 17 per cent mark but they had. How could they have gotten there? I thought the Central Bank had restrictions on any individuals owning no more than 5 or 10 per cent. Anyway they had it.'

It was not the family's only stock-market investment. John Clegg Jr was a half-brother to Jayne Riley. He trained as a lawyer with Nabarro Nathanson, a leading City of London law firm. At the age of twenty-five, and in the true spirit of the era, he purchased Wace, a tiny, near-bankrupt company, and used it as a 'shell' to make a string of acquisitions of graphics and imaging companies. By the time he was finished, the suave city lawyer had built Wace into the world's largest provider of pre-press photographic and design services to the advertising and media industries.

The size of the Clegg stake in Anglo was not a concern to Fitz-Patrick at the time. Quite the opposite. He pushed to have John Clegg Jr appointed to the board of the bank to represent the Jayne Riley interest. 'They seemed to have a huge amount of money and he seemed to be a very smart guy, very impressive guy to meet, and had very good connections in the UK.'

It was a critical juncture for Anglo. FitzPatrick knew that if the bank was to grow, it needed to raise more capital, and the Cleggs could play an important role. 'We were going to have lots of rights issues, as I saw it, as it was the only way to build the bank. [Clegg's] 17 per cent was a phone call away.' When putting together a rights issue, a Clegg commitment would represent a very useful vote of confidence that would help convince other investors to commit. 'If you had 17 per cent going out to the institutions, you could say you had got a commitment from 20 per cent of the shareholders. Already it was a big pull factor.'

When John Clegg Jr was appointed to the board of Anglo Irish Bank, on 25 April 1988, he was only thirty years of age. 'Rather than having him outside pissing in on us, I felt it was good to have him inside where we could control him,' says FitzPatrick, who describes Clegg as having been 'very sophisticated and debonair'. It was just one month after John Clegg Jr was appointed to the board that Anglo Irish Bank purchased the Cleggs' Dublin stockbrokers, Porter & Irvine.

In April 1989 the bank raised £21.5 million in a well-supported rights issue, by far its largest ever. In early December 1991 FitzPatrick announced that Anglo planned to raise £28 million by way of a rights issue. Three weeks later, on Christmas Eve, the bank revealed why: it was in talks to purchase Hill Samuel, the Irish business banking operation of Britain's Trustee Savings Bank (and the firm that Michael Sheehan and Gerry Watson once left to take over IBC).

FitzPatrick described the deal as a 'once-in-a-lifetime opportunity' and the 'most momentous occasion' in the bank's history. The acquisition would bring the Anglo loan book to almost £1 billion, the fifth largest in the country.

Gerry Murphy told shareholders at the Anglo annual general meeting in early January 1992 that the bank was 'buying a book with a sizeable investment in property and construction against the background of a slowing economy. We are doing a very careful due-diligence investigation.'

The rights issue was completed by the last week in January. On the Friday of the same week, as he was preparing to leave the office, FitzPatrick got a call from Bernard Somers, a Dublin accountant. Somers, who had trained at Craig Gardner at the same time as the Anglo boss, became finance director of the troubled Goodman Group in 1990. When Goodman, Ireland's biggest meat company, encountered difficulty raising finance to steer the company through examinership, Somers had turned to Anglo. The bank lent Goodman £40 million on a short-term basis. This was a huge piece of business: at the time Anglo's total loan book was worth not much more than £200 million. Anglo not only got its money back but was well paid.

Somers's phone call on that January night had nothing to do with Goodman, however. Somers had been talking to Pat Heneghan, the well-known Dublin PR adviser, Fine Gael party activist and adviser to Larry Goodman. Somers said Heneghan was aware that the *Sunday Telegraph* was working on a big story about Wace and the Clegg family.

'I didn't sleep Friday or Saturday because there was going to be big headlines,' says FitzPatrick. 'I knew [the story] would be about Clegg but I didn't know [exactly] what it was going to be about.'

The article, co-written by Irish journalist Alan Ruddock, was sensational. It claimed that the Clegg family had been involved in insider trading, buying shares in companies that were later purchased by the

Wace Group. It also stated that there were rumours that the family were under investigation for laundering money and gun-running for the Irish Republican Army.

FitzPatrick was shocked by the details of the article. 'I flew to London that night with Michael Jacob [a fellow Anglo director] and said to Clegg: Out. He said: What? I said: Out. I can't be having you. We got rid of him by the Monday.'

Clegg protested his innocence, claiming that the article was part of a smear campaign. He proclaimed to be 'stupefied' by the IRA allegations. It mattered little to FitzPatrick. 'This was a time when we were just surviving, trying to keep going, and making a few more bob. This wasn't a case of saying to institutions "Look at what we have built" or anything like that. That didn't come until much, much later.

'This was about survival. Suddenly we had this guy who was going to threaten our survival. Imagine linked in with the IRA. Imagine insider dealing. You had to get rid of the guy.'

Clegg was also forced to stand down at Wace. 'He blamed me afterwards, said that I had set him in motion and ruined his career,' says FitzPatrick. 'You could argue that I did. I was saying the primary thing here is to save the bank, not you, not me, the bank.'

Clegg's resignation was not the end of the affair. The family still held 17 per cent of the company, and this acted as a drag on the share's performance. To sell the Anglo holding, the family felt, would be interpreted as an admission that the rumours linking Wace with the IRA were true.

The Clegg affair was a huge distraction at a time when Anglo was trying to acquire Hill Samuel from Trustee Savings Bank. Negotiations broke down in April 1992 after Anglo reduced its offer on foot of its assessment of the Hill Samuel loan book. Hill Samuel did not agree with the assessment. Hill Samuel's minimum price is understood to have been between £25 and £27 million; Anglo was not prepared to go above £22 million. Anglo held on to the capital it had raised for the acquisition, FitzPatrick says, and 'used it to expand'.

Meanwhile, efforts to get the Cleggs to sell their stake in Anglo dragged on for over a year. Every press report that mentioned

Anglo also mentioned Wace, Clegg and inevitably the IRA and money-laundering. In a bizarre twist, a letter purporting to have been signed by Jayne Riley was sent to Anglo's institutional share-holders in January 1993. 'I wish to inquire if you are interested in selling your total holding in Anglo-Irish Bankcorp. If so, I would be pleased if you will let me know the price you require.'

The letter was sent from an office in Chicago from which the Clegg family operated. Nothing came out of the approaches, which were seen merely as a means of putting Anglo 'into play', prompting one or more bids for the bank from potential buyers who might pay a premium for the Clegg shares.

A huge amount of management time was spent trying to get the family to sell its stake. FitzPatrick eventually flew out to Durban, South Africa, in the spring of 1993 to meet John Clegg Sr, and finally convinced him to sell. Investment Bank of Ireland purchased the shares from the Cleggs and then placed them in an orderly fashion with a number of investment funds.

Getting rid of the Cleggs was a lucky escape. A six-year investigation by the Serious Fraud Office into the Wace Group would later reveal the true extent of the Clegg family's insider-trading activities. John Clegg Sr and John Clegg Jr and Albert Clegg used no fewer than twenty-nine different aliases to secretly buy shares in Wace and companies that Wace would purchase. Some of the names were acquaintances of the Clegg family that had been dead for more than fifty years.

Albert Clegg had previous convictions for forgery and theft. John Clegg Sr had used false names in the past to avoid creditors. Yet it emerged that John and Albert Clegg effectively ran Wace while pretending to work as janitors in the Wace offices. In total, it was estimated that the family had enriched itself to the tune of stg. £60 million through illegal share-buying. Jayne Riley was almost certainly unaware that she had ever held a 17 per cent stake in Anglo Irish Bank. By the time the 300-page SFO report came out, none of the Cleggs were living in the UK, and none were ever charged.

The British authorities had taken the money-laundering and paramilitary allegations seriously enough to convene a secret meeting at the London Stock Exchange in the summer of 1991. Present were representatives from the Royal Ulster Constabulary's C13 anti-racketeering squad, the Serious Fraud Office, the Bank of England and the exchange's own insider-dealing unit. The inquiry, however, was shelved, no evidence was ever found to back up the gossip, and the SFO discounted the allegations.

In a statement at the time of the Clegg stake sale, Anglo chairman Gerry Murphy welcomed the development. 'Many of our existing shareholders have upped their stakes,' he said. 'As far as we are concerned, this is a very positive day. We were never very happy with the idea that one individual or one family would hold so many shares.'

The words would have an extraordinary resonance in Anglo's subsequent history.

The Clegg affair had little real effect on Anglo's day-to-day business. Six months prior to the share sale, in the autumn of 1992, Murphy stood before Anglo shareholders at the company's annual general meeting and declared, in the manner of Sir Harold Macmillan, the former British prime minister, that 'We have never had it so good.'

Murphy reported that the bank was opening new accounts at a rate of 25 or so per day with an average balance of between £30,000 and £40,000. In other words, Anglo was raising in the region of £1 million a day in deposits. It was quite a performance against the backdrop of the weak, if improving, Irish economy. In September 1992 the country had been gripped in a currency crisis after the Irish pound was attacked by currency speculators. Short-term interest rates reached 22 per cent.

It helped that the bank could boast a settled and experienced senior management team. Tiarnan O'Mahoney, Bill Barrett and John Rowan had all been with Anglo since 1985. Peter Killen had been with the bank since 1982. A more recent arrival in the management team was Willie McAteer, who joined the bank from Yeoman, a leasing company, in 1993.

Bill Barrett, head of lending, did important work in maintaining ties to key clients in the wake of the currency crisis. House builder Gerry Gannon, for example, was holding a number of sites near Celbridge,

Co. Kildare, that he was unable to sell, and his firm was in serious trouble. Anglo stood by him until the market turned, and within fifteen years Gannon went from being close to broke to being considered a billionaire.

FitzPatrick relied heavily on his top lieutenants. 'I wouldn't have been seen as a great lender,' he says. 'I wasn't technically good. I didn't see myself as a banker. I was the entrepreneur. I was the businessman. I was the guy hiring people, getting good people in to run the show.'

He is frank about the unorthodox criteria he applied in making hiring decisions. 'I didn't have respect for hugely intelligent people, that was probably one of my shortcomings,' he says, though later he clarifies that he means academic intelligence. (In Ivor Kenny's book *Leaders*, he described this more positively as a 'healthy disrespect'.) 'I was more into people that could relate to other people, that could talk in the ordinary way. People that could go out and have a pint but didn't have to drink the whole night. Who could meet people from different levels and walks within organizations and relate to them, talk to them. That is what we wanted more than anything else in people: a hunger and wish to succeed.'

He may well have been describing himself.

Anglo continued to buy loan books, both in Ireland and the UK, as a means of building its customer base. In August 1993 Anglo bought a distressed UK loan book from Chemical Bank, then part of Manufacturers Hanover Trust, an American bank. It contained 118 loans, all of them secured on property. The deal boosted Anglo's nascent UK book to stg. £150 million.

In January 1995 FitzPatrick finally purchased the Hill Samuel Irish loan book, for £100 million – or £75 million more than Trustee Savings Bank had been prepared to accept three years previously. He regretted taking such a tough negotiating stance then, but by 1995 the Irish economy was recovering strongly and Anglo had grounds for greater confidence. Hill Samuel's loan book had also grown considerably bigger and healthier in the intervening years.

'Our acquisition policy is quite clear,' FitzPatrick told the *Wall Street Transcript*, a specialist publication, the same year. 'We only want to buy entities, or indeed loan books, where we would have done those loans in instances ourselves.'

FitzPatrick recalls that Anglo was very careful about such acquisitions, and worked hard to increase the amount of business it was doing with the new clients on its books. 'We went in and did due diligence. Looked at every loan in the book. Tom Lyons: What loans has he got? What is the property? What is the income from it? How much of the loan did he put in? How much will we pay for the loan and do we have to provide for it? . . . We would just get Tom Lyons up on the screen, see how was the loan going, is he repaying, he hasn't paid for six months, let's make a provision of whatever, or he hasn't ever missed a penny for five years.

'So you had a really good sense of where it was going and then what you did was you went and met [the borrower] and you said, OK, Tom, have you any other business? Do you want to refinance? Any other stuff you have got.

'Then they started building their own portfolios and we started lending to them and it was word of mouth that passed it on.'

In 1995 Anglo made its first acquisition beyond Ireland and the UK, purchasing the Royal Trust of Canada's operations in Austria. A private bank, the business took deposits from wealthy clients. Fitz-Patrick describes this new deposit base as 'manna' that helped the bank widen its lending in Ireland.

By now demand for loans was strong. The new loan books were important, but 65 per cent of all new loans in 1995 were coming from existing customers. Anglo went from having just 1 per cent of the Irish business lending market in 1986 to 7 per cent by 1995. Its ambition was to double that share by the turn of the millennium, again by a mixture of acquisitions and increasing its business with existing customers.

The Irish economy was surging. After the chaos of the currency crisis, interest rates plummeted. The country started to enjoy a boom in foreign direct investment as American firms pitched up to set up subsidiaries. This had a huge trickle-down effect.

'The environment in which we're operating in Ireland is very positive at the moment,' FitzPatrick told *Wall Street Transcript*. 'It's positive because we are, and have been, experiencing for the last eighteen months historic low levels of interest rates. Base rates today are around about 6.5 per cent on the one-month inter-bank market, and inflation is under control and it's running at around about 2 per cent here in Ireland, and has never really passed that in the last four or five years.'

FitzPatrick noted Ireland's position as a 'gateway to Europe' and its young, well-educated population. 'So you're talking about a developing and newish breed of Irish entrepreneurs that are very well represented in the professional sector, our special services, i.e. accountants, corporate financiers and lawyers, with whom we do a huge amount of business.'

Anglo, FitzPatrick said, had a highly personalized culture. 'When you deal with Anglo Irish Bank, you don't deal with the bank, you deal with the individual . . . the final decision-maker. So we tend to be different to the other banks in the sense that we hold out our managers as people who can actually make decisions. And we find that people want to deal with our people on that basis.'

FitzPatrick also gave a glimpse into another facet of the culture of the bank: a growing reputation for being ruthlessly performance-driven. 'There's a continual sort of reassessment of people we have. We take in a number of graduates each year and we try to focus them in and try to align them to our particular culture, and sometimes we over-promote people, and indeed throughout the bank if people are not getting on, we face up to that.

'We are the only non-unionized bank in Ireland, and that is not by accident. And that will be seen as part of the culture within this bank to deal openly and up front with personnel problems. Personnel problems in the sense where people are just not pulling their weight. We don't have any statutory pay levels. In other words people don't automatically go from one grade to another grade at the end of the year.'

The significant growth in the bank was not raising any concerns within the Central Bank of Ireland, FitzPatrick told *Wall Street Transcript*: 'I mean, big brother is always there, and while we might complain about their ever-increasing appetite for internal controls, internal figures and things like that, we realize that we need them and we're dealing with peoples' monies, and they entrust us and give them to us for trust, and so they've got to be looked after. So while there might have been from time to time gripes with demands from big brother, we don't see it as a big problem, and we don't see that gaining momentum and becoming prohibitive.'

Anglo continued to pick off smaller banks, buying Ansbacher in 1996 and Smurfit Paribas in 1999. Through its acquisitions up to that point, FitzPatrick had entered into business relationships with some of the most influential and ambitious property developers in Ireland. Anglo also increased its exposure to the construction sector considerably. The Bailey brothers, Mick and Tom, had been clients of the original Irish Bank of Commerce. Joe O'Reilly, who would later build Ireland's largest shopping centre, Dundrum Town Centre, had been a client of Hill Samuel. Donegalman Pat Doherty, who owned a string of shopping centres in provincial Irish towns such as Portlaoise and Letterkenny, had been a client of Ansbacher. Sean Quinn, the cement tycoon who would go on to become Ireland's richest man through a business empire that also comprised hotels and insurance, banked with Smurfit Paribas. By the dawn of the new millennium, they were all Anglo clients.

FitzPatrick spread the net by poaching lending executives from other banks. Ulster Bank was building quite a portfolio of house builders, including Seamus Ross and Sean Reilly. FitzPatrick waded in and hired Kieran Dowling from Ulster, and Dowling brought the clients with him. Ross's company, Menolly Homes, would become the country's largest house builder by the middle of the next decade.

It was not just technology that boomed in the Ireland of the 1990s. One powerful manifestation of the Irish economic resurgence was the International Financial Services Centre. Built on derelict docklands, the IFSC attracted the back office and administrative functions of large global banks and insurers happy to avail of Ireland's keen 10 per cent corporation tax rate. This was the unheralded side of the boom. Technology jobs such as those created by Microsoft, Intel and Apple, and a plethora of investments by pharmaceutical companies, tended to dominate media coverage of the Irish economic story, but foreign direct investment in financial services, from 1979 to the end of the 1990s, matched that of US manufacturers.

In 1997 a new body, the Dublin Docklands Development Authority, was established to oversee the further redevelopment of 520 hectares in the docks. The original board included Jim Lacey, chief executive of National Irish Bank. With a few months, Lacey was forced to resign his job over a scandal involving the marketing of offshore investments to clients. He stepped down from the DDDA, and FitzPatrick was asked if he would consider joining the authority.

'This wasn't any big deal for me,' FitzPatrick recalls. 'Truly. I would have been underwhelmed to have been asked. I didn't see it as a big honour or anything.' FitzPatrick says, 'It was only when I met with Lar' – Lar Bradshaw, the DDDA chairman – that he saw the possibilities of the Docklands Authority. 'He was saying this was huge, look, we can build so many buildings down here. We can actually create a big vibrant community down here, a business community, and a living community.'

The Anglo boss decided to accept the post after meeting Bradshaw, and had lunch with the minister for the environment, Noel Dempsey, at the Commons restaurant on St Stephen's Green to discuss the job. FitzPatrick would become close friends with Bradshaw, and in 2004 invited him to become a director of the bank. The fortunes of agency and bank would overlap considerably in the years ahead, and in time the connection would become controversial.

As the millennium came to a close, the banking landscape in Ireland was changing. Bank of Ireland entered into merger talks with Alliance & Leicester, only for the deal to fail after news of the talks was leaked prematurely to the media. Irish Life, Ireland's largest life assurance company, purchased Irish Permanent, the country's largest building society.

Building societies were mutual organizations, owned by their members for the benefit of their members. But as the societies grew, and became more like banks, there was a drive to demutualize and float on the stock market, creating windfall gains for members. In the

1990s two building societies – Irish Permanent and First National, later renamed First Active – took this path.

After Irish Permanent was snaffled up by Irish Life, FitzPatrick trained his eye on First Active. Rumours of a possible deal first emerged in July 1999. The society was a sitting duck. Unlike Irish Permanent, its shares had performed poorly since floating on the market, and senior management, led by long-time chief executive John Smyth, were under pressure. Broadcaster Eamon Dunphy and Senator Shane Ross, both shareholders, began a popular campaign to oust management. At the company's annual general meeting in early 2000, Ross raised the market whispers about Anglo's interest in First Active.

'Everyone here has lost money,' Ross was reported in the *Irish Times* as telling the meeting. 'People would be much better off being looked after by the directors of Anglo.' Smyth resigned shortly afterwards, which served only to make First Active more vulnerable. Later in the year the two banks announced that they were in merger talks.

'It was very, very simple,' FitzPatrick says. First Active 'had a big load of retail depositors and a whole branch network right throughout Ireland. We weren't keen on branches but we were keen on its big, well-spread retail deposit book. We reckoned if we could get [the depositors], we wouldn't lose them, even if we closed branches. The plan was that Anglo would trim down the First Active branch network and cut the cost out at head-office level.'

It was also, FitzPatrick says, an opportunity to diversify. The bank was backing house developers such as Sean Mulryan of Ballymore and Seamus Ross of Menolly Homes. With First Active's core building-society business, it could also lend to the ultimate house buyer.

Above all else, though, the move was opportunistic. Anglo's share price was high and First Active's was foundering. The relative sizes of the two banks meant that the deal, under accounting rules, could be considered a merger rather than a takeover, but Anglo would be the dominant partner. The other benefit of a merger was that there would be no cash outlay: Anglo would effect the merger by offering First Active shareholders shares in Anglo.

'It was going nowhere at a cheap price and it could be a paper deal with very little cash involved,' says FitzPatrick. 'We could use our paper. They didn't have a managing director in situ. They didn't have a finance director. Cormac McCarthy was there, who I got on extremely well with during that period. It was an attractive deal for us.'

But the markets, and the media, hated the deal from the outset. Why was high-flying Anglo getting down and dirty with a former building society? Margins on home loans were far slimmer than in business banking, and were eroded further with the arrival of Bank of Scotland into the Irish mortgage market in 1999. The British bank had a hugely disruptive effect on the mortgage market, selling tracker mortgages over the telephone that massively undercut other players. It made no sense to many analysts that Anglo would want to get into mortgage lending.

'The media and the analysts took it negatively,' says FitzPatrick. 'They saw it as a switch in direction. We were sort of saying it wasn't a switch in direction . . . We were going to have two platforms: Anglo Irish Bank there and we were going to have this retail branch network there. We were going to do the [business] lending in the normal way.'

FitzPatrick believed that investors could be won over. The problem lay in convincing the boards of the two organizations that it was a good deal. Under the proposal, Anglo would basically take over the management of the group. FitzPatrick would become chief executive of the merged bank; Willie McAteer, finance director; and Tiarnan O'Mahoney, operations director. To coax the First Active board, its chairman, John Callaghan, was offered the post of chairman of the merged bank.

This proved a sticking point for the Anglo board, who were unhappy with the deal. Tony O'Brien, the chief executive of Cantrell & Cochrane, had been appointed chairman of Anglo a year previously, replacing Gerry Murphy, FitzPatrick's long-time mentor. O'Brien was a respected figure in the business community. Callaghan, a former partner in KPMG, was under fire, not just from Ross and Dunphy.

FitzPatrick approached Tony O'Brien. 'I had breakfast with him and I said, Lookit, Tony, you have got to do the big thing here. You have got to resign. He said, Sean, that is not up to you, it is up to the board. I said absolutely. The board said no, we want O'Brien as chairman.'

FitzPatrick tried to get Callaghan to accept the chair for a six-month period, after which he would stand down and make way for O'Brien. He refused. 'I discussed it with the executives and we just said we weren't going forward with [the merger]. We pulled it.'

There would be other opportunities. Months after the talks with First Active ended, FitzPatrick got a call from Phil Flynn, chairman of ICC Bank, a state-owned development bank. The government had put ICC up for sale, and a clear favourite was emerging in the form of Bank of Scotland. Flynn tried to get Anglo to enter late into the bidding and create a bit of bid tension.

Bank of Scotland's bid was being managed by a familiar foe. Mark Duffy had left Anglo to head up Equity Bank, a small niche lender. At Anglo, Duffy had been seen as being very good at structuring deals, but until he took over at Bank of Scotland (Ireland) he was not considered much of a threat to Anglo's runaway growth. Buying ICC would represent a big step up, however. The development bank backed some of the most successful entrepreneurs in the country. It also lent to hoteliers and publicans, one of Anglo's hunting grounds.

FitzPatrick quickly assembled a team of advisers to mount a rival bid. Peter Crowley of Investment Bank of Ireland, solicitors firm Arthur Cox and accountant Hugh Cooney were hired to devise a strategy. It was February 2001.

'We were sitting in the boardroom of Anglo Irish Bank, wondering what sort of bid would make a knock-out bid to take out Bank of Scotland. We were all sitting around, twelve people in a big room. My wife was ringing me at 6.30 p.m., asking me what time will I be home, we are having people for dinner tonight.

'I am saying, I won't be home until all hours. She was saying, How can you do this to me? I was saying, This is the way it goes. We are trying to buy ICC and you are going on about a dinner party. I can't legislate for that. I have too many things to do. I am right up to my eyes here. Leave me alone.

'So about three minutes past seven, she rings me and says, I am just after hearing the seven o'clock news. You are telling me you are going to buy ICC? It has just been sold to Bank of Scotland. So I arrive back in to the whole table, and say, By the way, guys, you know all this fucking work we have been doing? It is all over, my wife has told me, she has heard it on the news. That is gospel truth. We all burst out laughing and that was the end of the deal.'

3. The Magic of Anglo

'I was a fairly fastidious guy but it was easy and it was loose. I never read papers. If people weren't good, I shot them or fired them. If people were good, I kept them.'

By 2001 the bank that FitzPatrick built had become the lender of choice for a new entrepreneurial class in Ireland. The clients it had helped during the slump of the early 1990s were now building the office blocks that housed the technology companies that were driving the boom. And Anglo was lending money to the house builders who were selling homes to the workers who were working in those office blocks. The bank was booming. For the financial year ending 30 September 2001, total loans grew by more than 40 per cent year on year, and there was a commensurate rise in profitability, with earnings before tax rising by 42 per cent.

FitzPatrick received a once-off additional bonus of €950,000 to reward him for the bank's performance over the previous five years and also for signing a new agreement to remain on as chief executive for a minimum of three years. The bonus brought FitzPatrick's total pay package for the year to €2.1 million, making him by far the highest-paid banker in Ireland that year. He received more than the AIB and Bank of Ireland chief executives combined.

His star was firmly on the rise. *Business and Finance* magazine reported in May 2001 that FitzPatrick was one of a number of bankers who had been approached about the vacant position of chief executive of Bank of Ireland following the retirement of Maurice Keane. It is not known if the approach was a formal one; in any case, FitzPatrick did not entertain a career move.

There were some clouds on the horizon. The Irish economic miracle, as it was reported internationally, had been fuelled in part by a surge of investment in the country by US computer hardware and software companies. As the technology bubble burst and the Irish economy started to lose some of its steam, Anglo prudently increased its provisions for future loan losses by €55.3 million to €146 million. It was a purely precautionary measure. There was no sign of stress in its own loan book, the bank said in its annual report.

Amid all the hoopla, there were sceptics, at rival banks and among the media. Michael Murray, a banker-turned-journalist, noted, in the *Sunday Business Post*, Anglo's 'canny ability to spot winners' and 'then go the extra mile to share the risk and the reward on individual projects'. This was a recipe for success – 'unless of course the extra mile is the most dangerous one. In banking, it often is.'

Murray also began to probe the Anglo loan book. In a presentation, FitzPatrick highlighted a pie chart that showed that 20 per cent of Anglo's loans related to property lending. A further 19 per cent, however, was classed within the category of lending to 'professionals' – architects, solicitors, accountants and others. Murray suggested that much of this lending was also property related. A further chunk of the loan book was categorized as bridging loans; again, Murray asked, what proportion of these loans was also property related? He felt that Anglo was muddying the water in how it classified its loans, and that property loomed far larger in the mix than the bank was letting on. Whether FitzPatrick would prove the sceptics wrong, Murray concluded, would depend on what precisely was in the 'rich and varied pie'.

The rich and varied pie now included some of the biggest names in Irish business. Denis O'Brien remembers being backed by Anglo in the early 1990s when, coming off the back of the failure of a home-shopping channel, he needed cash to launch a radio station, 98FM. O'Brien personally guaranteed the loan, but he later recalled that it was a 'gutsy' loan for Anglo to give and recounted how the bank had 'stuck by us'. As with a great many Irish business people, loyalty ranks high among O'Brien's guiding principles. O'Brien became a billionaire through his telecom interests in Ireland and the Caribbean, and Anglo would become one of his main personal lenders.

The bank was also an early backer of Dermot Desmond, the founder of NCB Stockbrokers and one of the country's most successful – and controversial – businessmen. One of Desmond's most high-profile and successful investments was a 20 per cent stake in Esat Digifone, the company set up by O'Brien to bid for Ireland's second mobile telephony licence. When O'Brien submitted his bid with the Norwegian telecom operator Telenor, the bidding consortium was to include a number of financial institutions. In the end, however, the sole financial institution to take a stake in Digifone was Desmond's International Investment and Underwriting. When presenting his financial bona fides to the Department of Communications, Desmond noted the availability of a £10 million loan facility from Anglo Irish Bank.

FitzPatrick would say that he never saw backing risk-takers of the calibre of O'Brien and Desmond as risky. It was a question of trust and knowing your customer. Talking to Ivor Kenny for his book *Achievers*, FitzPatrick said: 'I can lend to people into whose eyes I can look deeply and who's screaming at me "Sean, I need the money and I won't let you down." I have done that and have I been let down? Of course I have, because I didn't know my customer. And that's sore. It's betrayal. I've no problem lending to a person, knowing that there was risk in it, and if the risk goes wrong so be it. But where a guy screws me, I get really uptight.'

To ensure that Anglo was not betrayed, FitzPatrick became a pioneer of the personal guarantee in the Irish banking sector. This allowed the bank to seek recourse to a borrower's personal assets if the value of the underlying security dipped below the value of the loan.

'I would have been the driver of personal guarantees within Ireland,' he says. 'I never lent money without a personal guarantee. I used to say to the guys: if you are lending money to Tom Lyons, you have to have a situation where he dies before we die. We should be really well capable of bankrupting Tom Lyons, if he is not playing ball with us.'

The personal guarantee was designed to be a supplement to the normal security, and to concentrate the mind of the borrower. 'The personal guarantee was a mental thing,' FitzPatrick says. 'It was to keep the borrower focused all the time. It wasn't a case to say let's just take the personal guarantee and bugger the paperwork and bugger the due diligence ... Tom Lyons could say, Here you are, you are asking me for a personal guarantee, and I want to borrow €1 million off you and I am giving a property worth €3 million. I am giving you back-to-back on a deposit of €300,000 and now you want a personal guarantee. Why do you want it? We would say exactly, why would we need it? If you have all of that [security], why are you worried about giving it?'

Not everybody was happy to give a personal guarantee. Fitz-Patrick says that, in certain cases, the bank sought and received what he calls 'silent' personal guarantees: side letters from borrowers, personally guaranteeing debts to Anglo. The side letter would be kept separate from the ordinary facility letter, and was therefore unknown to other lenders. It was a highly questionable practice.

In any case, the personal guarantees – whether formal or 'silent' – were rarely called in. The economy was performing far too well, and Anglo's clients were making far too much money.

Noel Smyth, the well-known property and tax lawyer, was a long-standing Anglo client. He was an adviser to the Dunne family, owners of the Dunnes Stores retail group, and confidant of its senior member, Ben Dunne – who called Smyth his 'gunslinger'. Like many professionals, Smyth invested much of his considerable wealth in property. He bought up development sites across Dublin and invested in the UK property market. In 1995 he purchased Ben Dunne's shares in Dunloe plc, a quoted property company, and became its executive chairman; in 1998 he merged it with Ewart plc, a Belfast property company.

Dunloe Ewart owned prime development land, including a plot at Sir John Rogerson's Quay in Dublin's docklands, and Cherrywood, a large land bank in South Dublin, which was co-owned with British Land. But by 2002 Dunloe Ewart was a company under siege. Two dissident shareholders, property developers Liam Carroll and Philip Monahan, blocked Smyth's attempts to buy back shares in the company. Both men had gripes with Smyth. Carroll, a prolific and controversial builder of tiny apartments in Dublin city-centre, was underbidder for the Sir John Rogerson's Quay site. Monahan, who had been a client of Smyth for many years, felt the solicitor had pinched Dunne's stake in Dunloe from under his nose.

A third adversary arrived on the Dunloe share register in the form of Dermot Desmond. In the summer of 2002 Carroll, Monahan and Desmond voted to block a move by Smyth to buy out British Land's interest in Cherrywood. Cornered, Smyth decided to launch an all-out bid to take over the company. He turned to Anglo and FitzPatrick for help.

'This is gospel truth,' recalls FitzPatrick. 'I was going down to a Dublin Docklands Development Authority board meeting. It went on from four until seven thirty and I knew there was a meal afterwards, so I wouldn't be finished until half past nine. Noel Smyth rang me about half two and said, Sean, I need to talk to you urgently about Dunloe. I said, I can't. He said, Well, can you see me tonight? I said I could. I would be passing a pub out near where he lives. It is on the way out near Merrion Road, near Foxrock. The Galloping Green.'

When FitzPatrick arrived at the pub, Smyth asked him if he'd like a pint; FitzPatrick asked for a Budweiser. 'This was 2002, I had no problems having a drink,' he says. (FitzPatrick later developed diabetes.) 'He said, Lookit, Sean, I want to do something with Dunloe. You know I own 22 per cent of Dunloe. Dermot [Desmond] is in there and Liam Carroll is in there as well. I am now going to make an offer for it, to buy out every one of them.' FitzPatrick recalls: 'I am looking at him and I ask him: How are we fixed with you at the moment?'

As it happened, Smyth was 'fixed' well with the bank. He had loans out on various personally owned properties, but the value of the properties exceeded the amount owed on the loans, giving Smyth net equity of €30 million with Anglo.

'I said, Would I be able to see that easily? He said, Yeah, no problems at all. Lookit, Sean, I have been speaking to Bank of Ireland and if I am going to make an offer of 42.5 cent [per share], I have got to raise €170 million for the other 75 per cent [actually 78 per cent]. I have got it underwritten to the tune of €153 million and I need

another €17 million. You know yourself, Sean, it's the last €17 million
that is always the hardest to raise.

'I am suddenly looking at him in a different way because I am
totally relieved. I said, Noel, if you have €30 million of equity in
there and if we get a second charge on a couple of other things you
are going to give us, there is no problems. We will give you the €17
million.

'He said, I don't actually need the cash, I just need the guarantee
from you guys that you will give the €17 million.

'I said, Absolutely guaranteed. I will talk to the guys [in the bank]
tomorrow and I might even be able to come back to you tonight. It
was about 10.30.

'Now, he said, Sean, what about fees? I said, Yeah, we won't charge
you a penny. He looked at me and he said, What? . . . Why, Sean? I
said, You know what, Noel, we have been doing business for a long
time . . . and I didn't really like Noel Smyth at this time, but I said,
There are very few roads with no turns. It will come back.'

The men shook hands. Smyth's surprise was genuine: Anglo's
business model was based on earning big fees, which it could com-
mand in return for quick lending decisions; other banks charged
lower fees, but lost business to Anglo because they did not move as
quickly. Now FitzPatrick was deviating from the model. He rang
Peter Butler, a senior lending executive, and asked: 'Will you meet
Noel Smyth tomorrow? I think it is a good deal for us. [Butler]
said, Yeah. I said, By the way, no fees. Peter said, What? Ah, Sean.
I said, Lookit, Peter, there will be more deals and this is the way
we'll get them.'

Smyth made his offer for Dunloe Ewart on 25 October. One hour
before the offer was submitted to the Stock Exchange, Desmond
went into the market and purchased 9 million shares in the company.
The timing of the share purchase became the subject of a Stock
Exchange investigation, but nothing untoward was found.

It was clear, though, that Desmond was intent on torpedoing
Smyth's bid. Over the next two weeks he increased his stake to 16 per
cent, buying at a price above the Smyth offer. Desmond did not make
a competing bid, but, as he continued to buy at over 42 cents, Smyth's

lower offer became less attractive. Desmond also called for Smyth and the non-executive directors who had recommended his offer to stand down. Smyth, he said, was trying to get Dunloe on the cheap.

FitzPatrick says that Desmond rang him in late October, just as the Dunloe Ewart battle was reaching its climax. Celtic, the Glasgow football club part-owned by Desmond, was playing away to Blackburn Rovers in a UEFA Cup match on 1 November. Desmond was flying a party over to England for the match by executive jet.

'He said . . . Come out to the airport, about five or half five or six. We will be flying to Blackburn. There will a few guys coming. Do you want to bring your son or daughter? I said, I would love to bring my daughter. He said, Great, I will bring my son.

'It was lashing out of the heavens, coming down in torrents. I said to him, Is this match going to be on? He said, Yeah, yeah, it's bad here in Ireland, so you want to leave a bit early for the airport. I got Sarah in and we made the airport by 5.30 or 5.45. Got out to the airport and met Dermot. He said, Paschal Taggart was supposed to come, but couldn't make it.'

Taggart is an accountant and deal-maker, a famously gregarious but shrewd individual, and a good friend of Desmond.

'We went to the match. We met Alex Ferguson [the Manchester United manager], and a great singer, a great Celtic fan, Rod Stewart. We met everyone. We were in the directors' box, the whole lot. We met [television pundit and former footballer] Mark Lawrenson. The lot. Great crack. In and out. It was one celebrity after another. We get back into the plane at 11.30 to fly back to Dublin. Dermot says to me, I want to ask you a favour. You are a member down in the K Club? I said, Yeah.'

According to FitzPatrick, Desmond told him that he was opposing Noel Smyth's elevation to the captaincy of the club and needed thirty votes from members to block it.

Desmond's animosity toward Smyth was well known. Smyth had revealed to the McCracken Tribunal that Ben Dunne had given Charles Haughey €1.3 million between 1991 and 1994. Haughey initially denied receiving the gift, but was later forced to admit accepting the money.

Desmond was a huge admirer of Haughey and had worked with the former Taoiseach on the creation of the IFSC. Smyth's role in Haughey's disgrace would have rankled. The two men also had differences over a £250,000 legal bill, which related to a previous tribunal of investigation that had probed Desmond's role in a Ballsbridge property deal.

A year previously Desmond had opposed Smyth when he put his name forward to become deputy captain of the K Club, the posh golf club and designated Ryder Cup venue where membership fees were close to €40,000. Smyth won the vote and became deputy captain. Desmond was now trying to block Smyth's automatic elevation to the role of captain.

'He said: Will you give me a hand with that, Sean? I said, Yes, I will . . .

'Next day, he rang me. He said, Sean, can you get two or three other guys? I said, Yeah. So I ring Fintan Drury [whom he had recently appointed as a director of Anglo]. He says, I was a member of the K Club but I am no longer. I ring another guy, he said to me, Sean, get out of this. This is going to be dirty. This is going to be very dirty. Don't ever tell Dermot you rang me, please. I said, OK, I won't.

'I got back to Dermot and told him, One guy said no, he wasn't going to do it, and Fintan Drury is no longer a member. But I am going to do it . . .'

The day after FitzPatrick and Desmond returned from the Blackburn excursion, it was announced to the Stock Exchange that Paschal Taggart – the missing guest on the football trip – had agreed to buy Noel Smyth's 27 per cent stake in Dunloe at a price of 45 cents per share. To the Dunloe watchers in the media, it was an entirely unexpected turn of events. Smyth said that he was selling the shares in the best interest of the remaining small shareholders. Taggart turned to Anglo to finance the deal.

'Paschal came in to me the next day. I went through the deal with him. I said, Paschal, what are you paying for the shares? I forget what he is paying, €25 or €30 million. [The actual figure was €45 million.] I said, OK, and then you are going to sell them on? He said, Yeah.

'I said, We are going to make a profit on this. I am going to charge you a 2 per cent fee. I said, You take it, or you don't take it. He said, OK, I will take it.

'They were drawing the money down and I said, Fuck this, I haven't spoken to Noel Smyth. He will know I gave you the money. I walked out of the room. I picked up the phone and I rang Noel Smyth. I said, Noel, two things. One, Paschal Taggart came in to me yesterday and said he has agreed with you to buy the shares. I am telling you, notwithstanding that we are guaranteeing you, I said we are going to lend him the money. He said, Sean, that makes me certain that I will get my money sooner than any other bank.

'That is the number one. The second thing I need to tell you is that I am going to a special meeting down in the K Club next week to vote against you. He said, Sean, remember you said to me about the roads and the turns. Sean, I know who has put his hand on your shoulder. You did me a favour that I will never forget. I have no problems with that at all.

'That was that. I said, Thank you very much, and that was it. We were very close after that, really friendly, not a meaningful friendship but a decent friendship.

'Now we had the money lent to Paschal Taggart. The next thing, Dermot rings me and says, Reorganize everything. Liam Carroll now is going to buy my shares and Paschal's shares.' Carroll, too, sought finance from Anglo. 'I met him. He came in and he had a notebook, open-necked shirt. I didn't like him at all. I knew I wasn't getting on with him, so instead of having a row, I got Kieran Duggan [a lending manager at the bank] to take him away and do the deal with him.'

By the end of November, Carroll had tabled an offer of 50 cents per share for Dunloe Ewart. Taggart accepted, as did the other Dunloe shareholders. Smyth had bagged a profit of €30 million on the sale of his shares. The solicitor also withdrew his candidacy for the captaincy of the K Club.

While the K Club may have been personal, Dunloe was strictly business. Taggart and Desmond made a very nice return on their investments. The whole affair was also very profitable for Anglo Irish Bank.

'We did the deal,' FitzPatrick says. 'We financed the whole of Dunloe. From starting off charging no fee for a €17 million guarantee to the whole buyout. We ended up getting fees and interest from Paschal Taggart and fees and a good interest rate from Liam Carroll for the whole deal.

'I told the true story to Noel Smyth, told him absolutely everything before the deal was done. I did everything right. You know why I told Noel Smyth? Because I knew it would come out at the end of the day. Why not front up with Noel Smyth? I would get the kudos from Noel Smyth, which I did not expect, but I did. It is the easiest thing in the world: telling the truth straight out.

'Noel Smyth walked away with a smile on his face and thinking I was a great guy. That was my talent.'

The Dunloe Ewart takeover was seen as a colourful affair. Taggart saw his part as that of an 'honest broker' and insisted that he acted independently at all times. He believed that he was trying to break an impasse between the factions at a public company.

It did not bother FitzPatrick that the bank was acting on both sides of the deal. When pressed on the transaction, he gets slightly agitated.

'There was nothing wrong with that at all . . . Here was a guy who owned 25 per cent and was trying to buy the other 75 per cent [actually 22 per cent and 78 per cent]. We said we will give you the money for that guarantee. Dermot Desmond scuppered the deal.

'Everyone made a lot of money including your man Liam Carroll. That is the whole point here. Deals could be done . . . done well, done efficiently. It was done clean and it was a done deal. That was the magic of Anglo.'

The magic was apparent in the next year's annual results. The giant lending machine continued to crank up huge profits in 2003.

Over the course of the year, Anglo's share price jumped 80 per cent. *IR Magazine*, which runs an annual poll to rate how public companies in the UK and Ireland communicate with investors, awarded Anglo Irish Bank its highest accolade, the Grand Prix. A Sunday newspaper poll of analysts rated FitzPatrick the country's best chief executive; the Anglo boss took 71 per cent of the total poll, well ahead of Michael O'Leary of Ryanair and Denis O'Brien.

The gospel was spreading. In 2000 less than 5 per cent of Anglo's big institutional shareholders had been based in the US. By 2003 that proportion had risen to 20 per cent. Anglo Irish Bank had broken America, where one of its rising young executives, David Drumm, had established an office in Boston and was furiously growing its lending book.

FitzPatrick, finance director Willie McAteer and the rest of the senior management relentlessly 'beat the street', meeting investors and getting the Anglo story across. 'We operate in greater Ireland,' McAteer told *Financial News* in an interview. 'London is eastern Ireland, Boston is western Ireland and then there's mainland Ireland. Culturally they are very similar regions; it would terrify us to lend money in France, for example.'

The success created huge wealth for FitzPatrick and his management team. Five directors reaped a collective €9 million paper profit when they exercised share options in 2003. FitzPatrick ended the year with 3.8 million shares worth close to €50 million. The following February, FitzPatrick took some money 'off the table' when he sold 2 million shares worth €27 million. At the same time, two other Anglo executives – Peter Killen, who was retiring, and John Rowan – also sold some shares, making €9 million and €3 million respectively.

FitzPatrick was now a very wealthy individual.

An analysis of the share register by the *Sunday Independent* showed that at least thirty people held Anglo shares worth over €1 million. These were just the individuals who held the shares in their own names; a great many private investors held Anglo shares through anonymous stockbroker accounts. Two sisters, Alice and Elizabeth Doyle, with an address in central Dublin, owned 1.86 million Anglo Irish Bank shares, worth almost €20 million at the end of 2003.

The Anglo staff, which by this time numbered 1,000 in total, also shared in the bank's success. A scheme launched in 2000 allowed employees to save a maximum of €317 per month out of their salaries to buy shares in the company at a 25 per cent discount on the market price that prevailed at the time the scheme was launched. Ninety per cent of staff participated, and 80 per cent of those availed themselves of the maximum saving. In total, at the end of 2003 this scheme held options in over 2.1 million shares. Employees had bought shares for as low a price as €1.79; by the end of 2003 the stock was trading well over €11. Separately, the granting of share options was also widespread within the bank. Again, by the end of 2003 staff held lucrative options to buy 6 million shares priced between €1.09 and €6.70, and were sitting on massive paper profit. Many staff also simply purchased bank stock in the market with their own money.

'People have been buying shares all along,' Willie McAteer told the *Sunday Tribune*. 'They identify with the company. We don't push people into buying.'

Staff, including management and directors, owned 9 per cent of the bank by the end of 2003. Their shares were worth €400 million.

Widespread staff ownership and performance-related pay were part of the incentive-driven and proprietary culture that FitzPatrick was keen to engender. It permeated every level of the bank's operations. Some 35 to 40 per cent of staff cost at Anglo in 2003 was variable – in other words, it consisted of bonuses linked to the amount of business written and the overall performance of the bank.

The ownership culture did not just relate to pay. Lending executives were made to feel that it was their own money that they were lending. Credit committee meetings were held in the bank's headquarters on St Stephen's Green every Thursday afternoon and Friday morning. Each lending team consisted of six members, and one member from each team attended the credit committee, where, in a highly pressurized atmosphere, every loan issued by the bank was discussed.

At other banks, loan applications worked their way through a series of stages, from branch to regional office to head office. At Anglo, the officer who took the loan application made a presentation directly to the credit committee, outlining why the bank should advance the money and how the borrower would be able to pay the money back. It was the job of other lending-team representatives to pick holes in the loan applications. Debate was rigorous and often heated. The process was designed to ensure that the loan officer took personal responsibility for the loan. He who writes the loan, owns the loan, was an Anglo commandment.

This ownership culture, FitzPatrick believed, also served to strengthen the relationship between the borrower and the bank, because it was the individual loan officers who sat down face to face with clients. And that personal relationship, he believed, meant that the bank had a better chance of getting its money back.

Junior loan officers were invited to attend credit committee, so they could become immersed in the culture of the bank. A former Anglo employee remembers how 'Sean would tear strips off you.' In an interview in 2007 David Drumm, who had succeeded FitzPatrick as chief executive, said of the credit committee meetings, 'It is terrifying, but it is the real world. It is the only way to learn how to lend. We don't like surprises here. If you have a problem, then share it. A problem shared is a problem halved. Hide it and you will get sacked, simple as that.'

Decisions were taken quickly. Famously, FitzPatrick would say that, unlike its larger rivals in the Irish market, Anglo did not do 'the slow no'. But Anglo also boasted of its diligence. In 2003 FitzPatrick explained to investors at a Merrill Lynch banking conference the 'three simple principles of basic banking': cash flow, security and recourse. Anglo, he claimed, lent only where the underlying asset generated cash, where the bank could take good security, and where it could seek recourse against the borrower's other assets through personal guarantees. International investors were convinced. Bear Stearns issued a research note to investors in late 2003 stating that the credit culture at Anglo was 'focused on accountability and due diligence' and 'has been crucial to Anglo's success'. This reads very ironically now, after the demise of both Bear Stearns and Anglo; but it reflected the general view of Anglo at the time.

In the early days of the new millennium, the bank was gaining a reputation for generous entertaining and corporate hospitality – golf trips and excursions to sporting and cultural events. Anglo was a workplace where the philosophy of work hard, play hard was actively encouraged. FitzPatrick tried to avoid most of the outings;

he says he did not want to upstage his lenders. But there was one event he never missed.

'We used to have a huge big golf outing out in Druids Glen [in Co. Wicklow] with the top people in Ireland probably,' he says. 'They were huge, enormous, you would have Gerry Gannon, Denis [O'Brien], David Drumm, Kyran McLaughlin [from Davy stock-brokers], [Derek] Quinlan. Sean Mulryan I am sure would have been there. You name them, all the top names would have been there.'

Every year after the golf outing Anglo hosted a dinner for clients. Michael Soden, the man appointed to succeed Keane at Bank of Ireland, was invited to the dinner in 2005. It was a year after Soden had been forced to stand down as the bank's boss for accessing Las Vegas escort sites on the internet while at work. 'I used to slag people,' FitzPatrick recalls. 'I brought Michael Soden to that one year after he was fucked out of Bank of Ireland. I actually arranged with him I was going to slag him. We agreed. I said to him, I think it would be better that way. Rather than pretend you are not here, say you are here. Say you came in at great expense from Las Vegas. That is what we did. There was laughter. Then we moved on. He thanked me afterwards.'

The annual dinner increasingly played host to the new elite, Ireland's burgeoning band of property developers. Contrary to popular perception, FitzPatrick says that he did not know all the developers well. This he put down to Anglo's culture of delegation. 'My job was actually creating the conditions for other people to work and thrive,' he says. 'I gave huge autonomy, genuinely, I gave a huge amount to people to do the job. If they were good, I gave them more power. If they were bad, I tried to fire them. I was huge into people . . . The difference between Anglo and, say, AIB was not the product – in other words, money. It was the people and the way they dealt with the customer base. That was the difference. That might have been the big mistake we made, but that was the difference.'

The bank went to considerable lengths to foster good relationships with its clients. Brian Carey can recall meeting an Anglo executive one April Monday morning. His weekend had involved a trip to Glasgow for a football match between Rangers and Celtic, followed by a quick flight to Milan to catch a Formula One Grand Prix and then a match at the San Siro football stadium. All of these events involved entertaining clients.

'I would bring staff in for breakfast. I would meet people every morning for breakfast and I would talk to them, not about the customers but about themselves,' FitzPatrick recalls. 'How they were getting on? How were the young people coming through? Could we get better people in? Were there good people in other banks? How were they getting on with other people? How were they getting on with their bosses? How were they getting on at home?'

The success of FitzPatrick's relationship-banking model did not go unnoticed by other banks.

Bank of Scotland (Ireland), led by former Anglo executive Mark Duffy, was making big strides into FitzPatrick's patch. In 2003 BoSI's pre-tax profits rose by 36 per cent to €157.1 million – twice what they were three years previously when the bank acquired ICC.

Loans were up 17 per cent to €8.19 billion. BoSI was setting aside only €18.4 million for bad debts, representing just 0.24 per cent of loans. BoSI never bothered building a deposit base to fund its lending; instead it financed its massive loan expansion through its parent and the wholesale money markets. By the time the bank closed in Ireland in 2010, its loan-to-deposit ratio was close to 500 per cent, compared to the traditional ratio of 125 per cent.

AIB, the country's biggest bank, was particularly rattled by Anglo's rapid advance. Chief executive Michael Buckley put Anglo firmly in his cross hairs.

In 2003 AIB's loan book grew by 28 per cent, despite the fact that deposits grew by only 9 per cent. In a February 2004 interview Buckley told the *Sunday Business Post* that he had set up a special 'win-back' team to recover business lost to Anglo.

'That's what you should do, isn't it?' he said.

Bank of Ireland started to make similar moves, albeit at a slower pace. Rival executives began to court developers in the manner of Anglo, flying them by private jet to golf tournaments and Premiership soccer games, and throwing lavish dinners in order to win their business. (AIB infamously chartered a jet to ferry eighty clients to the

2008 Ryder Cup in Kentucky at an estimated cost of €1.5 million, and this after the onset of the credit crunch.)

Chasing Anglo was the new name of the game. Ireland's investors and developers found plenty of uses for the wall of money now coming their way. If the hallmark of Ireland's boom during the 1990s was an unprecedented flow of inward investment, then the early years of the new millennium brought a dramatic flow of Irish wealth outside of Ireland. Most of the money found its way into property.

Irish property investors planted a big flag in the London property market, and Anglo was instrumental in this. Property consultants DTZ estimated that, in the mid 1990s, the level of Irish investment in European property markets was less than €100 million. In 2002 Irish investors put £1.2 billion into UK commercial property alone. In the first three quarters of that year, Irish investors were the most active players on the UK commercial-property scene.

By 2006 the Irish investment in UK commercial property had ballooned, according to estate agents CBRE, to €5.5 billion. Historically low interest rates drove the investment. Ireland's membership of the eurozone meant that interest rates were set by the European Central Bank in Frankfurt, and not by the Irish Central Bank. Upon Ireland joining the euro in 1999, interest rates fell from 6 per cent to 3 per cent. In 2005, as the investment boom raced towards its peak, rates fell as low as 2 per cent. Using an economic model known as the Taylor Rule, Davy economist Rossa White estimates that in early 2005 a more appropriate rate would have been 6 per cent, to take some of the heat out of the boom. Instead, because the ECB interest rate was set to meet the needs of the eurozone as a whole, Ireland had ultra-low interest rates that encouraged ever more borrowing. For investors, money from the bank was costing 4 per cent, while properties in London were yielding a rental return of 6 per cent. A wall of Irish money migrated to Britain. All the Irish banks were willing to finance what was erroneously viewed as the 'diversification' of Irish developers' and investors' portfolios. They were simply heightening their exposure to the same class of investments.

A consortium of Irish investors assembled by Kevin Warren, a tax

adviser, and which included Larry Goodman, the beef baron, purchased the offices of Goldman Sachs on Fleet Street. Sean Mulryan, a
house-builder client of Anglo's, originally from Roscommon, emerged
as one of the most prominent developers in the booming docklands;
his Ballymore Properties logo was visible right across the East End of
London.

Arguably, no Irish property figure made as big a splash in London
as Derek Quinlan. A former tax official, Quinlan cut his teeth setting
up investment deals for professionals in Ireland. Early in his career he
specialized in property transactions that carried generous government tax breaks, many of them introduced or maintained by
FitzPatrick's old accountant friend, Charlie McCreevy.

In the 1980s and 1990s the country needed car parks, hotels and
nursing homes, so the state created tax breaks to encourage their
development. There were also tax breaks for 'urban renewal' (a
broadly applied concept) and for the construction of the IFSC. It was
the packaging of these deals, which often involved helping clients
access credit, that made Quinlan's name. His clientele was a who's
who of Irish society.

His most high-profile deal in Ireland was arguably the funding
of Ireland's first five-star hotel, the Four Seasons in Ballsbridge,
which opened in 2001. Quinlan assembled a group of 'hinwris' –
high-net-worth individuals – to purchase the prestigious development,
with the help of Anglo. The hinwris included Lar Bradshaw, chairman of the Dublin Docklands Development Authority (and later an
Anglo director), and Dermot Gleeson, a former attorney general
who would be appointed chairman of the country's biggest bank,
AIB, in 2003. After the Four Seasons project ran into financial difficulties in 2000, Anglo stepped in to ensure the hotel was built and the
investors were not wiped out.

Anglo was a banker to a great many of Quinlan's clients and
financed many of his investment deals. Sean FitzPatrick was also a
Quinlan client. In 1998 FitzPatrick put £885,000 into the Mercury
Partnership, a Quinlan investment group that purchased an office
building in George's Dock in Dublin. Four years later he invested
€2.4 million in another Dublin docklands office block, Harbour-

master 3, with Kevin Warren. FitzPatrick describes these as 'tax deals', where investors made use of capital allowances that drastically reduced their income tax bill.

In April 2004 Quinlan landed what was arguably the single biggest property coup of the entire Celtic Tiger period. In buying the Savoy Hotel Group from Blackstone, the US private-equity company, Quinlan not only bought a slice of the British establishment; he also outmanoeuvred an immensely rich rival bidder, Prince Bin Alaweed.

What landed the deal for Quinlan ahead of the Saudi billionaire was the speed at which he assembled both his investors and his finance. The lead banker was Anglo, and FitzPatrick played a far more prominent role in the Savoy deal than newspapers at the time recorded.

Quinlan assembled a suitably powerful group to back his purchase of the Savoy. It included Paddy McKillen, the developer behind the Jervis shopping centre in Dublin city-centre and also part-owner of a retail centre in London's Covent Garden. The Green family, a rich Manchester merchant family, also agreed to invest, as did John McColgan and Moya Doherty, the creators of *Riverdance*. The final investors in the original group put together by Quinlan were Lochlann Quinn and Martin Naughton, the founders of Glen Dimplex, the global electrical-goods manufacturers. Quinn and Naughton also own a half-share in Dublin's Merrion Hotel, a five-star hotel that houses probably the country's most celebrated restaurant, Patrick Guilbaud's. Naughton and Quinn seemed ideal partners for the Savoy venture, but the two men cooled on the deal and decided not to proceed.

FitzPatrick says that Quinlan, who had placed a large deposit with Blackstone, needed total equity from investors of £110 million and would borrow £600 million, financed by Anglo as lead banker and with support from Bank of Ireland. There were, FitzPatrick remembers, four 'twenty-five millions' of equity from other investors, and Quinlan would invest only £10 million for his share. The financier's lower upfront investment reflected his 'carry', or finder's fee. With Naughton and Quinn out, the financier was short £25 million.

'What happened was Kieran Duggan came in to me,' FitzPatrick recalls. 'He said if they don't put the money up, now, by Friday, Quinlan loses his deposit. I said, Why don't you get the private bank involved? Get on to Tiarnan [O'Mahoney]. Rustle up ten guys at £2.5 million each or three guys with £8 million, whatever you want. We shouldn't just stand idly by, we should help the guy.

'[Duggan] rang the private bank. They said yeah, yeah, that sounds great. So then he went to credit committee. They said that's all very good but who are the guys in the private bank who are going to do this? I said I don't know but we will get someone. They said no, no, no, they want someone to underwrite it.

'So [Duggan] comes back to me and says, Will you underwrite it, Sean? I said, What do you mean? Do you want me to go in for it? Do you want me to become a partner? He said yeah.'

FitzPatrick's net worth at this stage was well over €50 million, including the proceeds of his February 2004 share sale, which was still sitting in the bank. 'I said, I don't want to become a partner for 25 per cent. I will get three guys. I rang Denis [O'Brien]: No. I rang Gary McGann [Smurfit Kappa chief executive and an Anglo director]: No. I rang Lar Bradshaw. He said, Yeah, but I have no money. I said, Don't worry, I will look after you on that.

'I rang Pat Doherty [a Donegal developer]. He knew nothing about it, but he said, Yeah, you can count me in . . . I said, Right, there we are, each of us is in for a third of £25 million. It was just the three of us.'

FitzPatrick says that the strategy agreed between the members of Quinlan's consortium was that the Savoy Hotel, the flagship property, was to be sold on almost straight away. Two other hotels in the group, the Berkeley and the Connaught, would be sold at a later stage, and the consortium would keep Claridge's, another five-star hotel. With this approach, FitzPatrick recalls, the consortium calculated that 'We would all get our money back and we would each have a 20 per cent stake in Claridge's for zilch. I said, I am your man, I will do that.'

Quinlan, a connoisseur of fine food and wine, hosted a meeting of investors at Claridge's. Geraldine McKenna, the Savoy Group's director of marketing and sales, made a presentation to the investors. 'She was saying this is a great buy, a great purchase. We are going to get on great. This is our marketing team. I will introduce you to them . . .' FitzPatrick remembers that he asked what kind of people stay in Claridge's, and that McKenna mentioned the name of a well-known Middle Eastern sheik. 'She said oh yeah, he would come across during the summer to get his appendix done or to get out of the heat and the sun. He would bring his family and entourage, which would be 300 people or so, and they would take the whole top floor.

'I could see nothing but difficulty in all this. I know nothing about hotels. I am looking around the place. Paddy McKillen said [he] was down in the car park last night and you know what, the ceiling is eighteen feet high. I said, What does that mean? He said, What does that mean? That means that we could put a gym or bar in there, Sean, instead of a car park.

'And then you know we have Joe Bloggs in there cutting hair, fuck him out and we get in Fabiola. Then there is a jeweller down there called John Doe, fuck him out and we will get in Cartier. The guys were bang, bang, bang.'

The investors had developed a taste for the luxury-hotel business. The Savoy was to be sold to Bin Alaweed, the underbidder for the group, and the proceeds would be used to reduce debt taken on in the deal. But it was clear to FitzPatrick from the presentations and from conversations with fellow investors that the strategy had changed. The intention now was to retain the other three five-star hotels and perhaps even buy more at a later stage.

'I said, I don't like this, I want out. I rang Lar and he said, OK, I agree with you. Pat Doherty? He was just so far away from the deal, I hardly told him what was going on. I said to Lar, we should just get our money back plus maybe £2.5 million or £2 million.'

FitzPatrick recalls that Bradshaw, citing the size of the profits the Quinlan group stood to make as a result of acquiring the Savoy Group, wanted to push for a return of £15 million, or £5 million for each of the three members of the group, for providing the final £25 million the consortium had required to do the deal.

'I said, Lar, look, 15 million is too rich, we should settle for 10 or maybe 9 million. Three million each. He said no, no, no. I said, Lar, lookit, we are being stupid here. I hear what your arguments are, and, as you say, they are robust. But they are academic. That is all they are, Lar. They haven't even sold the Savoy. We don't know what these other hotels are worth.'

FitzPatrick took over the negotiations. Quinlan, he recalls, 'got down to £11 million' pretty quickly. I said, Well, you know, we will sell [our stake] to you for £13.5 million. I nearly got him to that. I couldn't believe it. He was dead simple to deal with. We ended up doing the deal for £12.1 million. Lar got a third of that, I got a third of it and your man [Doherty] got a third of it. We got that without putting a penny out.'

The three men had made £4 million each in a matter of months, their shares in the Savoy Hotel Group deal purchased by the other members of the consortium. In retrospect, FitzPatrick accepts that it was highly unusual for a bank's chief executive to rescue one of the bank's deals with his own money, and that this was not good practice.

'I was trying to help Quinlan out of a problem,' he says. 'And then I was sucked in because they needed it underwritten. I tried to pass it around to a few guys. No one would take it. That was my first introduction to doing a deal with Lar. It was the first big money Lar ever made. The first big money I ever made in some ways.'

He insists that it was not his original intention to flip the shares so quickly, and that he'd decided to do so only after the investors' strategy changed. 'I said, That was not the deal I went into. I am looking around and saying I couldn't see a hotelier among any of these people, in Quinlan or Paddy McKillen or any of them.'

FitzPatrick says his involvement in the Savoy deal was not inconsistent with the culture of the bank. 'I was a fairly fastidious guy but it was easy and it was loose. I never read papers. If people weren't good, I shot them or fired them. If people were good, I kept them.

'It was very much lending your own money and all that. It sounds frivolous but that was what it was. I was ready to put my own money up . . . I had the cash and that was it. Then I said I want out of it and I got out of it and I made a lot of money.'

The Savoy deal must have planted ideas in FitzPatrick's head. He had already signalled to the market in late 2003 that he was planning to step down as chief executive of Anglo by the beginning of 2005 to concentrate on his personal interests. Ireland was bristling with money-making schemes and high rollers. Money was cheap, and the appetite for risk seemed bottomless.

FitzPatrick felt it was time to create a little bit of his own magic.

4. The Succession

'The real thing in life was not to be bright, it was to be lucky.
I was lucky.'

The ballroom of the Four Seasons Hotel in Ballsbridge, the country's
wealthiest suburb, was packed to capacity. Sean FitzPatrick was
retiring as chief executive of Anglo Irish Bank and moving 'upstairs'
to become chairman. No longer would the man who had built Anglo
run the bank's day-to-day operations. Anglo's top executives, biggest
clients and well-known figures from business, accountancy and
politics gathered to celebrate the career of the man who had helped
many of them become millionaires.

Some of what happened that night, 28 January 2005, is captured
on a commemorative DVD produced by the bank. To the strains of
Frank Sinatra's rendition of 'My Kind of Town', the camera scans the
room. FitzPatrick – confident, tanned and relaxed – fills the screen;
then the camera peels away from him to pick out the great and the
good of Irish business. Denis O'Brien, Dermot Desmond and Derek
Quinlan were present, as were John Magnier, the bloodstock mag-
nate who had built up a stake in Manchester United, and Bernard
McNamara, then one of Ireland's leading developers.

Willie McAteer, Anglo's finance director, was captured on the DVD
sipping champagne; Gerry Gannon, the developer, wore his trademark
fedora even at the dinner table; Donal O'Connor, then managing partner of PricewaterhouseCoopers, and various Anglo executives from
down the decades could also be seen among the guests.

The DVD freezes a moment in time: Sean FitzPatrick – the man
one newspaper termed 'the greatest banker of his generation' – on
top of the world.

Peter Murray, in his final engagement as chairman of the bank,
compèred the evening's festivities. 'This is, of course, primarily a

celebration of one man's extraordinary career,' Murray said. 'But it is also a celebration of what you, the employees, the customers, advisers and generally the friends of Anglo have achieved in building the greatest Irish business story of the last twenty years.'

Amid cheering he introduced Gerry Murphy, his predecessor as Anglo chairman, to say grace. White-haired and mischievous, Murphy talked about FitzPatrick's qualities.

'He had a great belief. One of his great strengths was that he surrounded himself . . . with the very best people he could get. He paid them well . . . He didn't interfere. And provided they didn't make a total balls of it, he let them get on with it,' he said. 'He also had the great ability that whenever there were problems, he didn't duck them. He didn't hide them. He tackled them.

'He was able to turn an awful lot of ordinary people into wealthy people and you can ask no more than that.'

Murray turned to a big screen behind the podium in the ballroom and introduced a specially made film recounting memories of Fitz-Patrick and his exploits. Charlie McCreevy, the European commissioner and former finance minister who had trained as an accountant with FitzPatrick, was first up. Sitting in his office in Naas, Co. Kildare, McCreevy told the camera how 'Seanie' had taken a job in the Irish Bank of Commerce only to get a mortgage to allow him to buy his first home.

'He has made millions and millions and is still as mean now as he was then,' McCreevy said. 'He is still thinking of getting the 1 per cent gain ahead of everyone else. I am now more or less kind of destitute and I have now my wife out there standing in the streets collecting money. So I am looking for some of Seanie Fitz's money and he can have my job!'

McCreevy, whose introduction of tax breaks as finance minister had helped create the property boom, was a popular turn in a crowd filled with bankers and developers.

Old pals reminisced about FitzPatrick at school and on the rugby field. Paul McNaughton and Ken Ging, luminaries of Greystones rugby club and both managers of Leinster in their time, performed their own mock tribute.

'I think his best attribute, which I think he has brought to Anglo Irish Bank, is he was a great delegator. He delegated everything – tackling, passing, running – and I think he has brought that to Anglo Irish Bank,' McNaughton joked.

Between each speech shown on the video screen, the camera flicked back to FitzPatrick. Flanked by his wife, Triona, daughter, Sarah, and sister, Joyce, the banker smiled and winked at the camera. His eldest son, Jonathan, and middle child, David, were also present.

Maurice O'Connell, the wispy-haired former governor of the Central Bank, who held office until March 2002, was next up to laud FitzPatrick. O'Connell recalled meeting FitzPatrick to discuss his acquisitions of banks in Vienna and Geneva.

'I now began to realize that little Anglo Irish Bank wasn't so little any more,' O'Connell said. 'And then they acquired a box in Croke Park and I said, From now on, I must be nice to these people!'

The former Central Bank governor continued: 'I associate Anglo Irish Bank very much with the Celtic Tiger. In other words, this can-do attitude. Sean has a lot to contribute yet. I am glad he is not sailing away into the sunset and that he is going to be around for a long time.'

Pat Molloy, the revered chief executive of Bank of Ireland from 1991 to 1998, also paid lavish tribute. '[FitzPatrick] was a really professional banker, a very decent guy to compete with,' he said. 'I have to say if you were to have your lunch eaten by anybody, I cannot imagine a nicer person to do it.'

Chris Riley, perhaps Ireland's most successful ever fund manager and stock-market investor, recounted the series of Anglo rights issues in the 1990s – 'all of which seemed to be at 50p' – and wished aloud that all the other stocks he had backed could have performed as well as Anglo's.

There was a special cheer when Peter Killen appeared on the video. FitzPatrick's longest-serving colleague had retired a year earlier, and the bearded Killen spoke to camera from on board a yacht in an unspecified port in South America, part of a world tour undertaken on his retirement.

Tiarnan O'Mahoney, a member of Kilmacud Crokes GAA club,

was the last to speak. Filmed in a seat in the stands of Croke Park, he said with tongue in cheek that John Clegg sent his regrets that he was unable to attend, and went on to say that 'Sean was at his best always when in a tight spot. He always kept his sense of humour there.'

David Drumm, Anglo's chief executive in waiting, did not speak during the event. He features for just thirty seconds in the hour-long DVD, presenting FitzPatrick with a painting by the artist David Rooney. It depicts him as the conductor of an orchestra made up of Anglo bankers and clients.

As the meal drew towards an end, FitzPatrick was invited on to the stage. The screen lit up with the Anglo logo, an image of a smiling FitzPatrick in his prime, and a quote: 'We started on a great voyage . . .'

FitzPatrick, glasses perched precariously at the end of his nose, began his speech. 'Thirty years ago I joined Anglo Irish Bank, on the first of April 1974. Thirty years just go in a flash. It is hard to believe thirty years of doing great business, fantastic times but tough times also.

'I was brought up to believe that to have a passion was what it was all about. To have a passion about work was the recipe for a successful life.

'The real thing in life was not to be bright, it was to be lucky. I was lucky. I was lucky in many facets of my life . . . When I look back on the thirty years I was very lucky to work with such a talented group of people that I worked with in Anglo Irish Bank, who also had a passion for work, who also had a belief in people, who also had a belief in relationships.'

After presenting his wife with flowers, FitzPatrick brought his speech to a close. 'I said to Tiarnan, What's a good finishing line? He said, Ah, you give them what Pope John XXIII said on his death-bed, when he turned to the cardinals and the bishops and he said my bags are packed and I am ready to go.'

The room erupted into cheers.

FitzPatrick never found time to watch the DVD of his own retirement party. He dug it out after he was asked by Tom Lyons for any material that might help tell his story.

The morning after his retirement as chief executive of Anglo was the opening of a new chapter in his life. 'It was great,' he recalls. 'I had achieved what I had achieved. I was now finished. There was a great legacy to leave to a guy [Drumm] that was going to take it on. The same people were there. There was very good people all around the place. There was very good people and a very good future and it would continue and be built on.'

After the celebration, FitzPatrick asked himself, 'Right, now what am I going to do? I am going to get on with my own life. My own life now was free in the sense that I could do things. I didn't know what I was going to do, but I was going to invest.'

There was no inkling, under the crystal chandeliers in the ball-room of the Four Seasons, of what was to come: that many of the people present were about to lose millions, some even billions, in the oncoming Irish economic meltdown, and that the bank that had helped to make them so rich was about to go spectacularly bust.

FitzPatrick had first 'kicked around' the idea of leaving Anglo Irish Bank in 2002. He was restless after almost thirty years, and decided he wanted to step down as chief executive after his fifty-fifth birthday, in 2003. But as his fifty-fifth birthday came and went, FitzPatrick did not step down. The Anglo board wanted him to stay on and at first succeeded in talking him out of retirement. The itch did not go away, though. He was by now a very wealthy man, worth comfortably more than €50 million, and he wanted to pursue other directorships and to spend more time concentrating on his personal investments. He wanted to become a player.

Though still physically fit, FitzPatrick had developed diabetes, and this was another factor in his thinking. He had pushed himself hard during his years as chief executive. By 2004 he felt it was time for one of the 'young Turks' in the bank to take over.

He met with Peter Murray, the bank's chairman and an old friend, to discuss stepping down. He recalls that Murray asked whether he would consider becoming chairman.

FitzPatrick recalls: 'I sort of said, Well, yeah, I would like to stay on in some ways. But there was the whole issue that if [I was] staying on [was I] going to control the board? The other guy coming in [as chief executive], would I just use him as a puppet? I was very conscious of that, really, really, very conscious of that. I really had to make a clean split between an executive role and a non-executive role. This is very convenient for me to say in such clear terms to you, you might say, but I promise you that is exactly what was there.'

Anglo had what was considered at the time a strong board. It was staffed with confident, entrepreneurial figures. All of its directors were multimillionaires from their shares in Anglo, or from outside business interests, or both. They all sat around many other boardroom tables and been rewarded by the government with prominent positions in Ireland's semi-state companies.

Gary McGann was not only the chief executive of Smurfit Kappa, one of the world's biggest packaging companies, but also the chairman of the Dublin Airport Authority. The government had hired him to run Aer Lingus in April 1994 and, as a measure of his standing within the business community, McGann was elected president of IBEC, the employers' representative body, in 2004. The tough and uncompromising McGann was chief executive of Smurfit when it was taken off the Dublin stock market in a deal with Madison Dearborn, a private equity company. He merged it with Kappa, another packaging company. As FitzPatrick mulled his future options, McGann himself was busy preparing the combined entity for a stock-market flotation.

Another Anglo director, Paddy Wright, had a similar track record. He had been chairman of Smurfit Kappa's previous incarnation, the Jefferson Smurfit Group, in Ireland. The state at various points had appointed him chairman of RTÉ and the fisheries board, and deputy chairman of Aer Lingus.

Michael Jacob was deputy chairman of SIAC Construction, one of the country's biggest road builders. He had served as president of the Royal Dublin Society, a 280-year-old institution involved in the promotion of science and commerce.

Ned Sullivan was a former group managing director of Glanbia, one of Ireland's biggest food groups. He was chairman of Greencore, the biggest sandwich maker in Britain. Sullivan also worked in the UK in a senior role with Grand Metropolitan, the multinational food and drinks group that later merged with Guinness to form Diageo.

Fintan Drury – a college friend of Brian Cowen, who was then minister for finance – had worked as a news journalist with RTÉ, then founded and sold Drury Communications, which acted as public-relations adviser to Anglo. A director of Paddy Power, the bookmaker, Drury worked as a manager for sports stars and would play a central role in bringing the Ryder Cup golf tournament to Ireland in 2006.

Peter Murray, Anglo's chairman, was a chartered accountant who had trained with KPMG and then become managing director of Crest Investments, the investment arm of the wealthy McGrath family of Irish Sweepstakes fame. In 1989 he became chief executive of Irish Glass, a McGrath-backed company and the monopoly supplier of glass bottles to the Irish market. He had been a director of the bank from 1993 and its chair since 2002. He knew the bank and its culture inside out.

FitzPatrick says now that he could have looked around the boardroom table in Anglo Irish Bank in 2004 and told himself this was an independent board. It was, he felt, more than capable of ensuring that if he was allowed to become chairman, he would let go of the executive reins.

The Irish Association of Investment Managers, the representative body for institutional shareholders, did not agree. FitzPatrick had been a powerful chief executive. It was a clear breach of best corporate governance practice for chief executives to move 'upstairs' and become chairmen of listed companies.

The Higgs Report on corporate governance in Britain, compiled by businessman Derek Higgs and published the previous year, explicitly recommended that a chief executive should not go on to become chairman of the same company. The report led to changes in the so-called combined code of practice for British companies. The IAIM wanted Irish listed firms to follow the same code.

There was some resistance to these voluntary codes within the cloistered world of Irish business at the time. Ireland's two most successful businessmen from the generation prior to FitzPatrick's, Tony O'Reilly and Michael Smurfit, had both served concurrently as chief executive and chairman of their media and packaging companies respectively. Smurfit got something of a rough ride when his company's share price was in the doldrums, but when times were good there were few calls by shareholders or regulators to enforce good corporate governance practice.

FitzPatrick met with the IAIM and the bank's largest shareholders to reassure them of the merits of letting him stay on. 'We told them this was anti-good corporate governance but we think it is right going forward,' he recalls. 'They didn't like the idea of it all . . . but they could understand in this particular case why it could be seen to be good.

'I couldn't turn around to you and say everyone said that is a fantastic idea. There was not one day when the board turned around and said [I] should be chairman and that is definitely what we are going to do. It was an evolution and sounding out. That is the way it came about.'

Anglo shareholders – who had seen the value of their shares rise dramatically under FitzPatrick's leadership – did not make any real effort to block the move. Privately, many investors thought the voluntary code of corporate governance was a box-ticker's charter, and that universally applying rules to companies was not a good thing.

In August 2004 IAIM secretary-general Ann Fitzgerald told the *Sunday Business Post* that, for FitzPatrick, the association was prepared to make an exception – provided Anglo appointed a strong, 'independent' deputy chairman as a counterbalance. 'The IAIM would have reservations in principle about any chief executive becoming chairman of that company,' Fitzgerald said. 'However, each company must be considered on its own merits. Given Sean FitzPatrick's contribution to Anglo Irish Bank and the company's intention to appoint an independent deputy chairman, the IAIM understands the company's rationale to appoint him as a chairman.'

Anglo never did appoint a deputy chairman to FitzPatrick. It was a decision both shareholders and FitzPatrick would come to regret. But, over the coming five years, the matter was never raised at shareholder meetings or by the IAIM. It was quietly forgotten.

With FitzPatrick's appointment as chairman rubber-stamped, the board set about the task of picking a successor for the post of chief executive. 'It was decided very clearly that I would have no role, hand, act or part in the whole process,' FitzPatrick says. 'The only role I would have would be as a facilitator to the board to allow them to actually run the process.'

The selection process kicked off in July 2004. The board decided to draw up a four-man selection panel that would not include Fitz-Patrick. Three of FitzPatrick's closest friends on the board – Peter Murray, Fintan Drury and Michael Jacob – were appointed to the selection committee. The fourth member, Donal O'Connor, whom FitzPatrick describes as having been 'a very good personal friend of mine and an admirer of me and the bank', was senior partner with PwC, the consultants. O'Connor was hired expressly to bring an external viewpoint to the panel, in line with good corporate practice.

Anglo only briefly considered looking outside the bank for his replacement, according to FitzPatrick: 'There was a universe [of internal candidates] to pick from, talented people that were immersed and sunk within the culture of the bank.' The only candidate who was not an Anglo executive was Gary McGann, a non-executive director of the bank. McGann quickly dismissed the idea and remained at Smurfit Kappa, preparing to float that company on the stock market.

When asked by Tom Lyons on 27 April 2010 if he thought it odd that Anglo did not include a single person on the selection panel who was not close to the outgoing chief executive, FitzPatrick said: 'Maybe that is a fair criticism. [They were] not the strongest characters in the world but not people who would be pushed over . . . It was [independent], I believe. But I can understand what you are saying.'

To gauge what was needed to run Anglo, the selection panel called in the bank's top eighteen executives. They were each asked what qualities they thought the new boss should have and who were the potential candidates.

'The thing that kept coming back all the time was the standing of the culture within the organization,' FitzPatrick recalls. 'That could not be in any way jeopardized.'

The final shortlist comprised four candidates: Tiarnan O'Mahoney,

chief operating officer; John Rowan, the boss of Anglo's UK business; Tom Browne, head of wealth management; and David Drumm,
who had come back to Ireland as a lender after setting up Anglo's
North American division.

O'Mahoney was, from the outset, the clear frontrunner. He had
joined the bank in 1985 as head of treasury, having been headhunted
by FitzPatrick from Irish Bank of Commerce. His task was to go
out and source the money that Anglo could then profitably lend,
pushing its deposit-gathering and wholesale money market activities. Under his stewardship the bank's funding base grew from €100
million to €40 billion. He founded Anglo's private banking division, oversaw acquisitions and helped deal with the Clegg crisis.
During the critical fundraisings of the early 1990s, O'Mahoney was
ever present by FitzPatrick's side, fielding questions and briefing
investors.

Whitehead Mann, a British executive recruitment firm, was hired
to assess the four candidates. It described Rowan as a 'strong candidate', but there were concerns that after spending fourteen years in
the UK he did not know the bank's Irish clients well enough.

Browne, a former Limerick inter-county Gaelic footballer, was
commended for his 'people skills' and was a 'safe choice'. However,
Whitehead advised, 'he lacks the steely edge and single-mindedness
of many successful chief executives'.

The recruiters came down heavily in favour of O'Mahoney, who
was described as a 'very strong candidate'. O'Mahoney's 'prickly,
edgy approach' meant he wasn't popular with everyone in the bank,
and he would need to 'build some bridges' internally if he was to
succeed, the Whitehead Mann report stated. However, it concluded:
'[O'Mahony] has all the drive, determination, intellectual horse-
power and rigour to take the organisation forward. He has a clear
vision for the future.'

Whitehead Mann said it would not even have shortlisted Drumm
for the role. It found him to be 'naturally cautious, not willing to take
bold decisions or to take decisions that cannot be supported by logic or
reason'. (The observation that Drumm was 'naturally cautious' would
not be borne out by later events.) The report concluded that the

thirty-seven-year-old Drumm was 'someone of great potential who could be the next chief executive but one'.

O'Mahoney was liked by his own team in the treasury department, but was not as popular on the lending side of the bank or among top management. FitzPatrick says, 'Most people at executive level would not have had empathy with Tiarnan . . . He was a tough guy.' But Fitz-Patrick could see a more human side behind the analytical and tough-minded exterior. He says O'Mahoney was the person in the bank he most trusted, and the only one he would confide in if he had real difficulties either in the bank or in his personal life.

'[O'Mahoney] was much brighter than me,' he says. 'I felt that Tiarnan was the deepest and the most sensitive of all of them . . . but equally I was also aware that most people didn't like Tiarnan.'

Each of the four candidates gave a presentation to the selection panel. Each had to outline what he saw as the main issues facing the bank and how he envisaged its growth.

O'Mahoney's slide presentation, a copy of which FitzPatrick later found in his files, set out ambitious growth targets for the bank: annual pre-tax profits of €1 billion within five years. (The most recent reported figure, for 2003, was €346 million.) The Irish loan book, he said, would be 'of diminishing importance in terms of size and growth', with the UK coming to account for the largest portion of the bank's loan book as a whole. The US, where the bank's total book was just €1.38 billion in 2004, he said, would be the 'fastest growing'.

In his final slide, O'Mahoney described himself as 'the only candidate who can achieve [annual profits of] €3 billion in ten years'.

Drumm's presentation was equally bullish about the prospects for Anglo: he, too, set out a vision of growing profits to €1 billion within five years. By the end of August it was becoming clear, despite the reservations of Whitehead Mann, that the panel favoured Drumm.

'They said we think this guy is the best guy,' FitzPatrick says. 'He is young. He is bright. He has done well in North America. He built that up. He has come back to Ireland [as a senior lender] and he has done very well.

'I think the decisive factor was [that Drumm] was articulate. He had a proven track-record. He was well liked, or not heavily disliked. He was not well known in treasury, as he had never worked [there], but the lending guys would have known him from when he went to the States, how good he was.'

The four-man selection panel put their recommendation of Drumm to the bank's nomination committee – which included directors Ned Sullivan, Paddy Wright and FitzPatrick – who approved it and forwarded it to the full board. The board confirmed Drumm's appointment. On 22 September 2004 Anglo announced its choice.

FitzPatrick says he believed O'Mahoney was passed over because he did not fit Anglo's culture of lending as well as Drumm did. 'The bank was about lending. Tiarnan was treasury. Treasury got the money in, and the lenders were centre forwards. Treasury was about full backs, centre halfs, goalkeepers and wing-halfs. The lending guys were all about Lionel Messi [the Argentine forward]. They were all strikers. They were the pop-stars. They were the guys who were making the fucking money. They didn't worry about how the money was got to give to them. As far as they were concerned they were the guys lending money and that was where it all was. That was where the culture was as well.'

Incredibly, despite living and breathing Anglo since he joined it in 1985, and dragging it through some of its toughest times, O'Mahoney was now regarded as an outsider in the gung-ho Anglo of the new millennium.

'I think what killed Tiarnan [was that] we needed to continue the culture,' FitzPatrick says. 'People on the board loved the culture within the bank, they would get presentations [from the executives] every board meeting and they would just go, Jesus Christ! I know you smile now but genuinely that's what it was. They were seen as a level above everyone that they knew in their own firms. It was that good. So, that had to be maintained because the only product we had was money . . . It was to do with the people that were in the organization.'

FitzPatrick says he did not know Drumm well at the time of his appointment. 'I had never been out to his house. I didn't know his wife. I had never met his kids. I didn't know who his friends were or anything like that.'

Drumm's background mirrored FitzPatrick's in certain respects. He was one of eight children, the son of a truck driver, and grew up in Skerries, north Co. Dublin. His upbringing was comfortable but in no way privileged.

Drumm left school, De La Salle in Skerries, at sixteen, with his Leaving Certificate and a desire to make money. He was offered a place at Dublin City University but turned it down. Instead he took articles at a small Dublin accountancy firm. Within a week of joining the firm, he was working on the liquidation of a small shoe shop in Dundalk. This was 1980s Ireland and insolvency was one of the country's few growth businesses.

'I remember all these Northern bank guys going up and down on the Belfast train, saying "there's the liquidator" and pointing at me, this seventeen-year-old kid with glasses and spots,' Drumm told the *Sunday Times*.

Eager to progress, he soon wrote to the Institute of Chartered Accountants of Ireland to have him released from his articles so that he could switch to another firm. He sent out 150 letters to possible employers and got just one response. That reply came from Deloitte & Touche. Drumm was allowed to transfer to Deloitte and was despatched to work alongside John Donnelly, a legendary insolvency practitioner. Drumm remembers getting his job brief from Donnelly in a lift.

After four years in Deloitte, Drumm qualified as a chartered accountant, coming first in Ireland in one of his exams and fourth in another. He got a job working for Enterprise Equity, a state-backed venture-capital company based in the border counties. For all of its proximity to the Troubles in Northern Ireland and poor infrastructure, that part of the country was bursting with entrepreneurial talent. Companies such as Moffett Engineering and Monaghan Mushrooms were among the most progressive and successful ventures anywhere in the country. Drumm was 'the dog and devil' at Enterprise Equity, processing applications for investment and sitting on the boards of companies. It was to be a brilliant grounding in business.

He told the *Sunday Times* about one board meeting where the owner of the company turned up in a new Jaguar. Within a year, the company went out of business, and the equity company had lost its £200,000. He said that the main lesson he learned from Enterprise Equity boss Declan Glynn was intellectual honesty: never be afraid to ask the stupid question.

In 1991 Drumm returned to Dublin to work for Bastow Charleton, an ambitious second-tier firm of accountants, but he never settled in the job. Within a year, he took a 40 per cent cut in salary to join Anglo Irish Bank as an assistant manager.

Drumm, intense but personable, rose through the ranks. The people skills he'd learned 'tramping across the border counties' served him well. He was a good fit for the bank's culture of backing risk-takers, and he had a voracious appetite for work. Nowhere was the trait more visible than in the work he did for Anglo in Boston.

The bank's entry into the American market was more down to serendipity than to strategy. FitzPatrick was spending more and more time in America, courting US investors.

In the mid 1990s FitzPatrick joined a committee formed at UCD, his old alma mater, to raise funds to pay for sports scholarships to the university. Aidan Browne, a UCD alumnus and lawyer based in Boston, invited him to America to meet with businessmen to try to raise funds to support the project. While there he met a developer called Jimmy Pappas. FitzPatrick listened as Pappas complained about how hard it was to find good bankers.

FitzPatrick recalls that Pappas said that it was 'such a pity you are not out lending here.' Pappas told him he had a good site on Morrissey Boulevard in Dorchester, where he had already lined up a solid anchor tenant, Star Market, part of a chain of grocery stores. He also had a 1.4-acre site in South Boston that was strategically placed close to the planned development of the Boston Convention and Exhibition Center. All he needed was a bank that was prepared to take him on. FitzPatrick sent a team to check the deal out. They concluded that both sites had potential, and Anglo decided to back Pappas. The bank was now lending in America.

FitzPatrick was keen to do more deals in the States, starting in

Boston. Tiarnan O'Mahoney was against it. 'What do we know about the market? We are not on the ground,' he argued. But Fitz-Patrick pushed on. Robert Kehoe, an executive in the bank who later became a developer, had overseen the bank's initial move stateside, but Kehoe did not want to move there full time. FitzPatrick then asked David Drumm to pick up the Boston baton.

Drumm was not considered a great lender within the bank at this stage, but he was brilliant at picking apart holes in a company balance sheet. He was not as charismatic as FitzPatrick but was more numerate and analytical, and he communicated well.

Anglo asked Drumm to scope the market. The choice was between continuing as a 'suitcase banker', picking off an occasional deal in America, or setting up an office there. After six months Drumm reported back: 'Go for it.' Drumm worked out of his apartment before opening a small office in downtown Boston in 1997.

Within one year, Pappas had filed for protection under Chapter 11 of the US Bankruptcy Code. It was his second time doing so. Pappas listed $109.2 million in liabilities and only $10,863 in assets. Anglo was listed as the largest of Pappas's creditors, owed a total of $31.7 million on the two development projects. (FitzPatrick says he could not recall Pappas going bust. 'We certainly didn't lose any money. I'd remember that,' he says.)

From the beginning, Drumm pitched Anglo as a boutique lender to some of Boston's best developers. 'We didn't do any speculative stuff,' FitzPatrick says. 'We always wanted a tenant already signed up before we funded anything.'

Just as FitzPatrick had in Dublin in the late 1980s, Drumm strived to pick up smaller bits of business with the developers before trying to convince them to give the bank bigger projects. Anglo ended up financing much of the South Boston waterfront, including the $300 million Mandarin Oriental Hotel and the Fan Pier luxury apartment development.

'They were given a large hunting license to negotiate and do deals, and David was the top dog,' Kevin Phelan, president of Colliers Meredith & Grew in Boston, a real estate services firm, told the *Boston Globe* in 2010. 'They started off slow but then had some of the first-team clients in Boston. They did a hell of a job as a lender.'

Tom Alperin, chief executive of National Development, the region's largest commercial builders, told the *Boston Globe* that in the days after the 11 September 2001 terrorist attacks Drumm ensured he got a $27 million loan to build a Marriott Hotel in Boston at a time when American bankers were pulling back. 'Given the impact on the hotel and tourism business, they easily could have withdrawn that loan,' Alperin said. 'But they stayed with us.'

On investor roadshows in America with FitzPatrick, Drumm's fluency and numeracy convinced American funds to buy into the bank's shares. Drumm grew to love America, and bought several homes there. Even after going back to Ireland, he would travel to Cape Cod each year for his holidays, and he stayed in touch with Anglo's American clients by hosting an annual golfing bash for them in Kerry.

After a five-year stint in Boston, Drumm returned to Ireland in July 2003 to be in charge of Anglo's Irish and USA banking units. His selection as chief executive just over a year later came as a complete surprise to media commentators and most of the market. He was, after all, only thirty-seven, and he was not yet a director of the bank.

The *Financial Times* quoted an unnamed Dublin broker as saying of the appointment: 'We have had a number of inquiries from UK clients asking "David who?" He is an unknown quantity to lots of them.' FitzPatrick had become synonymous with the bank; few other executives were well known outside of its walls.

There was no sign of tension between FitzPatrick and Drumm at the announcement of the latter's appointment.

'We've got an open and straightforward relationship,' FitzPatrick told reporters soon after the Drumm announcement. 'I believe I can stand back and act in a non-executive manner.'

Drumm was equally upbeat: 'I don't expect unwelcome interference because that wouldn't be Sean.'

After Drumm became chief executive, he kept his distance from FitzPatrick and vice versa. 'He pushed me back a bit,' FitzPatrick recalls. 'I was happy he pushed me back a bit. I had to look [at my senior executives] and say I am gone. I was saying, Lookit, David, my measurement is going to be how well I remove myself. I saw that as a real important measurement of me and the board would have said to me individually, Jesus Christ, Sean, I did not ever think you would pull back as far as you did.'

The pressure on the new chairman to be seen to be hands-off, to keep a safe distance from the new chief executive, created an unhealthy dynamic between FitzPatrick and Drumm. FitzPatrick says that the kind of working relationship that he had enjoyed as chief executive with previous chairmen never developed. This is, he says, one of his greatest regrets.

Drumm might have taken a pay cut to join Anglo originally, but he was part of a bank that had become accustomed to rewarding its top executives handsomely. In his last full year as chief executive, Fitz-Patrick was paid €2.7 million: this consisted of a basic salary of €775,000, a pension contribution of €294,000 and a €1.6 million bonus. O'Mahoney was paid €1.7 million, which included a €1 million bonus. Rowan was on €1.5 million, McAteer on €1.4 million and Browne on €913,000. Murray, in his final year as chairman, made €217,000. The top five executives at Anglo all earned more money that year than Michael Buckley, the chief executive of AIB, a far bigger bank.

Drumm's starting salary as chief executive was €2 million. Soon he purchased a house in Abington, an exclusive development in Mala-hide, north Co. Dublin, built by an Anglo developer client. Ronan Keating, the pop singer, was a near neighbour.

In his final set of results as chief executive in November 2004, FitzPatrick reported another extraordinary performance. The out-going chief executive took a conference call with investors, with Drumm seated beside him as his designated successor.

Anglo's pre-tax profit had jumped to €504 million in the year to the end of September, up from €346 million a year earlier. The qual-ity of the loan book, according to FitzPatrick, 'remained very robust'; just six tenths of 1 per cent of the bank's loans were non-performing.

FitzPatrick reported that the bank had 'work in progress' worth €4.1 billion. Work in progress was not a term that other banks spent a lot of time talking about. It meant loans that had been approved by

Anglo's credit committee but which had not yet been drawn down. The work in progress was spread across all its geographic markets. The bank was firing on all cylinders.

FitzPatrick then handed over to his successor, who talked about the future of Anglo. 'There's no change in the mix,' said Drumm. 'There's no change or shift in gears, or no move from the strategy of the model that we've been adopting for many years, so very, very sustainable earnings going forward, and really what we're saying about the €504 million of pre-tax profits, it's hooked up to [a] very real basis going forward into the future.'

Anglo, Drumm said, had grown lending by €6.3 billion in the past year – a steep rise of 35 per cent. He spoke of 'sticking to our knitting, if you like, sticking to the same model'. He projected profit growth of 15 to 20 per cent per annum over the next five years.

Anglo's board incentivized Drumm to grow the business aggressively. After it delivered its end-of-year results in 2004, it granted him 500,000 share options at a strike price of €15.93. Anglo's shares tipped €17 for the first time on 19 November 2004, meaning that he was already quite handsomely in the money.

Banking analysts were wholly comfortable with the stock at these levels. Seamus Murphy of Merrion Stockbrokers tagged a price target of €18.50 on the shares, making Anglo his 'top pick' among the local banks. Eamonn Hughes of Goodbody gave it a target of €17.75.

There was no evidence of concern among Dublin's well-paid banking analysts that Anglo might be growing too fast. All the experts were upbeat about the bank's prospects. Every year from 2004 to 2008 Anglo Irish Bank had won the Grand Prix prize at the annual *IR Magazine* awards for best overall investor relations as judged by portfolio managers and analysts in the Irish market.

On his last full day at the office as chief executive, FitzPatrick did an interview with Brian Carey, then business editor of the *Sunday Tribune*, in the banker's small office perched above St Stephen's Green. The piece was published on 30 January 2005.

The bank on his final day was valued at €6.3 billion – compared with a valuation of €1 million when FitzPatrick launched it to the stock market in 1986. Anglo was the fifth-largest company on the Dublin stock market and the country's third-largest bank after the old behemoths AIB and Bank of Ireland. In Britain it was the sixth-largest lender to the investment property market.

It had more millionaire employees per square foot of office space than any other company in the country, with 1,000 staff holding stock worth more than €550 million.

As he headed towards retirement, Ireland's highest-paid banker said there had been no secret formula. 'Pure survival,' he mused. 'Living from day to day, that was always the main ambition.'

Anglo, Carey's article said, was 'forged from a unique culture, rooted in humble beginnings and fostered by collegiate spirit, hard work, self-belief and a fair dollop of "us against the world".'

'Peter Killen left at fifty-six, Bill Barrett left at fifty-six, now I'm leaving at fifty-six,' FitzPatrick said. 'None of us wanted to be prisoners of Anglo Irish Bank. I wanted to get out so I could live another life, do other things. But it is also to facilitate onward and upward movement by other executives. That was part of the deal, part of the culture.'

FitzPatrick praised Dermot Desmond, a businessman he admired. 'We were both outsiders. He was Northside, I was Bray. NCB was outside the establishment and so were we. As companies, we both worked hard to get where we got and took risks. We didn't take as many risks as we were perceived to have done, but we did take risks.'

FitzPatrick had no concerns that Anglo was overheating or that its share price was too high. The stock market, he said, had been 'three years too late' in getting the Anglo story. It was only when Anglo began to sell itself in the United States that fund managers realized this, he said. Irish institutional investors, he implied, just hadn't got Anglo.

FitzPatrick laughed when asked what kind of chairman he would be and said: 'Ask David Drumm in a year's time. I know the bank inside out and if David wants my advice, I'll respond. But I am not going to be an executive chairman. I've had my fun.'

Amidst the drama of FitzPatrick's move upstairs and Drumm's appointment as chief executive, other personnel changes at Anglo had gone relatively unnoticed. Bill Barrett, the experienced head of lending, had retired in July 2002. Peter Killen, Anglo's head of risk, had retired in February 2004 after cashing in shares worth €9 million.

Pat Whelan, who joined Anglo in 1998, took over from Killen as director of group risk and operations but he was left off its board. He was only appointed to the board by Drumm in July 2006. It was a sign of Anglo's priorities that for two and a half years it could lend without having a representative from risk at board level.

In September 2007 Whelan moved from risk and became managing director for Ireland. Responsibility for risk was then passed on to McAteer, the group's finance director. No one – either in the bank or in the Financial Regulator's office – raised the conflict of interest inherent in McAteer's having responsibility for both finance and risk. McAteer was expected to act as both poacher and gamekeeper.

Perhaps not surprisingly, the bank's treasury division suffered most upheaval in the regime change. O'Mahoney, disappointed at being passed over for the top job, left to set up a new venture, International Securities Trading Corporation (ISTC), a specialist lender to financial institutions, in 2005. O'Mahoney received a payoff from Anglo of almost €4 million. The bank's annual report for that year described the hefty payout as being 'in recognition of his substantial contribution'. Paul Somers, a ten-year veteran of Anglo's treasury team, left to join O'Mahoney the following year.

Drumm appointed Brian Murphy, an executive in his late forties who had previously worked in treasury for Citibank and ABN AMRO, as Anglo's new head of treasury. Murphy and Drumm never established a good working relationship, and Murphy resigned in June 2006. A spokesman for Anglo described Murphy's departure to the *Irish Independent* as 'something of a cultural thing'. Murphy, the spokesman said, had joined Anglo from 'a big bank environment and was more used to the slightly slower attitude to business in such organisations than that which he found in Anglo'.

Drumm never replaced Murphy, who went on to work under Michael Somers in the National Treasury Management Agency as chief executive of its state infrastructure expenditure advisory division.

Instead Drumm instructed treasury's key divisions to report directly to him from then on. Apart from the ill-fated Murphy appointment, Drumm failed to make any appointments to high-level executive positions from outside Anglo. And, of course, despite the express wishes of the Irish Association of Investment Managers, there was no strong deputy chairman appointed – or deputy chairman of any description.

Drumm brought three new non-executive directors on to the board: Anne Heraty, the chief executive of CPL, a recruitment company; Noel Harwerth, a former chief operating officer of Citibank International in the UK; and Declan Quilligan, the head of Anglo's business in the UK. Harwerth was the only outside banker on the board.

FitzPatrick believes that Quilligan was brought on to the board to be Drumm's ally. A controlling bloc of the bank's board – Gary McGann, Fintan Drury, Lar Bradshaw and Peter Murray – were all, on FitzPatrick's own admission, the chairman's 'friends', and he accepts that he still controlled the board, even after Drumm's three appointments.

The board lacked a strong figure to represent the treasury and risk-management elements of the bank for considerable periods of time. FitzPatrick agrees, in retrospect, that over time Anglo's attitude towards risk had changed. 'Maybe we had an overbalance. Maybe we did not have an equal rating, if you like, between risk and the structure of balance sheet all the way,' he says.

The entire organization had tilted towards the Lionel Messis. 'I would find it hard to fight with you on that, in hindsight,' FitzPatrick says. 'I did not see it at the time and maybe that is the proper way to describe it. I myself, and maybe other members of the board, did not pay enough attention to that.'

The status of risk management within the company, and on the board, had fallen dramatically. In 2002 Anglo's board had a four-man risk committee made up of two non-executive and two executive directors. This committee's role, according to the bank's annual reports, was 'to oversee risk management and to review, on behalf of the board, the key risks inherent in the business and the system of control necessary to manage such risks and to present its findings to the board'. Back then the committee was chaired by Michael Jacob, a business veteran. Killen and O'Mahoney, two of Anglo's most experienced banking executives, were both members. Drury, who was appointed to this very important committee in his first year as a director, was its only relatively inexperienced member.

By 2007 Drury, a public-relations man who had never run an international business or worked in a bank, was chairing Anglo's risk committee. The other members of the committee were Lar Bradshaw, a management consultant, and Ned Sullivan, an experienced food-sector executive. At this point Anglo stopped listing the specific executives who sat on the committee – the body that should have acted as a crucial check on the bank's lending at the peak of the boom. The bank was ill-equipped at board and management level to meet the challenges of the times ahead, or to curb the hunger of a new management team keen to prove itself.

Nevertheless, Anglo managed to get the imprimatur of the toughest international debt-ratings agency in the business. In March 2007, at Drumm's insistence, Standard & Poor's initiated coverage of the bank. FitzPatrick, when chief executive, was wary of going for an S&P rating, as the company was considered the most rigorous of the four main credit-rating agencies. Drumm worked hard with McAteer to secure the rating, which was seen as essential if the bank was to continue to raise money to fuel its expansion into the US and Europe.

The agency gave Anglo an 'A' long-term rating and an 'A-1' short-term rating, both below Bank of Ireland and AIB but still very credit-worthy.

Anglo was, in the eyes of the agencies that decided these things, a safe and secure institution.

5. The Player

'Listen, Angela. I have got a lot of cash. The very next deal you get,
show it to me and I might do a deal with you.'

The resort of Saint-Jean-Cap-Ferrat, on the French Riviera, has,
since the start of the last century, been frequented by European
royalty and its cultural elite, including King Leopold II of Belgium,
Charlie Chaplin, Jean Cocteau and Winston Churchill. In more
recent years, the new rich arrived: Russian oligarchs such as Roman
Abramovich, owner of Chelsea Football Club, Philip Green, the
British retail billionaire, Microsoft co-founder Paul Allen and the
advertising guru Maurice Saatchi. Bono, the U2 lead singer, and his
manager Paul McGuinness have holidayed there, as have Dermot
Desmond, Denis O'Brien and the financier Paul Coulson.

Derek Quinlan, the tax-inspector-turned-property-wheeler-dealer,
outdid them all. Quinlan spent €45 million buying a waterfront villa
with private beach in Cap Ferrat and another €20 million doing it up,
adding artwork, a lift and a lawn-tennis court. At the end of his private jetty, Quinlan moored a €5.75 million luxury motor yacht, a
102-foot Falcon.

Sean FitzPatrick was not part of the Cap Ferrat set, but he knew
from his friends that there was money to be made in Europe's most
prestigious property market if the right residence could be found.
One such friend was Angela Cavendish, a Dublin businesswoman.
Cavendish made her first fortune selling high-end property in Dublin and her second buying, selling and renovating homes for the
super-rich in the South of France. She was discreet, tough-minded,
hard-working and had excellent – and expensive – taste: perfect for
dealing with millionaires and their mansions.

FitzPatrick and Cavendish had both served on the board of the Dublin Docklands Development Authority. Cavendish's tales of the luxury

homes market, and the eye-popping prices paid for houses on the French Riviera, pricked the banker's interest. 'So one day I said, Listen, Angela. I have got a lot of cash. The very next deal you get, show it to me and I might do a deal with you.'

According to FitzPatrick, a property immediately came to Cavendish's mind. She said there was a great property on the market for €11.5 million in Cap Ferrat that could be worth even more if it was refurbished to billionaire tastes. FitzPatrick liked what he heard, and the two arranged a meeting at Anglo headquarters.

FitzPatrick's account of his approach to the deal is illustrative of his general approach to his personal investments. 'I sat with her for maybe ten minutes,' he recalls, 'and I said, I will get the loan, you guarantee it and I will guarantee it. They will be looking at me because they know my net worth.' FitzPatrick would use his huge personal net-worth statement to bankroll the deal with a loan from Anglo, and any profits would be split evenly between them. He recalls that Cavendish estimated that it would cost about €3 million to bring the property up to standard: 'We get in gold taps, nice baths, all the fancy stuff for the Russians, good security and a big swimming pool.'

According to FitzPatrick, he and Cavendish never drew up a formal contract to set out the terms of their joint investment; instead, he noted the key points, by hand, on a single sheet of paper, unsigned, which he kept on file. Each of them would own half of the Cap Ferrat property. Cavendish would receive €300,000 from the loan in return for 'doing all the work and getting it all organized'. FitzPatrick says that he told Cavendish: 'I don't want to see another thing, I don't want to get any paperwork from it or anything like that at all, and I will provide the money.'

The informal agreement was reached in February 2007. A loan from Anglo was taken out to buy the house in May 2007. Additional money was later drawn down to extensively refurbish the property. During one of his interviews with Tom Lyons, FitzPatrick dug out photographs of the property from a file in his spartan office: stunning views of the bay, bedrooms on an epic scale and a beautiful swimming pool. Cavendish's large wolf-like dogs could even be seen in some of the photographs, playing in its tastefully decorated rooms while the property was being renovated.

FitzPatrick's interest in the property was strictly as an investor. 'I have only seen the place once,' he says. 'I have never stayed in it. Not for more than maybe an hour. Why the fuck would I want to stay there?'

It was doing deals that interested FitzPatrick, trying to get a return. 'The deal itself and backing Angela and making it right – that was what I could do. Then she had to do the rest.' The two let out the property in August 2009 while they tried to sell it. 'It was let last for €250,000 a week.'

FitzPatrick did not see grounds for concern in his having this kind of business relationship with a fellow director in the DDDA. The deal was completed in February 2007, two months before both FitzPatrick and Cavendish retired from the Authority after serving their terms. 'It never struck me that we needed to put our hands up [within the DDDA] and say by the way we have a business relationship,' FitzPatrick says. 'We are investing in a sweet shop in Cavan or wherever it is, or we buying a palatial building in London – what has that got to do with being a member of the board [of the DDDA]? It has nothing to do with the Dublin Docklands, good, bad or indifferent.'

Cavendish, FitzPatrick says, handled all the paperwork on the deal. 'I wouldn't have got involved in that. She did a great job. That is the type of person she is. I have no paperwork. I was not terribly interested in that. I trusted her completely . . . That is the deal. That is the way I did deals all my life in Anglo. I never got involved in writing letters of offer. I have no idea what is in a letter of offer. I hired people who were able to do that.

'There wasn't a huge amount of analysis put in. A person came to me and said, I want to buy a property for €11.5 million. I said, Where? I am buying it sight unseen. I never went down there. I didn't say are you sure you are getting the pool right? Would it not be nicer this way? Why are we knocking out that lovely window there when it could be that one over there? Nothing at all. Why? Because she is the expert, not me. That was it.'

FitzPatrick says he never hired any specialists to advise him on Cap Ferrat or any other deal. 'Look, the reason why I am doing this [i.e. giving these interviews] is not to give you anything other than the truth, but also to put across to you the way I operated. Then you can understand what was driving me. You might find it hard to accept. You might say, How can a guy like that build a bank? Or maybe it's because of a guy like that, the bank is [now] the way it is. You can come to whatever conclusion. But that is the way I was. That is the way I am. That is me.'

FitzPatrick's career as an investor started long before the heady days of the mid noughties.

Over a period of two decades FitzPatrick invested mostly in Anglo shares. As chief executive, he felt it important to show other shareholders that he was confident in Anglo, and he participated in the periodic rights issues the bank undertook to raise cash. He borrowed money from Anglo to fund these purchases, as did other senior executives. Anglo also operated a share-option scheme for employees. FitzPatrick borrowed from the bank to finance both the purchase of his share options and to pay off any related taxes.

He constantly dabbled in other companies' shares and in property, but on a relatively small scale. As Anglo grew, so did FitzPatrick's salary, and by extension his ability to make bigger and bigger investments. In 1996 he was approached to participate in two property syndicates, the Clonmel Partnership and the Gowran Partnership. At the time such syndicates were a popular way of investing. Groups of well-heeled investors pooled their cash in order to be able to borrow more money from banks and do bigger property deals.

To participate in these two consortiums, both of which invested in shopping centres, FitzPatrick borrowed €593,000 and €844,000 respectively from Anglo. Put together by BDO Simpson Xavier, a firm of accountants, the two deals were driven by tax incentives that allowed investors to write off their investment against their tax bill over a set period, usually seven years.

FitzPatrick's participation in the investment partnerships led to unforeseen complications. As Anglo's financial year-end drew closer, the bank's accounts department met with FitzPatrick to discuss how the syndicate loans should be treated in its annual accounts.

'In my particular situation, I had a particular percentage in a partnership and, in some cases, Anglo had provided the main funding to the partnerships, so the question arose as to what figure should be used for me,' FitzPatrick recalls. 'Let me give you an example: say the bank lent €4 million to a property partnership and the partners contributed €1 million [in cash], of which my share was 20 per cent, or €200,000. Let's assume that all partners were jointly and severally liable. What is disclosed in the financial statements? Is it the €200,000 that the bank lent to me directly [to put up the cash to invest] or is it €200,000 plus €800,000, which is 20 per cent of the total loan? Or is it the €200,000 plus €4 million, which is the total of the loan?'

If the total loan figure was used, it would appear that FitzPatrick had borrowed €4.2 million. Technically, as he was potentially liable for the full amount, this is the appropriate figure. But for FitzPatrick to become liable for that amount, the value of the property would have to fall to zero and the rest of the syndicate would have to renege on repayment. FitzPatrick therefore took – and continues to take – the view that his exposure, in this hypothetical deal, was just €200,000, and that that would be the appropriate figure to be noted among the directors' loans in Anglo's accounts.

It was, of course, open to FitzPatrick to make a full disclosure as to the nature of his borrowings, to fully explain why the loan figure was so large. He could have told the shareholders, in a footnote to Anglo's accounts, that the reason why his personal borrowings were so high was because he was an investor in various property syndicates. Or he could simply have funded his personal investments by borrowing from other banks, as lots of other bank directors did.

But to do this he would have had to sacrifice privacy; his personal investment dealings would have become open to scrutiny by the media. Very few people knew, for example, that he made money when his stake in the Market Cross shopping centre in Kilkenny was sold in 2006 at a hefty profit. FitzPatrick was already being quizzed by the press about his sizeable pay package. He could certainly have expected more questions if his borrowings were seen to be going through the roof.

'There may also have been an element of laziness,' a senior Anglo source said by way of explaining FitzPatrick's use of loans from Anglo. 'All the paperwork was in Anglo. He had a young assistant in the bank who would pull it all together and even present his loans at credit committee. Going outside the bank would have created a lot of hassle. Sean liked to move fast and hated paperwork.'

After discussions with Anglo's accounts and lending departments, FitzPatrick decided to make both the accounting and disclosure dilemmas go away. The Anglo chief executive entered into what is known in banking as a 'warehousing' or 'bed-and-breakfast' arrangement. It was agreed that FitzPatrick would transfer his loans to another institution – Irish Nationwide Building Society – for a short period of time around Anglo's year-end so that the bank's auditor, Ernst & Young, would not include the loans in the annual accounts. FitzPatrick says he did not come up with the idea but that he allowed it to happen after he was assured internally that it was all above board.

'That appeared to be the best and simplest way of dealing with the [accounting] problem [of investing in property syndicates] so as not to give an exaggerated figure of my indebtedness,' FitzPatrick says. (His other borrowings from the bank were officially declared in the bank's annual accounts, among its other directors' loans.)

Although they never appeared in the Anglo accounts, the warehoused loans – which would eventually precipitate his resignation – were not secret inside the bank. When the loans were later reviewed, after FitzPatrick left the bank, more than twenty names of Anglo employees were discovered over eleven years as having signed off on, or otherwise processed, the warehousing arrangement with Irish Nationwide. Outside the bank, too, FitzPatrick made little effort to hide the fact he was a prolific investor. Investment advisers habitually sent him prospectuses and invited him to investor meetings to attract his money. It was also well known that he was an investor in property syndicates. He listed, for example, his stakes in four property syndicates in documents prepared in 2006 for the floatation of Aer Lingus, where he was a director. In addition, Anglo continued to file quarterly reports to the state's financial regulators that detailed the true amount of its directors' loans. It appears that neither the regulators nor any of Ernst & Young's accountants noticed what was going on.

Despite the unorthodox nature of the annual transfers, FitzPatrick claims he never discussed them with Michael Fingleton, the powerful boss of Irish Nationwide. 'Never once did I discuss it with Fingleton ever,' he says. 'I hardly ever met Fingleton. I did not know Fingleton. To the best of my recollection I never actually spoke to any director, manager or any employee of Irish Nationwide.'

FitzPatrick showed Tom Lyons loan documents from Irish Nationwide that are signed by mid-ranking employees of the building society and not by Fingleton. However, he does not dispute that Fingleton, who micro-managed even relatively small loans from the society, must at some level have approved the deal.

FitzPatrick says the warehoused loans were never discussed at any Anglo board meeting, but it is possible that other directors knew about them before they emerged publicly. He says Drumm knew of the loans but never questioned the arrangement with Irish Nationwide.

In the late 1990s, following his initial borrowings to participate in property syndicates, FitzPatrick took two more loans from Anglo for similar purposes: a deal called An t-Oileán Orga involved a loan of €726,000 in 1998; and he borrowed €1.2 million to participate in the Mercury Partnership in 1999. These loans, like the earlier ones, were warehoused annually at Irish Nationwide.

In 2001 FitzPatrick for the first time sent a loan over to Irish Nationwide that did not relate to a property syndicate: a €528,000 loan relating to a family property investment. FitzPatrick was now warehousing borrowings at Irish Nationwide not out of any perceived 'accounting' concerns but purely to disguise them from shareholders. The following year, however, he warehoused only his property partnership loans at Anglo's year-end.

A key turning point in FitzPatrick's investment activities was his decision to sell 2 million shares in the bank for €13.35 each, thus raising €27.6 million in February 2003. After paying tax, he had between €24 million and €25 million cash in his bank account. He still had another 5 million shares in the bank and the value of these was rocketing by millions every year. He was now a very rich man, and this allowed him to borrow more in order to invest more. He could of course have simply bought assets with cash, but in the leverage-addicted culture of the time it was easy to borrow the money, and the potential returns were higher.

In 2003 he borrowed €762,000 from Anglo to fund the purchase of a stake in the Beacon Hospital, a private hospital being built with tax breaks in Sandyford, South Dublin. With other high-rolling clients of Quinlan Private, he invested in the Four Seasons Hotel in Prague, and borrowed another €6 million for his family to buy high-end apartments and houses in Dublin, London and America.

All of these loans, even the non-syndicate family loans, were also warehoused with Irish Nationwide at the end of the financial year. By 2003 the total being transferred over was just under €15 million. FitzPatrick never missed an interest payment while the loans were with Anglo and he paid an extra premium to the building society for its warehousing services. In this respect he did not receive special treatment from his bank.

FitzPatrick characterizes his investments prior to stepping down as chief executive of Anglo as 'Mickey Mouse stuff'. Offhand he recalls putting about €5.5 million into various property syndicates; €1 million into an apartment development in Barbados; and €4.4 million into shares of companies other than Anglo.

A list of his assets shows he also made other investments while in charge of the bank. These include the purchase of a 10 per cent stake in the syndicate that bought the DHL building at Dublin Airport. In 2003 he stuck €250,000 into developing a five-star hotel, retail premises, offices, apartments and a medical clinic in Cape Town central business district. The project was developed by Frank Gormley, a prominent developer who had co-founded Howard Holdings.

In 2004, with Brian Davy, the chairman of Davy stockbrokers, he put €2.25 million into trying to develop a 350-acre golf resort along the Danube, about seventy kilometres outside Budapest. Fintan Drury, his fellow Anglo director, was employed to help promote the project and get it off the ground on site.

Among the investments made by his family around this time was the purchase of an apartment in London, which was then rented to the bank. Despite the practice having gone on for several years, it was not declared until the bank's 2008 annual report (after FitzPatrick had left), where it was said to be a 'related party transaction'. The report claims the apartment was used by Anglo employees 'rather than hotels . . . on a temporary basis'. Rental income, paid to an unnamed member of FitzPatrick's family, was €31,500 in 2008. The bank then halted the arrangement.

FitzPatrick's investment appetite was constrained by two things when chief executive: time and money. Once he retired, he had plenty of both. 'I wanted to change my life,' he says. 'I was down there 24/7 in the bank in different ways. I was coming in early and going home late. Travelling. Meeting guys at seven o'clock for breakfast, meeting more junior people. I was just going non-stop. It was my whole life, everything. I just sold all the time. When I was out with people I was talking about the bank. I was a hail-fellow-well-met . . . I was so different from the other bankers. I wasn't playing at that. That was the way it was.

'I didn't have time [for extensive personal investments]. It was not that I had no interest but I was running a bank. That was my job and that was what I wanted to do. Now I was relieved from the position of a 24/7 job.' The plan at that point, FitzPatrick says, was 'to cut loose and have a bit of fun'.

The transition from full-time banker to full-time investor was seamless, and was fuelled further by a decision to unlock funds in his pension scheme.

FitzPatrick's Anglo pension guaranteed him two thirds of his salary of €1 million a year upon retirement; this equated to a fund value of about €25 million. Upon stepping down as chief executive, Fitz-Patrick transferred this pot into an Approved Retirement Fund. ARFs, another innovation of his former accountancy colleague Charlie McCreevy, allowed company directors to take control of their pensions when they retired. Rather than putting the money into an annuity, a savings product that guaranteed a steady income, ARF holders could continue to invest in their fund by playing the stock and property markets, thus making themselves even richer.

So, at the start of 2005 FitzPatrick had €50 million in cash from share sales and his pension, as well as 5 million shares in Anglo (which would be worth over €80 million at their peak). With that kind of wealth, and in the frenzied lending culture of the mid noughties, any bank would have lent to him. He could easily have refinanced his existing loans and borrowed whatever he wanted from any bank other than Anglo. Yet FitzPatrick continued to keep his loans with Anglo before warehousing most of them every year with Irish Nationwide. The scale of his borrowings rocketed almost fourfold, from €27 million in 2005 to €129 million in 2007. FitzPatrick could not seem to stop himself investing and borrowing.

'You can call it unlucky. You can call it foolhardy. You can call it mistaken,' he says. 'I mean, looking at it back now, here I was in a situation where I had €27 million on deposit in 2004 . . . There was very little leverage by me in 2001, 2002, 2003, 2004, then it really got going after I resigned.'

It was not about the money, FitzPatrick insists. It was about the deal. He made decisions on investments based mainly on intuition. He put his money with people he liked.

'I wasn't a smart guy . . . but I wasn't seen as stupid either. What did I want in life? Did I want to end up dying with €50 million to pass on to my kids? No, I didn't . . . I was no longer in the bank so now I was free to do what I wanted to do. I would invest here, there and everywhere. I put money into this, that, €2 million or €3 million. I was not trying to increase wealth and I was not trying to spend it. I was just doing what I was doing. It sounds terrible but it is the honest view.

'I had no ambitions to become the richest man in Ireland because I was a rich man,' he says. 'The difference between having €50 million and €500 million made no sense to me. Would I have liked €500 million? Of course I would. So would I aim to that? No, that wasn't there.'

In 2001 FitzPatrick was one of a group of business people asked by the *Sunday Business Post* for his favourite sources of personal finance information. 'For information, one of the best sources is FT.com,' he said. 'For analysis, read the *Economist*. But for the real McCoy, you can't beat the nineteenth hole on the golf course.'

It was not quite that simple, but the truth was not too far away. FitzPatrick liked to listen to presentations, get a feel for the person doing the deal, but he ignored the details and rarely read contracts or lengthy investment brochures.

A small team in Anglo helped him manage his investments by filling in the paperwork and updating him on their performance. They were junior members of staff. 'You didn't question Sean,' a former mid-level employee recalled. 'Nobody could tell him what to do or not do.'

FitzPatrick simply felt he did not need professional advisers or managers of his wealth. 'That [wasn't] my style,' he says. 'I should have done, when I reflect on it . . . I was doing this as part of my life: "This [is] interesting, I am going to do it." It was not a case of "Will this make great sense?" It was no, no, I want to do this. I like the guy.'

The cash-rich FitzPatrick was a popular man. There was a queue of people offering him opportunities to invest his money. He seemed to find it hard to say no. 'People were all the time meeting me, saying, What do you think about this? Do you want do something here or not?,' he recalls. But the person ultimately driving it all, he acknowledges, was 'me, me'. All the top investment names in the country took his money and charged him fees for doing so, including Quinlan Private, Claret Capital, Davy, Bloxham, Goodbody. His investments ballooned. In his office at Anglo, cabinets of paperwork were filled tracking his various deals. Each time FitzPatrick borrowed to invest, his application went through the bank's credit committee. Each of his loans was backed by cash and his seemingly gilt-edged Anglo shares. He says he was never once told to scale back his risk-taking. 'No. No one did that at all. That should have been done. Absolutely. No one did that.'

During his time on the board of the Dublin Docklands Development Authority, FitzPatrick had become friendly with Lar Bradshaw, its former chairman.

Bradshaw ran a venture-capital company called Cove Capital, a small group of business people who pooled their expertise, contacts and resources to make investments in start-ups. The other members of the group were James Osborne, the former managing partner of A&L Goodbody Solicitors and a director of Ryanair; Denis Tinsley, a former McKinsey management consultant; Clive Kilmurray, a former manager with IBI corporate finance and director of Deerbay Properties; and Lorcan Tiernan, a solicitor with Dillon Eustace. Maurice Cox, also an ex-McKinsey consultant, was also involved in some of Cove's investments.

'I was seen as the rich guy,' FitzPatrick says. 'I had all the money and I put €3.5 million to €4 million into that. They would have brought the deals and we would have made decisions. I said, Yeah, yeah, that sounds great, put me in for that.'

Through Cove Capital, FitzPatrick took stakes in a wide array of business sectors. He had a slice of Great Irish Pubs, set up in 2004 to run a chain of Irish-themed bars in Florida; shares in Clear Power, a green energy company; and a stake in Fresh Mortgages, a Dublin sub-prime lender that lent money primarily to taxi drivers to buy investment properties. He invested in Sweetwell, a Belgian company that has developed a non-sugar sweetener. He also took a piece of System Solutions, which makes software for pharmacies in Ireland.

The Cove investors ran up liabilities of about €18 million, owed to AIB and Anglo. FitzPatrick signed a personal guarantee of €10 million in relation to his investments.

Claret Capital, led by Domhnal Slattery, a former aviation financer, also courted FitzPatrick. A private-equity group based in the Oval Building in Ballsbridge, Claret was backed by a number of well-known business people, including Fergal Quinn, a senator, who had made a fortune selling his supermarket chain Superquinn. Slattery himself had become wealthy through selling his start-up aviation leasing business to Royal Bank of Scotland.

'I never met them before,' FitzPatrick recalls. 'They just rang me up.'

Soon he was investing in a number of highly leveraged deals, originated by big investment banks such as Merrill Lynch. FitzPatrick's biggest investment with Claret was the $5 million he put into a fund that backed what was then the biggest buyout in corporate history, the acquisition of Hospital Corporation of America for $31.6 billon.

HCA was the largest private-healthcare operator in the United States. Kohlberg Kravis Roberts and Bain Capital, the private-equity giants, led the deal.

Also through Claret, FitzPatrick put $3 million into Aeolus Re, a Bermuda-based re-insurer, in May 2007, and another $3 million with a Merrill Lynch property fund. The Merrill Lynch fund gave him exposure to one of his more exotic investments: a stake in a casino in Macau.

FitzPatrick was a long-time investor in shares of Riverdeep, an educational-software company founded by Pat McDonagh, a serial entrepreneur, and Barry O'Callaghan, a thirty-something invest-ment banker. The company floated on the Stock Exchange but its time there was not a happy one: in the dotcom bubble fallout River-deep saw its share price plunge, leaving it vulnerable to a short-selling campaign.

O'Callaghan took the company off the stock market and then set off on one of the most ambitious acquisition sprees ever undertaken by an Irish company. He borrowed $4 billion to purchase two of the top five American school publishers, Houghton Mifflin and Harcourt Education, and merged them with his small software company to create the Education Media and Publishing Group.

'It was a big success,' FitzPatrick says. 'Barry O'Callaghan was a good guy and I liked him . . . I was taken by him. I liked the look of him and he sounded very good. I wouldn't have done huge research [before investing]. I was quite intuitive as an investor. I spoke to a few people and it seemed a very good deal.'

FitzPatrick says he invested 'five million bucks' with O'Callaghan in 2006.

Apart from his brief and highly profitable involvement in the Derek Quinlan-led purchase of the Savoy Hotel Group in 2004, FitzPatrick made a number of investments over the years with the tax inspector-turned-financier.

In 2001 FitzPatrick put €700,000 into the €70 million purchase of the five-star Four Seasons Hotel in Prague. Gay Byrne, the former presenter of the *Late Late Show*, was among the other high-net-worth investors in this deal. A few years later FitzPatrick invested €5 million more through Anglo Irish Assurance company in the Quinlan NOREF fund, which owned a stake in a large portfolio of properties in Europe.

In February 2007 he stuck €1.5 million into an equity pool of €65.7 million to purchase Maximilianhöfe, two adjoining buildings on Maximilianstrasse in the heart of Munich. The total deal was worth €286 million. Five months later he stuck €1 million more into the highly geared buyout of Jurys Inn, a group of twenty three-star hotels, bought for a jaw-dropping €1.1 billion.

In June 2006 Bank of Ireland's pension fund sold its iconic headquarters building on Baggot Street for €200 million to a consortium put together by Quinlan. The financier was short €2 million in cash to fund the deal. Kieran Duggan, a former director of lending with Anglo, asked FitzPatrick if he would step in and make up the difference.

FitzPatrick looked at the plan. The Bank of Ireland headquarters consisted of three separate blocks. Its handsome design by Irish architects Scott Tallon Walker, with bronze manganese cladding and tinted windows, was influenced by the great modernist architect Ludwig Mies van der Rohe. Quinlan and his partner in the deal, the developer Paddy Shovlin, wanted to add two new floors on to two of the building's blocks and one on to the third block. This would add almost 16,000 square metres of floor space, nearly doubling the overall gross floor area.

Bank of Ireland was outgrowing the building, but its lease's break clause could not be activated until 2013. The Quinlan/Shovlin plan was to use those years to get planning permission to expand the building – and then get Bank of Ireland to move into the extra space.

It sounded like a 'great deal' to FitzPatrick. He had never met Shovlin but knew his reputation after he built the Beacon Hospital and a hotel, apartments and retail area in Sandyford, south Co. Dublin. Shovlin was taking 50 per cent of the deal. Quinlan was in for 25 per cent. FitzPatrick decided to take 3 per cent of the remaining 25 per cent, along with a group of other businessmen. (FitzPatrick dismisses the suggestion he wanted to be the landlord to Bank of Ireland, his old rivals.)

Bank of Scotland (Ireland), ACC and Danske funded the deal. FitzPatrick believed the money being lent to buy the building was on a non-recourse basis – in other words, his personal exposure was limited to the €2 million he put in. 'I didn't realize at the time that the first €25 million [of borrowings] was recourse, but I found that out when the deal went bad. It was there. But I didn't even see it.'

FitzPatrick would pay a price for ignoring the paperwork. When the credit crunch came in 2008, the redevelopment became impossible to finance. Worse, Bank of Ireland scrapped its plans to find a bigger headquarters and began to look instead at moving into a smaller building. FitzPatrick would not only lose all €2 million of his investment, but would also face a demand for his portion of the recourse element of the syndicate's borrowings, which worked out at €750,000.

In November 2006 FitzPatrick stumped up £1 million, via Niall McFadden's Boundary Capital, to participate in the acquisition of the Club Company, which owned and ran a chain of ten golf clubs in the UK, for £96 million. That same month he put €500,000 into a Paris-based commercial-property fund.

Through CMC Capital, based in Cork, he put another €500,000 into a tax-efficient Luxembourg company that bought the Schloss Strassen Centre, a retail shopping mall in Berlin. The syndicate bought the building for €104 million and FitzPatrick had a 2.2 per cent stake.

Around the same time he put €2 million into a property fund that bought fifty-nine properties in northern Germany. FitzPatrick expected to be paid interest of 17 per cent for the two years that his money was in the fund, which was run by Bomac, a Galway company owned by Tim Bohan and Michael McDonagh.

He put €1.5 million into Danube Bay, a company that planned to build a €100 million riverfront project with 2,000 apartments in Budapest. Fellow investors on this deal included Tom Mulcahy, former AIB chief executive, Cormac McCarthy, the chief executive of Ulster Bank, Gary Kennedy, a former AIB director, and builder John Sisk.

In 2007, through Davy stockbrokers, he put €750,000 into a fund that backed the €12 billion leveraged buyout of Alliance Boots, the pharmacy chain, at the time Europe's largest-ever LBO. In October of that year he put $2 million into a Goldman Sachs hedge fund, and he also had €1 million in a Geneva-based hedge fund.

As late as November 2007, even as the property market started to wobble, FitzPatrick put £3 million into the acquisition, for £180 million, of an office block in the West End of London called 1–19 Victoria Street. The building, located 200 metres from the Houses of Parliament, is the headquarters of the UK's Department for Business, Enterprise and Regulatory Reform and the Department for Innovation, Universities and Skills. The deal was put together by D2, a property investment group, set up by Dave Arnold, a developer, and Deirdre Foley, who formerly worked with Quinlan. FitzPatrick ended up with a 6 per cent stake invested through a Luxembourg company set up by D2 to reduce taxes. The deal was described by *Property Week*, the UK's property investment bible, as a 'bold move'.

In July 2008 – by which time the world financial system was teetering and Anglo's share price had plummeted – he put €1 million into Mainstream Renewable Power, a wind-farm company, set up by Eddie O'Connor and chaired by Fintan Drury.

FitzPatrick owned shares in banks other than Anglo – he had invested €16 million in AIB and Bank of Ireland down the years and had stakes in HSBC and Lloyds – but he also invested freely in sectors he barely understood.

Did FitzPatrick want to move from being a banker to a financier like Dermot Desmond? 'I don't know what I was doing, is the honest answer. I didn't see myself as a Dermot Desmond type guy. I saw myself as a very wealthy guy who had plenty of money.'

Despite the sheer volumes of deals he was involved in, FitzPatrick says he never lost sleep over them. 'I was genuinely never worried about them. Why? Because I thought they were going to be OK.'

FitzPatrick says that getting older and health concerns were not factors in his decision to borrow and invest so much. 'I am going to have to be very careful with you and with anyone in mixing up the reality of today with where I was three or four years ago. I am not trying to justify it or play it down. I am being terribly open with you and honest with you by saying there was nothing that was driving me. There were no health issues. There were no blackmails. There were no affairs. There was no nothing in my life that was going on. I was just being myself.'

He was never concerned that the scale of his borrowings from Anglo would come out into the public domain. 'Why would I be? I was paying it all at commercial rates. There was nothing strange about it.'

But he was warehousing huge borrowings at Irish Nationwide. 'Do you know what the reality was there? If I had thought about it a bit longer, then I would maybe have said, Jesus, I should not have done that.'

When the FitzPatrick loans transferred annually to Irish Nationwide became very large, they were disclosed to the building society's board; but nobody on that bank's board ever appears to have questioned why year after year it was lending Sean FitzPatrick a large amount of money for a small period of time.

The Irish Nationwide board minutes were sent to the Financial Regulator, and FitzPatrick's loans should have been included in them. If the Financial Regulator saw these loans, it never acted on them.

Anglo, contrary to its apparent legal obligation, failed to keep a registry of directors' loans on site at the bank. The Financial Regulator never asked to see such a registry. (Anglo has claimed in legal correspondence with the Office of the Director of Corporate Enforcement that around 1990, just prior to the introduction of the new Companies Act that required the register, it received legal advice to the effect that it did not have to keep one.)

Of the myriad of FitzPatrick's post-retirement investments, none compares in scale, or strangeness, to his foray into the oil business.

In 2005 FitzPatrick received a phone call from a man called Jim O'Driscoll. FitzPatrick had known him for fifty years. His best friend in school, Jackie O'Driscoll, was Jim's brother, and FitzPatrick had played rugby with Jim in the same back-lines as a schoolboy in Presentation Bray and later as an adult with Bective and Greystones.

Jim O'Driscoll had spent the previous decades working as an engineer in exploration in Malawi, Zambia and Nigeria. Now he had an audacious plan to invest in developing an oil well in Nigeria that was believed to hold oil worth over $1 billion.

O'Driscoll had heard about the well from an English businessman called Michael Barnes. Barnes worked with a company called DWC Supplies, which managed to secure the rights to a marginal oil field about fifteen kilometres offshore from Bayelsa state, at the tip of the Niger Delta. DWC needed money to exploit the well. Barnes told O'Driscoll, who then immediately thought of his old school pal who had hit the big time.

FitzPatrick listened carefully to what O'Driscoll had to say. The find, called the OML 88 Ekeh Field Development, was first discovered in 1986. It was close to a huge discovery of hundreds of millions of barrels being managed by Chevron. The Nigerian government, in an attempt to lessen the power of the major oil producers, had decided to hand over smaller nearby oilfields to local businessmen. The fields typically had only 20 million barrels or so and were of little interest to international oil groups. But to local businessmen who could raise the money, they promised a bonanza. With oil climbing above $50 a barrel, such wells were becoming more and more valuable.

DWC secured the support of a group of Nigerian businessmen with strong political and military links to bid for the well. None of them, however, had the money to exploit the well.

O'Driscoll asked FitzPatrick if Anglo would be interested.

FitzPatrick recalls: 'I said, No, the bank would not be interested, but maybe I could try to get a few people that might be interested in it. I said, How much is required? Jim said, About $12 million. I said, What sort of deal could we get for that? He said, Well, you lend them money, you get a rate of interest on it, and what will happen is you will get an equity stake. I said, What type of equity stake? He said, Your man has 40 per cent of that and maybe you will get 10 per cent of that, or 25 per cent.

'I had never been [to Nigeria] before. I said, Have you any seismic sort of stuff? and he said, I have. I said, Well, I will never read it but do you know who I will get to read it is Lar Bradshaw.'

Bradshaw didn't know any more about oil exploration than Fitz-Patrick, but as a former managing partner in McKinsey, the international consultancy firm, he had contacts who did. He passed the relevant seismic data on to one of its experts.

'Lar came back and said, Yeah, it looks very good,' FitzPatrick recalls. 'I had €20 million on deposit in Anglo Irish Bank, cash. So I said, OK, Lar, do you want to put in half, and we will give Jim O'Driscoll and some other guy some money as well, some equity stake.' (The 'other guy' was Gerry Nashe, an Irishman living in Nigeria.)

FitzPatrick told Anglo of his plans, and it was agreed that the bank would give him what is called a back-to-back loan: a loan entirely secured on cash he held in his deposit account. The amount was $12 million.

In return for their money, FitzPatrick, Bradshaw, O'Driscoll and Nashe would get a 20 per cent stake in the oil well. DWC would also get 20 per cent and the Nigerian businessmen would control 60 per cent. A new company called Movido Exploration and Production Ltd was set up to manage the project.

'We gave them the $12 million out in pieces as they required it. They went out to the site and [. . .] they drilled the well and they found 16 million barrels, with the potential of 22 to 23 million barrels and maybe more.'

FitzPatrick's account of the methodology for extracting oil is reminiscent of the climactic 'I drink your milkshake' monologue of the oilman played by Daniel Day-Lewis in the film *There Will Be Blood*.

'I am not, as you know, an expert in anything and I am certainly not technically minded,' he says. 'But apparently if you have the big field there and this is your little field, if you go down the little field and you can actually take from underneath from the big field.

'It doesn't seem fair but that is apparently the deal. If the head is here, you can actually go [sideways] into other parts of the field. That was why it was 16 million there and with a potential of 25 million maybe up to 30 million . . . Pretty soon, pretty much straight away, we found we had oil.'

Less than six months after investing, FitzPatrick's luck was in. He was now an oilman as well as a banker. It seemed almost too good to be true. But this was Nigeria, where corruption is endemic. The issue of trust in his business partners must have been a concern.

'Well, I knew that Jim was telling me the truth – but did he know the whole truth himself? We didn't know. I didn't. I saw that as a two-faced coin. Nigeria is a very difficult nation, reputationally. People down there have a very bad reputation and therefore people would be less inclined to [invest]. I was kind of saying, Well, you could see that as a warning sign or you could see that as advantage.'

FitzPatrick admired entrepreneurs like Denis O'Brien, who had made a fortune selling mobile phones in tough markets like Haiti, and Aidan Heavey of Tullow Oil, who has succeeded in oil exploration in Africa. He clearly thought he could do the same.

'I saw it as an advantage. We would tread where other people were afraid to tread. Therefore we would get away with it. I had plenty of cash so there was no issue on that. I was prepared to put the money up. Lar hadn't got money so I said to Lar, I will lend you half my money and I will deal with you on an interest rate, and that is how we started off . . .'

FitzPatrick was the money man for the project. As the cash calls increased, FitzPatrick and his friends' stake in Movido, held through another company called SJL Ltd – the initials stand for Sean, Jim and Lar – increased. The Nigerians, meanwhile, kept their hands in their pockets. FitzPatrick says: 'They had got the licence and that was it.'

Having struck oil, the next challenge was to link the find by underwater pipes to an offshore platform owned by Chevron some distance away. But there was a hitch. The pipes didn't fit correctly, and the oil refused to flow. FitzPatrick flew to Nigeria in 2006 to try to sort things out. He had invested $12 million over nine months without ever having met his Nigerian business partners. He was relying on other people's word that oil had actually been found. Not even O'Driscoll was based in Nigeria on a full-time basis.

'This was an interesting hobby,' FitzPatrick says by way of explaining his lack of stress over the Nigerian deal. 'If you were to lose it, you were to lose it.'

According to FitzPatrick, his lenders at Anglo were equally relaxed. 'The credit committee was thrilled. They had back-to-back from me. They couldn't have better security [than the cash in my bank account]. They were thrilled, delighted with themselves.'

On his trip to Nigeria, FitzPatrick witnessed 'big rows between the Nigerians and the expats about the drilling and the money that went in. We were looking on aghast. We were told the Nigerians were difficult. They seemed OK to us, but we weren't down there.'

The Irish investors decided to bring their Nigerian colleagues to Dublin. FitzPatrick took them out to dinner. In Anglo's private investment office, he met with a representative of the Department of Petroleum Royalties, the Nigerian state agency responsible for exploration, and explained what the Irish investors hoped to do.

FitzPatrick's Nigerian business partners appeared to have influence and connections. They were impressive in meetings and seemed to have a good grasp of what needed to be done. Yet, for all their clout, they needed the chairman of a bank in Ireland to help them. Surely the local consortium could have raised the funds from a local bank?

FitzPatrick says, 'It was hard to get money from a local bank down there. And this was a proven formula . . . In other words, they would get the licence, they would keep 60 per cent and they would pass out 40 per cent to maybe a big oil company that would maybe provide the technical and the money. That was the model.'

Michael Barnes was a brother of Richard Barnes, the former chief financial officer of Waterford Wedgwood; but FitzPatrick and O'Driscoll knew little about him.

'We didn't do tremendous due diligence on it. We didn't have them all checked out. Here was Jim O'Driscoll, a friend of mine. I knew nothing about oil. I wasn't interested in oil. I knew nothing about Nigeria. I wasn't really interested in Nigeria. Jim came to me and said, Sean, here is a deal that could be really, really worthwhile. We could get maybe a 10 per cent stake in this oil field. It is a marginal oil field and it could produce 20 million barrels over its lifetime. If you take 20 million barrels, and just think about it – $40 a barrel. That is $800 million, and what we would get is 10 per cent of the $800 million, which would be $80 million, and whatever money we put in, the $12 or $13 million we put in, we would get an interest in that. I said, Yeah, let's go for it . . . Lar said, Yeah, good deal. That was it.'

While the rows continued, FitzPatrick's money kept on flowing into Nigeria. His investment grew from $12 million to $19 million. Eventually the disagreements about the pipes and the progress of drilling were resolved. SJL agreed to allow its investment to rise to $35 million in order to get things back on track.

It was now 2007 – the very top of the Irish property bubble. Fitz-Patrick's Anglo shares, the cornerstone of his wealth, were still trading well. Even if the oil investment had gone wrong at that stage, he says, it would not have been that big a deal.

'It was not going to bring me down. It was like a pension. I even thought at one stage about putting it into my pension scheme . . . Everything was backed 100 per cent back to back. All the way right through '05, '06, '07, '08. All backed by cash. Lar had now got the deposit against it as well. Lar had about €5 or €6 million [in part from his profits from the Savoy deal] and I had maybe €14 million.'

Inside Anglo his Nigerian investment was well known. 'Everyone thought it was a bit mad,' an Anglo source said. 'But nobody really questioned it. The security on the loan was cash, so why would we?'

As 2007 closed, the price of oil began to fall as it became clear the world was headed towards recession. FitzPatrick's team scrambled to get the pipes fixed and the oil pumping. Months passed, and the price of oil kept falling.

During an interview with Tom Lyons on 27 April 2010, FitzPatrick dug out a sheet of paper that had been prepared as part of his response to the various investigations into his loans. The page outlined the growth over time of his loans from Anglo, set against the growth of the bank's loan book.

The document indicated the scale of FitzPatrick's investment splurge – one source of his disgrace. It also revealed the seeds of the downfall of Anglo: a loan book that ballooned sixfold over the six years from 2001 to 2007.

Year of loan	SF loans book	Anglo loan book	SF loans as %
1996	€1.437m	€1.75bn	0.082%
1997	€1.428m	€2.2bn	0.065%
1998	€2.132m	€2.517bn	0.085%
1999	€3.286m	€5.613bn	0.059%
2000	€3.259m	€7.794bn	0.042%
2001	€4.004m	€10.952bn	0.037%
2002	€4.432m	€13.357bn	0.033%
2003	€14.439m	€17.269bn	0.087%
2004	€23.883m	€23.724bn	0.101%
2005	€27.326m	€33.6bn	0.081%
2006	€48.026m	€49.142bn	0.098%
2007	€121.599m	€66.949bn	0.184%

By the end of 2007 FitzPatrick's mind would be preoccupied not by the scale of his own borrowings or falling oil prices or ill-fitting oil pipelines, but by a far bigger problem for him and the bank. It took the shape of a border businessman with an insatiable appetite for risk.

6. The Mighty Quinn

'He was bringing me . . . because he always felt that Quinn regarded
me as a superhuman, as a superhero. He wanted Quinn to see how
disappointed I would be.'

Up to 2005, Sean Quinn and Sean FitzPatrick, two of the most
prominent business leaders in a country of just four million people,
knew each other only by reputation.

With an estimated net worth of $6 billion, Quinn was Ireland's
richest man. *Forbes* placed him among the top 200 richest people in
the world in 2008. FitzPatrick was easily the country's most flamboy-
ant banker and the main figure in one of Europe's fastest-growing
financial institutions, rapidly building an international reputation.

Quinn was to Irish industry what FitzPatrick was to Irish banking: an outsider, a maverick, whose rise to the top had been achieved
by getting the better of long-established rivals. Though a billionaire,
Quinn lived with his wife Patricia in a modest house in Ballyconnell,
Co. Cavan, on the border between the Republic and Northern Ireland.
He built the head office of the multibillion-euro Quinn Group, a
small two-storey building, right beside his late mother's house, and
just up the road from the local Teemore GAA pitch.

Every Tuesday night Quinn played a friendly game of cards with a
group of friends, all locals, in the back room of a house. He was the
quintessential local business hero who told the *Sunday Business Post* in
2001 that his motto was 'live poor, die rich'. Yet he had a formidable
business reputation well beyond his local bailiwick. He revelled in taking on big and powerful players in Irish business, and invariably he won.

Quinn had left school at the age of fourteen to work on the family's
twenty-three-acre farm in Derrylin, Co. Fermanagh. Twelve years
later, in 1973, he borrowed £100 to dig a hole on the farm's land to
extract gravel, which he then sold to local builders. Four years later,

he opened a second quarry in Williamstown, Co. Galway, to supply builders in the West of Ireland.

Quinn was a disciplined and talented Gaelic football player; for a period he was captain of the Fermanagh team. (His brother Peter, a business consultant, was also steeped in the Gaelic Athletic Association, rising to become president of the sporting organization from 1991 until 1994.) From quarrying, Sean Quinn expanded into making building materials. He used the cash from his burgeoning enterprises to build up a chain of pubs in Dublin, starting with the Cat and Cage in Drumcondra in 1985.

'Every time I used to come to Dublin, the pubs were always full, so I said to myself: "This has to be a simple business because they're charging a ransom for the beer, they get paid for the beer before they pay Guinness, so this seems to be a good business,"' Quinn said. The leisure division of the Quinn Group would eventually consist of eleven pubs and six hotels.

In the late 1980s he began a hugely ambitious project, a new stg. £30 million cement plant in Derrylin. It was a large investment for the border counties and heavily supported by the British government. Quinn told RTÉ television that his new plant would produce 500,000 tonnes of cement a year, to be sold at a price that would reduce the cost of building a new house in Ireland by £500.

The investment brought Quinn into the cross hairs of Cement Roadstone Holdings, a company well known for protecting its patch vigorously. CRH was many times larger than Quinn and easily the dominant cement producer in Ireland. Quinn claimed in an RTÉ documentary that CRH was determined to stop the Derrylin project. 'They used to fly an airplane over here about every six weeks or so to see how we are going,' Quinn told the programme. CRH used the aerial photographs, he claimed, to monitor the building works and to make sure that Quinn did not transgress any element of his planning permission.

Quinn would not be intimidated, and his timing was perfect. The house and road building boom took off in Ireland in the 1990s and Quinn Cement was a major beneficiary. Its trucks became a common sight up and down the country's roads.

The business generated huge amounts of cash, which Quinn continued to invest in his local area. Just 500 metres from his home in Ballyconnell, he built what was then one of the best hotels in the country, the four-star Slieve Russell, complete with championship golf course.

As his cement and leisure interests grew, Quinn became irked at the mounting cost of insuring his various businesses. In 1996 he decided to set up his own insurance company solely to manage his own risks. Once he understood the business, and saw the profits to be made, he launched Quinn Insurance under the brands Quinn Direct and Quinn Life. Quinn Direct would target the motor and commercial insurance market, Quinn Life the life and pensions market.

The cost of motor insurance rose 57 per cent in Ireland in the 1990s, driven up by the high cost of claims, particularly legal costs. Quinn believed that he could drive down general insurance premiums and take market share by settling legitimate claims early (thereby avoiding legal expense) and keeping his own administration costs low and selling directly to customers rather than through brokers. For almost a decade, he was proved spectacularly right. Quinn Life, meanwhile, was a cut-price assurance company that offered pension-type investments without the hidden charges so beloved of the industry.

With the insurance company up and running, Quinn's next target was another industrial behemoth. At the time, Irish Glass, later renamed Ardagh, held a domestic monopoly over the production of glass bottles for the drinks and dairy industries. Irish Glass operated from a down-at-heel factory at Ringsend in Dublin's south docklands. In 1998 Quinn built a large, state-of-the-art factory in Derrylin at a cost of €120 million, with a €26 million grant from the UK's Industrial Development Board. The factory, which employed 330 people, had the capacity to meet all of Ireland's glass bottle needs. Quinn now went head to head with Irish Glass. Within two years of opening Derrylin, Quinn was planning a second glass-bottle factory, this time in the north of England.

Quinn generally preferred to use banks with an established presence along the border, such as Northern Bank, and he was not an

Anglo client during the first phase of his feverish expansion. That changed in 1999, when Anglo acquired Smurfit Paribas Bank. At the time of the takeover, Quinn had relatively modest borrowings with Smurfit Paribas, but a year later the relationship deepened.

Quinn was a born risk-taker. On his instructions, Quinn Insurance made a number of large bets on technology shares in the middle of 2000. The dotcom investment bubble had just burst, and Quinn bet that a number of the top technology shares, battered in the sell-off, would bounce back.

This time, Quinn got it wrong. Quinn Direct lost €48 million on turnover of just €126 million in 2000. Poor investments accounted for €20 million of those losses in a year when other insurance companies were reporting investment gains.

In 2001 Quinn's bankers injected €70 million into Quinn Direct to shore up the stock-market losses and secure the business. It was not a rescue. The entrepreneur was asset rich but cash poor. Anglo, in its first significant involvement with Quinn, led the way in helping to raise the cash to plug gaps in the insurance business. FitzPatrick does not recall Anglo's 2001 involvement with Quinn in detail, but 'I do remember that there was a problem with him. He needed to get it right. And he got it right apparently. We were very good at helping him.'

The losses were grist to the mill for Quinn's rivals in the insurance business, who latched on to the opportunity to highlight the insurer's shortcomings to the industry regulator. But Mary Harney, the enterprise minister, and her civil servants backed Quinn. Harney pioneered reform of the insurance sector, and Quinn, which was bringing premiums down faster than anybody else in the market, was seen as a part of the solution.

In the wake of the dotcom fiasco, Sean Quinn stood down from the insurance company's investment committee; and, to help ease the minds of the regulatory authorities, Paddy Mullarkey, a former secretary of the Department of Finance, was appointed to the Quinn board.

In a rare interview with the *Sunday Business Post* in late 2001, Quinn shrugged off his losses. 'Quinn Direct is not in trouble,' he said. 'The only time that Quinn Direct will be in trouble is when Sean Quinn is in trouble. And Sean Quinn is not in any trouble.'

Having righted the insurance business, Quinn Group bounced back strongly. In 2003 it recorded a turnover of €593 million and pre-tax profits of €164 million. The cement business continued to perform well as Ireland's construction boom entered a new, more aggressive phase. The general insurance business also benefited from the boom. There were more cars on the road that needed insuring and Quinn offered the cheapest rates, particularly for younger drivers. Its share of the market grew rapidly.

Even the glass business was starting to turn a profit, and Quinn snatched contracts from Ardagh. Despite the concerns of competitors, Quinn added more and more manufacturing lines to the Derrylin plant. In March 2002 Ardagh raised the white flag, closing its Ringsend factory – the site would later be purchased in one of the most extravagant and disastrous property deals in Irish history – to concentrate on its British businesses. Quinn now dominated the Irish glass market.

The huge cash flow from all these businesses allowed Quinn to begin a second wave of investment. He backed the buyout of NCB Stockbrokers from Ulster Bank, taking a 20 per cent stake in the broker for about €3 million. Announcing the deal, NCB chairman Conor Killeen said: 'The people at Quinn are similar to ourselves. They are free-thinkers and independent, and like challenging the establishment.'

Quinn was impressed by Killeen, a former head of equities with investment bank Dresdner Kleinwort Wasserstein in London, and appointed him as a non-executive director to the Quinn Group's board.

In early 2003 Quinn launched a bid to get control of Ardagh and its substantial British businesses. Ardagh's chairman, Paul Coulson, defeated the Quinn bid with the backing of his banks – led by Anglo.

Undeterred by losing out at Ardagh, Quinn bought Barlo, a radiator and plastics company, in 2004. A decisive €85 million bid trumped an attempt by the company management team to buy out the group. As at Noel Smyth's Dunloe Ewart, financier Dermot Desmond was kingmaker in the bidding war, selling Quinn a large stake and putting him in an unstoppable position to take control of the group.

Barlo was a large business, with operations in twelve countries, and it greatly increased Quinn's international reach.

'The decision-making process within the organization is extremely quick,' said one source close to the company at the time of the Barlo bid. 'It is a hallmark.'

In 2004 Quinn bought a 13 per cent stake in Airtricity, the wind-energy company founded by Eddie O'Connor, for €36 million, complementing his own wind-farm business, which included a farm overlooking Derrylin. In early 2005 Quinn purchased the Belfry, a world-renowned golf resort and conference centre based outside Birmingham, for €275 million. The business was profitable in its own right, but it was also an ideal location to entertain the group's growing British client base. It would be a calling card for the Quinn Group, a potent indicator to customers that they were dealing with a company of real substance.

In Britain, Quinn Group was spending €400 million on two huge investment projects: building Europe's largest glass-bottling factory in Ellesmere Port in Cheshire and the world's biggest radiator plant in Newport, South Wales. It was planning a further €180 million investment in a chemical factory near Leipzig, to make raw materials for Quinn's plastics business.

Despite helping to provide the cash that got Quinn Direct over its funding 'hump' in 2001, Anglo did not emerge as a major financier of the Quinn Group. To fund its growth, the group tapped a syndicate of banks led by Barclays. It also successfully completed a number of bond offerings in America, attracting top insurance companies as investors. These lines of credit, and the massive cash generation of the manufacturing and insurance business, fuelled the Quinn Group's huge expansion plans.

Sean Quinn's personal investments were another matter entirely. Quinn was, by 2005, an extremely wealthy man. The family business was valued at up to €3 billion. This paper wealth allowed Quinn to open up a whole new front of entrepreneurial activity. This time, Anglo would most definitely be along for the ride.

In mid 2004, just five months before the Czech Republic joined the European Union, Quinn set a record price for a hotel deal in

Central Europe, paying €145 million for the Prague Hilton and an adjoining budget Ibis property. Anglo provided the finance. The Hilton was a fine hotel where, some years later, an uncomfortable-looking Quinn would be photographed with America's new President Barack Obama and his wife, Michelle.

The deal would become the first of many. Quinn looked east to get superior returns from property investment and set up a company called Quinn Investments Sweden to control his burgeoning interests. Based in Sweden for tax purposes, QIS invested in high-risk, fast-growth emerging markets; Quinn sent investment teams to scout opportunities in the emerging economies of Turkey, Russia, India and the Baltic states.

'We always followed the bigger return,' Quinn said in 2007. 'Some people go for a safe return – we go for a bigger return. We don't like the 3, 4 or 5 per cent returns. Any of the properties we ever bought, we only bought them on the basis that we'd receive a 10 per cent return, with one or two exceptions. In Prague, Bulgaria, Poland, Russia, wherever we went, we always got those double figures, and now of course we have to go that little bit further.'

That little bit further included a DIY store in Ufa, the capital of the Russian republic of Bashkortostan (just north of Kazakhstan), and land purchased with a view to developing a 500-bed hotel in Hyderabad, India. QIS also purchased a shopping centre in Kiev, the capital of the Ukraine, and a warehouse in Kazan, Russia.

By the end of 2008 Anglo had lent Quinn, through QIS, €500 million to engage in his personal emerging-market investments. Quinn's lending director at Anglo was Michael O'Sullivan, one of the most senior lenders in the bank.

Quinn was clearly impressed by Anglo, and he showed his admiration by taking what would easily be the largest-ever punt on an Irish stock-market company by a single individual.

It is impossible to look at the boom in Ireland, and Anglo Irish Bank's role in it, without understanding the primacy of leverage. In financial terms, leverage is the use of debt to amplify gain.

Imagine that you have €1 million in cash that you wish to invest. You borrow €9 million and, with the total of €10 million, you buy a property. If that property were to rise in value by 10 per cent to €11 million, the return you have made on your €1 million investment is €1 million, a gain of 100 per cent, or ten times the percentage gain you'd have made if you'd used your own money to cover the entire purchase price.

In a rising market, leverage is an extraordinarily powerful investment tool. But it can also be very, very dangerous. If the value of the same property were to drop by 10 per cent to €9 million, then your loss is €1 million, or 100 per cent of your total investment. Just as leverage amplifies gains, it amplifies losses. In short, leverage is an investor's best friend when a market is going up, and its worst enemy when a market is going down. Leverage is the ultimate means of getting rich quick, and getting poor even quicker.

In the early years of the new millennium, with markets rising, Ireland learned to love leverage. Real interest rates were negative – in other words, the cost of money trailed the cost of living – and this made leverage extremely accessible and affordable.

Anglo was a key purveyor of leverage in the property-investment market. It was not unusual for Anglo Irish Bank to finance the purchase of a property by an investment syndicate and also to finance the individual investments of the members in the same syndicate. Anglo might require the syndicate members to put up 30 per cent of the purchase price of the building, meaning that it was lending only 70 per cent of the purchase. Its loan-to-value ratio was therefore a conservative 70 per cent. But what was less apparent to the credit committee was that the bank was also heavily financing the syndicate members' investment in the same deal – in other words, much or all of the other 30 per cent – often through Anglo Irish Private Banking. The private bank did insist on taking additional security before it lent more money, but this was almost always more property. Old property was being used to fund new property, making the bank even more vulnerable to any crash. As long as the property market kept rising, these highly leveraged deals were spectacularly profitable for investors. Anglo comforted itself with cross-guarantees against the investors' other holdings, often made up of property, and its trademark personal guarantees.

The other get-rich-quick scheme during the boom was planning gain. Achieving planning permission sprinkled gold dust on car parks, warehouses and disused factories right across Ireland. Motor dealers and builders' merchants left their Main Street premises for the outskirts of town, selling out to property developers who sought to unlock the site value by getting permission to build apartments, houses, offices and shops.

Advancing prices for homes and development land fuelled the hunger for land, which in turn further fuelled price rises. An International Monetary Fund report in 2000 said Irish property prices were unlikely to continue to grow as strongly in the future as they had in the previous decade. All the evidence from other countries suggested that there would be no repeat of the rapid appreciation of prices. Yet the 1990s boom – prices rose by up to 75 per cent over the second half of the decade – was just a prelude. Between 2000 and 2006 Irish residential property prices tripled.

The housing market was being driven forward by a quantum leap in wealth and incomes, demographics (including high net immigration), the availability of cheap mortgages, and the widespread belief that most or all of these factors would remain in place, driving up prices further, for the foreseeable future. Anglo and other banks allowed developers to 'roll up' interest on loans to purchase land until planning permission was achieved. The extent of the interest roll-up was based partly on the client's other security and cash flow; but developers were often buying land on the never-never.

In the final three months of 2005 Sean Quinn began trading in the shares of the bank he had come to admire so much. Quinn made the investment through what is known as 'Contracts for Difference'. A CFD differs from traditional share trading in that it does not involve the purchase of the shares; rather, it is a bet on their price movement. The trader enters into a contract with the CFD provider, who agrees to pay the difference between the opening price and the closing price at the end of the contract. The big attraction for investors is the way it facilitates the use of leverage. In order to open a CFD position, the investor has to put down only a percentage of the value of the underlying shares, known as the 'margin'. The margin could be as low as 10 per cent. And, just as in the property market, the use of such extreme leverage meant that small upward movements in a share price could produce greatly amplified gains. Apart from the obvious attraction of leverage, trading in CFDs was exempt from stamp duty; and, as there was no actual share purchase involved, trading remained anonymous. The upside for the brokers was an attractive commission and interest charged on the value of the borrowed shares.

Cantor Fitzgerald and Davy stockbrokers were early promoters of CFDs in the Irish market. In the late 2005 Quinn used both Cantor and Davy to take a position on 8.9 million shares at an average cost of €11.32 each in Anglo. Quinn put up a margin of €20 million in cash to Davy and Cantor, in order to take control of shares worth about five times that. If Anglo's share price rose by 20 per cent – which it did – Quinn doubled his original investment; and, better still, he would pay no stamp duty on his profits.

By the time Quinn opened his position in Anglo CFDs, the bank's strong performance had been recognized internationally. At the start of 2006 Mercer Oliver Wyman, one of the world's top financial services strategy and risk-management consultants, named Anglo as the world's top-performing bank in terms of returns for shareholders from 2001 to 2005. The bank's share price had risen 300 per cent, from €3.14 to €12.90, during the period, and investors who had put all their dividends back into buying more shares were up an incredible 800 per cent.

In March 2006 the Financial Regulator paid a site visit to the headquarters of the Quinn Group and gave the group's systems, controls and corporate governance structure a clean bill of health. But the Regulator's remit did not extend to any of the family's investments outside the group, such as its owner's growing gamble on Anglo.

During the same month the Office of the Revenue Commissioners, then chaired by Frank Daly, announced its intention to impose stamp-duty charges on CFDs. Behind the scenes Ireland's powerful stock-broking community swung into action to convince the minister for finance, Brian Cowen, and his civil servants to oppose the move. The *Irish Times*, using the Freedom of Information Act, discovered that on 22 March Tony Garry, chief executive of Davy, e-mailed Tom Considine, a senior civil servant in the Department of Finance, saying the stockbrokers 'continue to get hugely negative feedback from overseas investors on the proposed duty changes'.

Two days later officials from PricewaterhouseCoopers, acting on behalf of clients, met officials from the department to lobby them to the same effect. A script note from the meeting records one unidentified participant saying that CFDs are used by hedge funds, 'not private clients', and that they are usually held for two or three weeks' duration. This was not entirely accurate. Cantor and Davy had been widely marketing CFDs to high-net-worth individuals, including Quinn and major developers, for the previous twelve months.

The same day a note was sent to Cowen informing him of what was said at the meeting. On the following Monday the Irish Stock Exchange met with the Department of Finance and the Revenue Commissioners. According to notes from the meeting, the Stock Exchange told the department that 'hedge funds account for around 30 per cent of overall activity and CFDs were their preferred instrument'. It warned that these players were likely to withdraw completely from the market if the tax break were removed. On 30 March, Cowen and his civil servants buckled under the pressure. Cowen announced a review of the measure and the Revenue withdrew its notice to the market. The review of the tax was buried and CFDs remained outside the stamp duty net.

At the end of March, with his earlier CFD bets already paying off handsomely, Quinn increased his exposure to Anglo by buying additional contracts worth €106 million, using Davy and Cantor again but also two other providers, IG Index and Merrill Lynch. Again, his margin was just 20 per cent. He also started placing CFD bets on other shares on the Irish stock market, including McInerney, the house builder, and Ryanair. Quinn's non-Anglo bets eventually reached hundreds of millions of euro.

But his main focus was Anglo, and he continued to stack up the bet. In June 2006 Quinn sold his stake in Airtricity, the green energy company, for €70 million – almost double the value of his original investment just two years before. The deal freed up more cash to

spend on Anglo. In the summer of 2006 he increased his bets with
IG Index and Merrill Lynch while maintaining his positions with
Cantor and Davy. He opened up his fifth CFD account, this time
with Bear Stearns, and took a position in another 9.8 million Anglo
shares at an average price of €12.79.

At this stage his CFD providers were getting a little concerned.
Quinn's 'margin' on the Bear Stearns trade was 35 per cent, far higher
than that imposed by any other provider. Undaunted, Quinn plunged
back into the stock that same autumn, putting up a margin of €25
million with Credit Suisse, Davy and IG Index to take out contracts
worth €101 million on Anglo shares. As 2006 closed, he went again to
Credit Suisse and placed his biggest bet yet, taking an additional €220
million exposure to Anglo, topped up with a small additional exposure via IG Index.

At the end of 2006 the value of Quinn's Anglo contracts stood at a
vertiginous €653 million.

The bank FitzPatrick built was now receiving worldwide recognition on a grand scale. At the World Economic Forum in Davos on 24
January 2007, Mercer Oliver Wyman lauded Anglo yet again in its
shareholder 'performance hall of fame' and rated it the best of the
170 banks worth over $10 billion it had surveyed globally. 'Anglo
Irish Bank owes much of its success to a concentrated focus on business lending, treasury and wealth management in the Irish, UK and
US markets. Business lending, its largest and most profitable seg-
ment, has grown by 38 per cent annually over the last ten years,'
MOW said. 'A centralized loan-approval process has helped the bank
maintain high asset quality and minimize the risk of portfolio concentration.'

MOW also praised the bank's low cost base, which it felt provided
a 'strong foundation for organic growth'.

Anglo's share price closed in 2006 at €15.71. Quinn was up tens of
millions on his highly leveraged bet. In gambling terms, those returns
kept Quinn at the table. He did not cash in any of his contracts, or realize his gains. Instead he allowed his bets to roll on into 2007, staking
more and more of his personal fortune on just one stock.

This obsession with Anglo was richly ironic. In 2006 Quinn Group was awarded *Business & Finance*'s Company of the Year. Picking up the award, Liam McCaffrey, group chief executive, stressed the group's motto, 'Strength through Diversity'.

Quinn Group, like Anglo, was turning in record-beating results. Quinn Direct, McCaffrey said, made a pre-tax profit of €123 million in the six-month period to the end of June 2006, an increase of 38 per cent over the first half of 2005.

As 2007 dawned, Sean Quinn continued the expansion of his business. He started the year by buying the Irish business of BUPA, the British health insurer. It decided to exit the Irish market after more than a decade, citing unfair competition from the state-owned VHI. Quinn spent an estimated €30 million to buy the business, which he rebranded Quinn Health.

The government was grateful: Quinn's move saved the jobs of BUPA's 300 employees, ensured continuing cover for 500,000 health-insurance customers and deflected any criticism over government policy in the area. Quinn Insurance now had almost a million policyholders, and the noisy upstart was officially the second-largest insurance company in the state.

The deal required the approval of the Financial Regulator, which sent a team to Cavan to pore over the Quinn Group's books; but, again, the proprietor's enormous share position in Anglo Irish Bank was not on the radar.

As the due diligence was going on, Sean Quinn kept betting on Anglo, bigger and bolder than ever. In the first three months of 2007 he took on a further €790 million in Anglo contracts – doubling the already enormous position built up over the previous fifteen months.

In a speech given to the Cavan County Enterprise Board at that time, in a packed Slieve Russell Hotel, Quinn gave a rare insight into his thinking. 'I suppose I was always very greedy,' he said. 'Whatever we had, I was never happy with what we had. And I was always looking for new opportunities. If it was sand and gravel, it was blocks and readymix; if it was blocks and readymix, it was roof tiles and the floor.

'We came from a very simple background and we tried to make business always simple. We don't believe in too much fuss, we never got a feasibility study done in our lives . . . I don't use a mobile phone, I play cards in a house at night where you have to go out into the front street to go to the toilet.

'I enjoy that. I live a very simple life and that's the way I want to continue living that life. I'm not overly shy, but I much prefer to just sit back and enjoy what I'm doing, with my two dogs, the Wellington boots on and dodging about the mountain.'

In the same speech, Quinn cited David Drumm and Michael O'Leary, the boss of Ryanair, as two businessmen he admired.

On 24 May 2007 Anglo's share price reached a record high of €17.31. Quinn's paper profit on his extraordinary investment was now probably in the region of €200 million.

It was something of a false position. One of the reasons that Anglo shares were bid up so high was that Quinn was so active in the market. Elsewhere in international markets, a credit crunch was setting in, property bubbles were being detected and scepticism was rising about Anglo and the Irish economic story. The quiet billionaire, who every month rolled a significant portion his fortune on Anglo, suddenly found the house moving against him. Ireland stood out as particularly vulnerable to a property shock, and Anglo stood out as a main lender to the sector.

In his book *Ireland's House Party: What the Estate Agents Don't Want You to Know*, Derek Brawn, a former head of research at Savills Hamilton Osborne King, recalls two meetings he held with hedge funds over the summer of 2007. Och-Ziff and Centaurus were both London-based clients of Davy stockbrokers. The hedge funds were keen to learn all about the Irish property market.

'I knew at once that they were fishing for data to support their view that the best way to "short" the Irish property market was to execute the trade by "shortselling" Irish financials, namely the four main banks,' Brawn writes.

A number of hedge funds were aware of Quinn's CFD position, though probably not the scale of it. As early as January 2007 the *Sunday Times* reported that Quinn had taken at least a 5 per cent stake in Anglo through CFDs. The market was awash with talk of his involvement, and estimates of the size of his holding rose throughout that year.

The knowledge that there was a single investor who had a big 'long' bet, i.e. a wager that the stock would go up, added to the stock's vulnerability. The short-sellers scented blood.

Throughout April, May and June, Quinn took on the short-selling hedge funds. In those three months he placed another €655 million bet using four CFD providers, including Lehman Brothers and Bear Stearns. Anglo's share price rose to a record high of €17.56 on 31 May 2007, propelled by Quinn's activity in the market. Anglo at this price was worth over €13 billion.

The shorts continued to gnaw away at the Anglo share price. Through the summer of 2007 it started to fall steeply. By 17 September the stock was down to €11.63, almost 34 per cent off its peak.

By now, the leverage that Quinn had embraced so enthusiastically to build up his massive position in Anglo was biting back. On some of his later contracts, entered into at near-record prices, Quinn was firmly in negative equity. When this happens, a CFD provider asks the investor to reinstate his margin by putting more money on the table. If the investor does not meet this so-called 'margin call', the CFD provider can sell the shares in the market to recoup its cash, with the result that losses are automatically crystallized for the investor.

Quinn was in a bind. He could have tried to wind down his position by selling off his CFDs. But he was now in so deep, with so many different CFD brokers, that any sell-off would have accelerated the downward spiral in the bank's share price and triggered even more margin calls.

It was a treacherous but still retrievable position. Quinn would have had to admit he was wrong and take his huge losses, estimated at €500 million, on the chin. The Quinn Group, still very strong, would have survived such a hit. Instead Quinn took his ultimate gamble. He decided to keep going, throwing more of his family fortune into Anglo during the last six months of 2007 in the hope that the share price would recover.

Quinn bet that the drop in Anglo shares was temporary, as the world's financial markets creaked and the contagion of America's sub-prime property crisis began to spread. There was also a widespread feeling among brokers and even bank management that Anglo was suffering from an anti-Irish bias among London hedge funds, happy to glory in a turning Irish economy. Quinn was driven by gain, but the buying was also being sustained by more than a little national pride.

Between June and September of 2007 he took on another €343 million exposure to Anglo. By now he quietly controlled over 20 per cent of the bank through CFDs.

Throughout the summer of 2007 Anglo management was becoming increasingly worried. Through data provided by Euroclear, the share clearing-house, the bank could see that the number of its shares out on loan was rising. Fund managers loan out stock for different reasons, not just to CFD investors, so Anglo could not gauge the level of CFD activity in the stock, but it had good cause to worry.

All that summer rumours kept swirling that Quinn had built a large stake in the bank. Newspaper reports gradually moved the estimate of his stake upwards, above 10 per cent. The speculation in the market was it could be much more. Anglo looked hard at its share register and estimated that up to 14 per cent of the bank could be held through CFDs. Gradually it dawned on the board and executives inside Anglo that, rather than dozens of different investors, the CFDs might be controlled by just one man: Sean Quinn.

The issue had to be confronted. If there was a potential 14 per cent shareholder out there, then the bank needed to know. Quinn was also one of the bank's biggest customers. If he was borrowing heavily to punt on the bank's stock, then that was also an unstable state of affairs.

Just after 9 a.m. on 11 September 2007, Sean FitzPatrick and David Drumm, Anglo Irish Bank's chairman and chief executive, walked into lobby of the Ardboyne Hotel, a Quinn Group three-star hotel in the centre of Navan, Co. Meath.

The men were greeted by Quinn and Liam McCaffrey, his trusted lieutenant and the chief executive of the Quinn Group. The men repaired to a meeting room in the hotel, which FitzPatrick describes as 'pretty sparse but with a table and chairs. They were sitting on one side of the table. We were sitting on the other. Quite informal: "Sean, Sean, David and Liam", and what have you.'

Quinn struck FitzPatrick as a 'real 1960s Irishman'.

'He was one of those hail-fellow-well-met, ah sure I will go down there and play the old cards, five or six lads for ten bob, or whatever it was,' FitzPatrick says. 'He was always producing all that and would nearly be blessing himself. Everything will be all right. He was very human, but . . . I didn't easily like him.'

Drumm had set up the meeting. He and Quinn had spoken on the phone about the market rumours about his CFD position, and both parties agreed that this matter was something best discussed face to face.

'David wanted to meet with him. David knew more than I did at the time. David was more up to speed clearly about the activities of CFDs. He was bringing me . . . because he always felt that Quinn regarded me as a superhuman, as a superhero. He wanted Quinn to see how disappointed I would be.'

According to FitzPatrick, the meeting was not long: 'There wasn't a lot to say.' The main question was: how big was Quinn's CFD position in the bank?

'What he said, I don't know whether it was 19 per cent or 22 per cent,' FitzPatrick says. 'That was more than we thought.'

FitzPatrick's recall of the precise number given at the meeting is vague, but the actual size of the Quinn holding at this time was at least 25 per cent. 'We were shocked,' FitzPatrick says. 'Both of us were. I certainly was because I was never led to believe it was that figure. And I believe David was also shocked. The point that they made then at that stage was that they were going to have to get rid of [the shares]. The problem then was they were losing money.

'[There was] no banging the table or anything like that. [But there were] voices raised. I mean: "Jesus, that is terrible dangerous!"

'I was physically shocked. I wasn't expecting that. I said: What! David said afterwards to me that he looked at [Quinn] and he just saw the surprise in Quinn's eyes at my reaction. How negative I was.'

Quinn assured the Anglo bosses that he had no plans to convert the CFDs into shares and take over Anglo, an option that had been widely speculated in the media and privately by brokers. 'He told us absolutely, no, he wasn't. He saw it as a good investment in a very fine bank which he was dealing with. He knew the bank, knew the style of operation and liked it.' FitzPatrick says he was 'pretty sure' at the time that Quinn did not want to take over the bank.

Quinn was very interested in how the bank was doing and wanted to be reassured that the market was wrong about Anglo.

'David would have said: The bank is going very well. We are going to have a very good year this year. It was September time and the results were coming out. We were saying things were good.'

The extent of the information that the Anglo duo gave was limited. 'Your man was not a shareholder. He was punter in the stock.'

Quinn in turn told the bankers that his businesses were also doing well.

'Here were two successful Irish firms, chatting away to each other about a particular issue that your man had with us – the CFDs,' FitzPatrick recalls. 'He didn't have an issue with us, but now we were aware of it and we didn't like it. We said this is wrong. Individuals can't have big stakes in banks. It is bad for individuals and it is bad for banks. We would like him to get rid of all of those [CFDs] and get it down below 5 per cent ASAP.

'I don't even know what the figures were but he was saying he was at a loss at this stage . . . I think he also felt listening to David, and possibly me as well, that things were going well within the bank. Therefore the rest of the world had got it wrong. Sean [Quinn] had got it right and time would show that he had got it right, and the share price would come back again.'

Quinn's disposition at the meeting clearly suggested that he wanted to manage his investment down on his own terms. 'He felt that [the bank's share price] was not a proper reflection in the minds of the investors as to how the bank was doing. He just felt that when that became quite clear to the investor community the share price would look after itself. Then he could unravel what he had created.'

Drumm, however, took a hard line, according to FitzPatrick.

Although he kept his temper in check, he was furious with Quinn's logic. 'David could see that coming and he was saying it doesn't work like that. We just said it is just unhealthy and it is wrong, plus the Central Bank will go wild.'

Of course, Quinn was also a substantial Anglo borrower. Anglo had advanced Quinn large sums of money for his property investment in Eastern Europe, but the chairman and chief executive did not press Quinn on how he might be financing any margin calls. FitzPatrick says that Quinn did not mention that he could not, even then, afford to meet his margin calls from his own pocket. 'No. No. There was no question of that.'

FitzPatrick recalls that he told Anglo board members – including Gary McGann, Lar Bradshaw and Ned Sullivan – about the size of Quinn's holding as he 'met them'; he waited to tell the full board at the next board meeting. (He is not sure of the date of this board meeting, but believes it was not long afterwards.)

'What you have to bear in mind is, Quinn was seen as the richest man in Ireland at that stage. [He was seen as] beyond any sort of financial strain. It was felt that it was a dealable deal, in other words, it was sortable out.'

After his secret meeting with Drumm and FitzPatrick, Quinn went back into the stock market and bought even more Anglo contracts. He was more convinced than ever that the market was wrong about the bank. He took a position on Anglo shares worth another €111 million at €10.15 a share via Bear Stearns, Dresdner, Lehman Brothers and Morgan Stanley. His stake was now up to 28.5 per cent of the company: 28 per cent through CFDs and half a per cent through directly held shares.

Anglo had no idea at the time that Quinn was betting again, according to FitzPatrick.

'What the fuck was he doing?' he asks. 'He just keeps on going. It was like a drug.'

Before long, this issue would prompt the biggest crisis in the history of the bank.

Three weeks after the meeting with Quinn, FitzPatrick flew to Germany for an operation on his prostate. Cancer had been diagnosed the previous June by doctors at the Blackrock Clinic, leading to a worrying summer for the banker.

In Germany, FitzPatrick collapsed on the operating table, a complication arising from his diabetes. He revived, and ultimately the procedure was a success.

7. Massacre

'Our exposure is not to the building, it's to the money that comes from the leasing of it. If the value of the property goes down, it doesn't matter. We still get our loan repaid.'

During the summer of 2007 the implosion of the US sub-prime mortgage market triggered a global credit crunch. The most high-profile early victim was the British mortgage lender Northern Rock, which faced a run on deposits and required £29 billion in emergency funding from the Bank of England.

Irish banks were quick to distance themselves from the Northern Rock crisis. They were not as heavily reliant as Northern Rock on funding from the mortgage securitization market, which had now seized up. The message from Irish banks and regulators was one of reassurance: there was nothing amiss here.

For one former Anglo Irish Bank executive, though, the events of the summer of 2007 would have profound consequences.

Tiarnan O'Mahoney had quickly brushed off the disappointment of losing out on the top job at Anglo to David Drumm in late 2004 by implementing an ambitious plan B. He established International Securities Trading Corporation in May 2005, a firm specializing in the buying and selling of bank bonds. O'Mahoney hired Goodbody Stockbrokers to raise funds from private investors to fund the venture and set an initial target of raising €50 million. By tapping his extensive contacts in the banking market, and Anglo's builder and developer clients, ISTC managed to raise €165 million: the largest-ever fundraising by a private Irish company.

The register of investors was a roll-call of the great and good. It included Denis O'Brien, former EU commissioner Peter Sutherland (then chairman of Goldman Sachs International and BP) and Lochlann Quinn, a former AIB chairman. Tellingly, though, the largest single shareholder, staking €10 million on the venture, was a house builder, Seamus Ross, who was also an Anglo client. Bernard McNamara was in there, as were Sean Mulryan of Ballymore, Johnny Ronan of Treasury Holdings, Gerry Gannon and Paddy Kelly.

In truth, the vast majority of these developer-investors had no in-depth understanding of O'Mahoney's business. But the former Anglo man was highly regarded by the bank's clients. '[Our investment] was driven by our relationship with Tiarnan and Anglo,' Paddy Kelly told the *Sunday Times*. 'He had this great idea and we liked it, and invested.

'Banks need to lend money to one another. I'm no expert but they always seem to need finance. Anglo used to do a lot of this and [O'Mahoney] was a specialist.'

ISTC became known as the banker's banker. 'The real attraction of this business is that you are lending to the highest-quality borrower that there is,' O'Mahoney said. But the banker's banker tag was a mis-nomer. In truth, ISTC was a highly leveraged investment fund. It used the shareholders' equity to borrow hundreds of millions of euro from a syndicate of eighteen of the world's largest banks to start trading in bank bonds.

The first two years were startlingly successful. Unusually for a business start-up, ISTC paid a dividend to shareholders in its first year after clocking up a €6.5 million profit.

The venture was so successful that Friends First, the Irish life-assurance company that is part of the Dutch Eureko group, advanced O'Mahoney €40 million through a bond that it then sold to Irish investors. The small-time investors included credit unions and some pensioners who were no doubt impressed by the banker's banker concept.

In May 2007 ISTC announced half-year profits of €5 million, a substantial increase on the same period in 2006. The company was now firmly on track to list its shares on the London stock market by the end of 2008, which was O'Mahoney's expressed target at the time of the company's fundraising. O'Mahoney launched a $150 million bond in the Far East to raise further finances; investor demand was such that ISTC ended up raising $235 million.

ISTC's reversal of fortune was to be swift and savage. Within three months of raising the bond in the Far East, the sub-prime crisis created a freeze in the market for bank-debt securities. There was fear in the markets. ISTC was finding it nearly impossible to trade. As part of its business model, it needed to cash in securities intermittently to service its own borrowings. With the markets closed, that proved almost impossible. The company started to face cash-flow difficulties.

O'Mahoney looked to his former employer to help ease his funding problem.

Anglo was hardly a stranger to the venture. Sean FitzPatrick had personally sunk €2.5 million into ISTC. A number of the bank's largest clients were investors, and Anglo Irish Private Bank had provided finance to many of the equity investors to buy their shares.

In late summer of 2007 O'Mahoney picked up the phone and rang FitzPatrick. 'I was at my niece's wedding down in Limerick,' FitzPatrick recalls. 'He said, Howya, Sean, can I meet with you? I said, Sure, Tiarnan. He said, Where will we meet? I said, I am down here in Limerick and I am at a wedding and it is on tomorrow. He said, What time is the wedding? I said twelve o'clock. He said, If I drove down for about 9.30 a.m. we could meet. I said, But I am down in Limerick. He said, I will drive down. I said to myself, God, it must be serious. He is going to drive all the way down from Dublin to meet me.'

The following morning in Limerick, FitzPatrick recalls, O'Mahoney told him that ISTC needed €15 million to solve its short-term liquidity problem and 'asked could the bank lend him money. I said, Jesus, I don't know, Tiarnan . . . I will tell you what, I will talk to David Drumm and Willie [McAteer].'

O'Mahoney had, in FitzPatrick's words, 'stolen a few guys' from Anglo's treasury department when setting up ISTC, a move that did not endear him to Drumm. McAteer had soldiered alongside O'Mahoney and would have been more favourably disposed to him.

Ultimately, Drumm and McAteer turned O'Mahoney down. 'They rang me and said, Sean, we are not going to do it,' FitzPatrick says. 'I said, Have you really looked at it? They said, We have, Sean, this deal is not good.'

For his own part, FitzPatrick put a further €2.5 million into the venture.

ISTC never got over its funding problems. When Moody's marked down the ratings on a number of bonds held by the company, it faced further calls for cash from its bankers. A late rescue attempt, involving Dermot Desmond's International Investment and Underwriting, failed to materialize. O'Mahoney's company collapsed in November 2007. At the time it was the largest business failure in Irish corporate history, with international banks owed €830 million. FitzPatrick's personal investment of €5 million was wiped out. A rescue was facilitated by a High Court examinership, and Collins Stewart, a London broker, took the business over, but the high-profile investors and the small-time players hooked in by Friends First were completely wiped out.

ISTC was the victim of an extraordinary set of unforeseen circumstances, but its failure was a sign of things to come. It was a concrete indication that what was still being called the 'sub-prime crisis', with roots in places like Nevada and Florida, had dangerous implications throughout the global financial system. International money markets were heading for lockdown. But few in Irish banking saw the demise of ISTC as anything more than an isolated business failure.

The ISTC collapse barely registered among the problems facing David Drumm in the latter half of 2007. Just before presenting the bank's results in late November, Drumm went to the dentist for root-canal treatment. It was, he told Brian Carey at the time, 'the most relaxing forty-five minutes he had spent in months'.

Drumm and his management had been fire-fighting rumours about the bank. The onset of the credit crunch and the slowdown in the Irish property market put Anglo in the spotlight. The bank suspected that London hedge funds were circulating stories about large corporate depositors and other banks removing funds from Anglo. One widely circulated rumour was that Ryanair, which generates huge cash flow and holds deposits of hundreds of million of euro at any one time, had pulled its money from the bank. The rumour was unfounded, but the extent to which it took root was telling.

On Monday, 5 November 2007, the bank took the highly unusual step – in advance of announcing its annual results – of indicating to Dresdner Kleinwort, the investment bank, that it was not facing a liquidity crisis. Anglo shares had lost almost 23 per cent of their value over the previous four weeks. A Dresdner research report, titled 'No liquidity or funding problems', said that Anglo had assured Dresdner that all was well at the bank. 'Anglo also clearly said that it had not accessed the ECB [European Central Bank] or Bank of England for emergency funding; it is a net inter-bank lender,' the investment bank's analysts told the market. 'We are now even more convinced that the fundamentals are safe.' Anglo shares bounced 1.4 per cent to close at €10.94 the day after the broker note.

Drumm did his best to kill the rumours when announcing a 45 per cent rise in pre-tax profits for the financial year 2007. The bank broke the billion-euro profit mark for the very first time. Drumm had achieved in just three years what he had committed to doing, on taking up the job, in five.

But the market's worries did not go away. On 28 January 2008, UBS, the investment bank, put out a research note on Irish banks predicting a '30 per cent downside risk to commercial-property values'. UBS predicted increases in impairment charges and downgraded all the Irish banks one notch; the recommendation for AIB and Anglo was reduced to 'sell'.

At Anglo's AGM on 1 February, FitzPatrick described this report as 'undeserved'. Before a gathering of 200 shareholders at Dublin's Mansion House, the Anglo chairman said: 'UBS is entitled to its views but I disagree fundamentally with it.'

Anglo was not concerned about the value of commercial property but rather about the ability of its borrowers to repay their loans, FitzPatrick declared. 'Our exposure is not to the building, it's to the money that comes from the leasing of it,' he said. 'If the value of the property goes down, it doesn't matter. We still get our loan repaid.' FitzPatrick was nothing if not consistent in this, one of his core philosophies. It sidestepped the fact that the building remained the core of Anglo's security. It also did not address a growing problem in Anglo's loan book: its exposure to development lending. The bank was increasingly financing medium- to long-term development loans using short-term funding from the wholesale money market. There was a funding mismatch.

A defiant united front at the annual general meeting belied simmering tensions between FitzPatrick and Drumm. Unlike the previous two chairmen of Anglo, FitzPatrick kept an office in the bank. Drumm later told friends that he became more and more irritated as Fitz-Patrick began to show up at the bank more frequently as the crisis unfolded. He felt FitzPatrick was using his friendship with the two biggest hitters on Anglo's board, Gary McGann and Ned Sullivan, to put pressure on him at board level. Sometimes, Drumm told friends, his impression at board meetings was that FitzPatrick had already thrashed out the issues with his allies beforehand and items on the board agenda were often faits accomplis. He also believed that FitzPatrick was talking with other executives in the bank. (FitzPatrick rejects this account of his dealings with the board and with Drumm.)

After being appointed chairman, FitzPatrick sometimes hosted a dinner the night before a board meeting for the Anglo directors. The dinner was usually held in Heritage House, a beautifully decorated Georgian house on Stephen's Green, owned by the bank and a couple of doors down from its head office. The dinners had been informal affairs when times were good. Drumm told friends that as the crisis unfolded, they became de facto board meetings where many of the issues facing the bank were discussed without minutes being taken. Drumm felt that it was becoming harder to get his point across at these dinners and at meetings to a board made up of directors who were largely removed from the running of the bank. He felt that the board did not understand how tough it was simply trying to keep the bank ticking over on a day-to-day basis during the crisis.

Drumm at one stage pondered having FitzPatrick removed as chairman but decided that doing so would only damage Anglo more. In any event he would never have got support from the board for such a move.

FitzPatrick's office on the executive floor of Anglo was the one nearest the lift, which meant that every visitor to the floor had to pass it on the way to Drumm's large corner office. FitzPatrick's office spilled over with papers and packed filing cabinets relating to his personal investments, while Drumm always kept his desk clear. It was only a slight annoyance that clients would sometimes pop in to say hello to FitzPatrick before seeing Drumm, but, as the relationship between chairman and chief executive cooled, this dynamic became more and more vexatious to Drumm. With the crisis ratcheting up, Drumm considered moving FitzPatrick's office out of the bank entirely and into Heritage House.

Anglo management was increasingly occupied in countering the rumour mill. In late February, Anglo discovered an e-mail sent by an employee of Mirbaud Securities, a London stockbroker, which said: 'Anglo-Irish: ML [Merrill Lynch] pull a $2 billion credit line? Rumour.' Anglo filed a lawsuit, never ultimately pursued, against Mirbaud to discover who had sent the e-mail, but it made no difference. The rumours persisted.

Around this time Sean Mulryan, a major Irish developer who operated largely in London, rang FitzPatrick directly to inform him that a Dublin stockbroker had told him Anglo was 'fucked'. According to FitzPatrick, Mulryan 'was absolutely outraged by it. He told us that they were badmouthing us.'

A furious Drumm sought meetings with the heads of two Dublin stockbroking firms, Davy and Merrion, and read them the riot act. Both firms denied that they'd been badmouthing Anglo. That the conversation was even taking place marked a dramatic turnaround in the bank's relations with the brokers, particularly Davy, which was Anglo's own broker.

The single biggest casualty of the sustained market attack on Anglo was Sean Quinn. But the falling share price would not be his only worry.

Early in 2008 a team from PricewaterhouseCoopers arrived in Cavan to conduct the annual audit of Quinn Insurance. It was shocked by what it discovered.

Quinn Insurance was part of the family-owned group, but as a regulated entity it was required to operate separately. Its by now substantial reserves could not simply be pooled with those of the rest of the group, but had to be kept separate to meet potential future claims. It had to meet strict solvency requirements set down the Financial Regulator.

In trawling through the books, PwC found that a total of €398 million had been transferred from the insurance company into the Quinn Group. The group then lent the money to external Quinn family companies, which in turn used the money to pay Quinn's margin calls on his Anglo CFD investment.

The transaction was described in the Quinn Insurance books and records as 'a treasury arrangement'. The €398 million was classed as a 'deposit' and therefore part of the insurance company's reserves. It was nothing of the sort. It was an inter-company loan.

The auditors also discovered that Quinn Group had raised a further €300 million in cash by selling property assets to Quinn Insurance. These property assets were now part of the insurance firm's pool of reserves. But no independent valuation of these property assets had been conducted.

PwC had little choice but to blow the whistle. It immediately revealed the irregular treasury arrangement and the purchase of the property assets to the Financial Regulator. Both were breaches of the most serious kind. PwC, with the Financial Regulator's backing, forced Quinn to get an independent valuation of the property assets his family had sold to Quinn Insurance for €300 million. This found that Quinn Insurance had overpaid by €89 million and insisted that Quinn Group adjust its books accordingly. The Quinn family, as owners of the Quinn Group, were set up as debtors to the insurance business for the full €89 million and told they must pay back the difference.

Quinn, when questioned on this issue in a June 2010 interview with RTÉ's *Prime Time*, said: 'I think we had valuations, but maybe the Regulator wasn't happy with those valuations.' He insisted that the assets had been 'transferred at a true and honest value'. When pressed on who other than himself approved the original transaction, he said he did not know. 'It was a company decision. I don't know who all was involved in it.'

PwC also forced Quinn to reclassify the money he had improperly taken out of his insurance company. It would appear in the accounts not as a cash deposit but as an inter-company loan. Quinn Insurance was also required to set aside money against the eventuality that the family would be unable to repay the loan. The annual insurance-company accounts would therefore show a much weaker picture to Quinn's bondholders than Quinn had intended.

It also emerged that neither transaction had gone to the Quinn board for approval. Quinn Insurance operated a board investment committee, which until the summer of 2007 was headed by Paddy Mullarkey, a former secretary-general of the Department of Finance. It was the investment committee's role to inform the board of all relevant transactions. However, the investment committee had not met during the period when the two controversial deals were done because of Mullarkey's departure from the board.

Sean Quinn's actions were shocking. It was only six years since he had put Quinn Direct in jeopardy by investing so aggressively in dotcom shares. The investment committee, and Mullarkey's appointment, were the direct result of the injudicious technology punting. These subsequent breaches were far more grave, and the company's insurance licence must have been in serious danger.

The Financial Regulator, headed by Patrick Neary, a Central Bank lifer, was in no mood to rock the boat, at least for the moment. Neary was well aware that Quinn had a 28 per cent CFD position in Anglo. Quinn also owed his bondholders and other banks billions. If his lenders had discovered that he had made a €2.5 billion secret bet outside the group, and used the insurance company to help fund the gamble, they could conceivably have pulled the plug on him. Breaches of regulations can trigger default covenants in loans and bonds.

Such a development would have had serious economic and political consequences – Quinn Group was a huge employer, and Quinn Direct was the most profitable part of the empire – and it had the potential to create terrible problems for Anglo and its share price. His case had to be handled with the greatest of care. There would be no immediate sanction.

FitzPatrick says that he was aware of 'shorters' attacking Anglo's share price during this time. He believes they were trying to 'flush out' Quinn, force him to dump his shares – a move that would in turn bring down the share price further and put the shorters in the money. For the bank, this attention was most unwelcome, and not just because of what it did to the share price. 'It had the impact of reducing the share price, which had the consequent impact of diluting confidence in the bank by ordinary shareholders and not only shareholders but by ordinary deposit holders as well,' says FitzPatrick. 'That actually gained some traction at some speed, which, again, we, as a bank, failed to recognize at an early stage.'

Reducing Quinn's exposure quickly now became an even greater priority. Anglo hired Morgan Stanley, the prestigious international investment bank, to advise it on how to handle the Quinn situation.

On 6 March Anglo issued an unusually detailed trading statement to the stock market. 'Anglo Irish Bank is strongly positioned with an unwavering commitment to asset quality, a robust funding franchise and excellent liquidity,' Drumm told shareholders. The chief executive warned that net new lending for the six months to the end of March would be about €6.5 billion, down from €9.3 billion for the same period last year. There was no mention of Quinn. As for problem loans, Drumm said the bank was 'actively managing' a 'limited number' of 'smaller relationships'.

The forecast was resolutely upbeat. It maintained earnings-growth guidance at 15 per cent and made the point that net new lending would be 'substantially funded' by customers, with 50,000 new deposit customers having placed deposits with Anglo over the previous six months.

Within days of the trading statement, Merrill Lynch published a survey of thirteen of Britain's seventeen biggest commercial-property valuers to get a handle on banking exposure to the then falling British commercial-property market. The survey found that the 'most aggressive lenders' were perceived to be 'Halifax Bank of Scotland, Royal Bank of Scotland, "Irish banks" generically, Anglo, AIB'. Merrill added that 'the UK commercial real estate bubble is bursting and the banks are going to lose money'. It said that bank earnings would be impacted by 'record capital value declines'.

The Irish banks were furious. AIB, which regularly outbid Anglo to fund major property deals in the latter years of the boom, was dismissive of the report. 'While we may have done some big individual deals, you need to look into the lending practice behind them, which you'll find is conservative,' a spokeswoman said. Under pressure from both Irish and British banks, Merrill rowed back.

On 11 March 2008 Morgan Stanley organized a trip to the Middle East for Drumm, McAteer and Matt Moran, the chief financial officer. Over three days they met representatives from sovereign wealth funds, investment companies that managed billions on behalf of oil-rich families. The purpose of the trip was to find investors to take up at least part of the Quinn stake – a strategy, Drumm told the investors, that had the support of Ireland's Financial Regulator. (This reassuring invocation of the regulatory authorities was ironic coming from Anglo. Not quite nine months earlier, FitzPatrick had given a speech in which he described state regulation as 'corporate McCarthyism' and declared: 'In my humble opinion, our wealth-creators should be rewarded and admired, not subjected to the levels of scrutiny which known criminals would rightly find offensive.')

The competition for sovereign oil money was intense. Barclays was active in the region at this time and three months later landed the support of the Qatari Investment Authority in a £4 billion fund-raising. Anglo was a relatively small property-based bank in a niche European market, and found it hard to stand out from the crowd. The Anglo executives' trip was unsuccessful.

At the same time Morgan Stanley also discreetly sounded out some of Anglo's existing institutional shareholders and asked if they might be interested in increasing their stakes. There were no takers. If anything, the approach may have unnerved them more.

Three days after Drumm landed back in Dublin from the Middle East, a very bad situation got appreciably worse. On 17 March the share price of US investment bank Bear Stearns, buckling for months under the weight of its exposure to the bombed-out sub-prime market, collapsed. The news rocked the Irish stock market, which lost €3.5 billion of its value in one day. The banks were hardest hit. Anglo shares fell 15 per cent in what was dubbed the St Patrick's Day

Massacre. Depositors, spooked by its share price collapse, were clamouring to withdraw funds. The board and management feared a run on the bank's deposit base.

During the panic Fintan Drury, a director of Anglo, advised FitzPatrick to call Brian Cowen and tell him what was going on. This was not easy. The minister for finance was thousands of miles, and many time zones, away on a trade mission to Malaysia, staying in the five-star Shangri-La Hotel in Kuala Lumpur.

FitzPatrick rang Cowen on his mobile. He recalls that he spoke 'about the whole issue of rumours going around about the bank that were unfounded'. According to FitzPatrick, Cowen didn't have much to say. 'He just said yeah. He was just taking it all in.'

FitzPatrick also mentioned the Sean Quinn issue. 'I told him that [Quinn] had it in CFDs, I think. I am not sure. What I said was what was really happening was that pressure was coming on from the shorters, these guys, the hedge funds, trying to get Quinn,' he says.

That same day, a spokesman for Cowen tried to reassure the market: 'This is an international development as opposed to a local development.'

The St Patrick's Day Massacre galvanized Anglo and the authorities into concerted action. The first task was to stabilize Quinn's personal finances – a project that had commenced a few days before the Bear Stearns meltdown. Between 14 March and 19 March, the Fermanagh entrepreneur's borrowings with Anglo shot up from €1.2 billion to €1.574 billion. Anglo described the money internally as an increase in 'working capital'; the reality is that Quinn used the money to help finance his margin calls, which became even more onerous after St Patrick's Day. The money was advanced despite an insistence from the Financial Regulator some months earlier that Anglo reduce its exposure to Quinn. It was a case of desperate times and desperate measures.

Separately, the authorities also finally acted. Anglo had engaged with the Financial Regulator for months on ways to combat the short-sellers. Drumm and other bankers had lobbied hard behind the scenes for an official statement to be made, quashing rumours of liquidity problems. On 20 March 2008 Con Horan, prudential director of the Financial Regulator, said the office was investigating 'false and misleading' rumours about the Irish banks. Horan launched a full-frontal attack on any short-sellers who might be spreading such rumours. 'Market participants who take unfair advantage by spreading false rumours while trading on the basis of those rumours are in breach of market-abuse regulations,' he said, 'and we will actively pursue those who may be engaged in this.'

The governor of the Central Bank, John Hurley, also chipped in. He said he strongly supported the actions being taken and stated that Irish banking 'remains robust'.

The subsequent investigation would unearth not a scintilla of evidence that Irish stockbrokers were spreading false rumours to profit from a falling Anglo share price.

The situation was rich with ironies. Apart from concerns about liquidity, there were also widespread rumours in the market concerning Quinn's mysterious CFD position. The Financial Regulator was well aware of the scale of Quinn's gamble, but it had no intention of sharing the information with the market or making a statement on the matter. Horan, the man who announced the investigation into the hedge-fund rumours, was also the public servant in the regulator's office monitoring Quinn's position in the bank. He knew just what was at stake every time Anglo's share price fell.

Horan's comments had the desired effect. The ISEQ surged by 5 per cent, and Anglo shares rose by 14 per cent.

On Good Friday, 21 March, FitzPatrick and Drumm drove into the underground car park of the Central Bank offices on Dame Street in Dublin. They parked their car, entered the lift and went straight to a small meeting on one of the building's upper floors.

The bankers were met by Patrick Neary, the chief executive of the Financial Regulator, and Horan, his prudential director. John Hurley, the Central Bank governor, and one of his senior officials, Tony Grimes, joined the meeting.

'A number of things were going on at that stage,' FitzPatrick recalls. 'We are talking about the background of the rumour campaign, the investigation into short dealing, the investigation into

Dublin brokers, the concern that David had about the deposits. All of that type of stuff.

'The very fact that we were meeting on a Good Friday with a group of civil servants shows how serious it was. That afternoon Willie McAteer drove out to Neary's house and met Neary to go through the detail of the [Quinn] margins and who he had them with.'

By this stage the bank, which had been on the receiving end of positive media coverage for years, had become highly sensitive to negative commentary. When the *Sunday Times*'s London business editor, John Waples, described Anglo as 'a building society on crack' in June 2008, it prompted a swift legal letter from the bank.

There was no shortage of people willing to talk down the Anglo story, but the bank still had a legion of supporters, especially in Dublin. Emer Lang, a banking analyst with Davy, described the Anglo sell-off as 'irrational'. 'We are pretty gobsmacked at how much it has been beaten up by the market,' she told the *Sunday Times*. 'To me it is a bank that is managing its way very sensibly through this crisis. It is now targeting a lower level of new loans, preserving its capital and liquidity, growing at a more measured pace and being careful about asset quality.'

Alex Potter, a bank analyst at Collins Stewart, a British stockbroker, reversed his 'sell' recommendation on Anglo, claiming once the price went below €10 it had gone too far. 'There are people who are attempting to shake confidence in the banking sector and companies like Anglo Irish specifically,' he said. 'That is unwarranted, unfair and tantamount to reckless.'

Drumm rang Potter to thank him for supporting the bank. But the doubts remained. 'Why would you ever want to own Anglo?' one New York-based fund manager who had sold Anglo shares told the *Sunday Times* in late March. 'You could say it's super, super cheap but there are tonnes of super-cheap things out there.' The manager said Anglo had a 'fifty-fifty' chance of going bust by the end of 2008. 'Anglo needs money from the credit market to fund itself. It is a small bank facing a big property bubble. I think it is fucked.'

The fund manager specified that this last view was not for publication. He did not want to help precipitate the very catastrophe that he was predicting.

On or around 27 March a meeting was arranged between Anglo and Sean Quinn in Buswells, the hotel situated across the road from Dáil Éireann and owned by Quinn himself. FitzPatrick and Drumm represented Anglo, and Liam McCaffrey, the Quinn Group chief executive, accompanied his boss.

The Anglo duo expressed a sense of extreme urgency that Quinn's position in Anglo shares be reduced. They discussed 'putting it away' – closing out the CFDs by buying the underlying shares, placing some of the stake with the Quinn family and some of it with an institutional or sovereign fund investor. With the share price having halved in the previous six months, this was a very painful option. Quinn would have to crystallize a loss on practically all of his CFDs.

The tenor of the discussion was different from that of the relatively informal meeting at the Ardboyne Hotel six months earlier. 'Now it was closing it out, getting full agreement, getting powers of attorney [i.e. giving the bank legal powers to sell his shares],' FitzPatrick says. 'We had a series of meetings with Quinn saying this can't go on. This has got to be dealt with.'

At one point, FitzPatrick recalls, he was left alone with Quinn in the meeting room for twenty minutes. The two men looked at each other. The multibillion-euro businesses they had built from scratch were now on the line.

'It wasn't easy for him,' FitzPatrick says. 'It was bad for him. It was a bad day for the bank. It was a bad day for everyone. It was a big call. It was a big, big call. They all left the room and they left him with me. He was very close to tears. He could see what was happening.'

FitzPatrick says he never discussed with Quinn the 'working capital' arrangements extended earlier in the month. 'I did know the bank was lending him money but I didn't know the bank was lending him money for his CFDs,' he says.

But how then did FitzPatrick think Quinn was covering his huge margin calls? 'I knew we were lending him money for his investments. I am not trying to be smart with you now. You can turn around and say, Ah, yeah, really what he was doing was he was getting money for that but he was using it for the other . . . yeah, could easily have been.

'You couldn't lend him money on his investment properties unless he was buying or doing something specifically . . . I am not trying to be evasive with you. I just don't know. I wasn't close enough to it. I was a hundred million miles away from it. I just didn't get involved. I didn't get involved in any of the lending. I had no idea what money we had lent to the guy at that stage in general terms.'

It seems odd that FitzPatrick did not know that almost €375 million had been advanced to Quinn over the course of just five days in March 2008.

'I certainly wasn't aware of that, nor would the board have been aware of that,' he says. 'We didn't look at this on a regular basis. Loans were never an issue for the board. It just didn't come up. There was a great trust and belief in the credit committee, that things weren't abused there.'

Did nobody ask how Quinn was paying for his CFD margin calls? 'Presumably he had facilities with lots of banks,' FitzPatrick says.

Presumably?

'I had no idea how he was [paying for his losses],' FitzPatrick says, adding that Quinn never confided in him that he could no longer pay up. It was only months later, during the summer of 2008, FitzPatrick says, that he learned the true extent of Quinn's borrowings from the bank.

FitzPatrick's recollection of his – and the Anglo board's – ignorance of the bank's lending of €374 million to Quinn between 14 and 19 March is hard to square with the fact that between 17 and 19 March the Anglo board held five conference calls to discuss Quinn and the impact of the bank's share-price collapse on its funding and liquidity. Quinn was demanding huge working capital facilities and this was discussed by the Anglo board, according to internal Anglo files. It is hard to believe FitzPatrick could have thought the money was being lent for anything other than funding Quinn's CFD position. Yet he insists this is the case.

Drumm, FitzPatrick and McAteer met with Neary and Horan on 27 March, around the time of the Quinn meeting, to discuss the crisis.

Hurley, the Central Bank governor, was unable to make the meeting, as he was in Germany at a meeting of the European Central Bank, but was briefed on his return.

Neary again urged Anglo to resolve the Quinn issue by getting the shares placed as soon as possible, and the bankers said they were working hard to do so. Over the following days, Drumm and McAteer were in touch with Horan several times a day. The bank was also still negotiating with Quinn and McCaffrey. On 31 March, Anglo forwarded to the regulator a 'memorandum of agreement' between it and the Quinn Group, which consisted of a plan to reduce Quinn's holdings. Anglo told the regulator that the aim of the planned share placing was to ensure that 'the market price of the company's shares [would] not be destabilised'; it also said that the terms of the agreement would be kept 'confidential' from other shareholders in the bank.

Under the agreement, Quinn was to take direct ownership of 18 per cent of Anglo's shares by effectively buying out the CFDs. The other 10 per cent of the bank's shares covered by Quinn CFDs would be placed with investment funds. Quinn would spread ownership of the 18 per cent stake among the members of his family, thereby avoiding the need to publicly declare his holdings. (Only shareholders holding 3 per cent or more of a company's shares must declare their holdings publicly.)

Anglo had taken advice on the plan from its legal advisers Matheson Ormsby Prentice and from Morgan Stanley. The Financial Regulator expressed no objections. The bank also told the Regulator in meetings that it would fund Quinn's share purchase. The Regulator did not object.

Anglo now had to find buyers for the 10 per cent of its shares covered by Quinn CFDs that Quinn would not be purchasing himself. FitzPatrick recalls the process as follows: 'We were looking to solve this. There was the Middle East [sovereign wealth funds], or our six largest or ten largest shareholders. It was getting extra new shareholders in from overseas. It was venture-capital companies coming in and taking a stake. There was a number of [possibilities] and actually then Quinn legitimizing [his position] and maybe putting [the stake] into his insurance company. All in all, we tried everything to take this cancer off our shareholding register.'

On 24 April, the minister for finance, Brian Cowen, arrived late for a private dinner at Heritage House. Fintan Drury, his old college friend and a director of Anglo, introduced him to the other guests. Cowen had a gin and tonic and chatted with a group of about a dozen Anglo board members and executives.

Cowen had always made time for Drury. Cowen's appointments diaries as minister for finance show he had at least ten meetings with Drury between September 2004 and May 2008. By contrast, the diaries – released to the *Irish Independent* after a Freedom of Information request – show he met officials from the Office of the Financial Regulator only eight times during his term in office. Neary, who took the top job at the Regulator in 2006, is listed as having met the minister just twice, in September 2006 and September 2007.

As Cowen sat down to dinner with Anglo, he had a lot on his political plate. Less than three weeks earlier the Taoiseach, Bertie Ahern, had agreed to step down following embarrassing revelations at a tribunal of inquiry into payments made to politicians. He would resign as Taoiseach and as leader of Fianna Fáil on 6 May. Cowen was the party's sole nominee to take the top job. The Lisbon Treaty referendum was to be held in June and was a 'must win' for the government.

At dinner Cowen drank red wine and chatted easily. FitzPatrick sat on his left and Drumm on his right. After desert FitzPatrick asked each of his key executives to give Cowen a brief update on the lending environment in their various areas. His non-executive directors, including McGann, Sullivan and Drury, also updated the minister on how they saw the economy.

Cowen was told that the property market had crashed to a halt because of the credit crunch. He was told the bank had funding issues because of fears in international stock markets, but that the problem was not urgent. Drumm repeatedly voiced his concerns about how difficult it was to hold on to deposits and raise new funding in the crisis.

'David did ask about the NTMA,' FitzPatrick recalls, referring to the National Treasury Management Agency, which managed the state's assets and debts. 'Anglo wanted [Cowen] to have a word about it placing some of its money on deposit with the bank. He said he'd look into it.'

There was, according to FitzPatrick, no discussion of the ghost at the banquet, Sean Quinn, or of FitzPatrick's urgent phone call to Cowen only six weeks before. To an outsider it seems extraordinary that the issue would not have surfaced at the Heritage House dinner or that FitzPatrick did not draw Cowen aside to update him.

'Sorry. I am not saying that it was right or wrong. I just didn't do those things. I never saw politicians as important in that way. Clearly they were important but I never saw them as to be used or anything like that. I never saw . . . It never struck me once in my whole life that Fintan [Drury] would be very useful because he was on our board and because he knew Cowen so well. It never struck me once.

'In my life, I never asked him to do anything with the minister for finance when he was on the board of the bank ever. Never even gone near it.'

Even in the exceptional circumstances surrounding the events of March 2008, there was no attempt to seek government support?

'No.'

Away from the fine dining of Heritage House, Sean Quinn was preparing a detailed presentation to his bondholders on the performance of the Quinn Group. He remained determined to keep his personal investment adventures secret. To do so, he would require the help of others.

On 8 May, David Drumm, fellow executive director Pat Whelan and Michael O'Sullivan, the banking director with responsibility for Quinn, met with Con Horan at the Financial Regulator's office to discuss a proposal for Anglo to release Quinn from a guarantee he had given to the bank in connection with loans worth over €250 million. Quinn needed to be released from the guarantee in order to improve his credit standing in the eyes of the Quinn Group bondholders. The regulator allowed Anglo to take the unusual step of relieving Quinn of the guarantee. On foot of this approval, the bank's credit committee approved this move.

Quinn Group finally completed and circulated an in-depth financial report to the bondholders in May 2008. The report admitted that 'certain equity investments outside the Quinn Group incurred triggering margin calls' and that these were funded by 'inter-company loans', which were 'originally treated as cash deposits'. It went on: 'The group's auditors disagreed with [the original] accounting treatment and instead held that they should be accounted for as inter-company loans and that on this basis they should have been notified to the Financial Regulator.'

Quinn Group told its bondholders that Sean Quinn had taken €398 million out of the Quinn Group, but that by May this figure had been reduced to €288 million, which the Quinn family intended to repay in instalments under a plan agreed with the Financial Regulator. 'Management now accepts that the decision to enter into the treasury arrangement (now inter-company loan) was not undertaken with proper due diligence on the regulatory impact of the transactions.'

The report also admitted that the Quinn family, as owners of the Quinn Group, had sold property assets to Quinn Insurance for €300 million without undertaking any independent valuations and that, at the insistence of PwC, independent valuations had now been carried out that put their worth at just €211 million. Quinn blamed the huge difference between the two valuations on 'falling property values' during the months it took for the independent valuations to be completed. Property values had indeed fallen, but a 30 per cent fall in a number of months was most severe. There was no excuse, in any case, for the lack of independent valuations.

Crucially, Quinn could report to bondholders that PwC had eventually signed off on its 2007 consolidated accounts without any qualification. 'As part of the sign-off process PwC received comfort from the Financial Regulator that it will not take any action against the company that would affect its ability to continue as a going concern,' the Quinn Group said.

This was an extraordinary concession by the Regulator, given that it had still not completed its investigation into the group.

It did not stop there. The Regulator also gave the Quinn Group a 'special derogation' that allowed it to include more property in its insurance company's reserves than normal – and this despite the imploding property market that Quinn's own report had cited.

For its part, Quinn Group said it was 'committed in writing' not to take any more money out of the group until it had 'sufficient head-room' under its agreements with its lenders to do so. It also outlined a range of changes it would make in its corporate-governance structures. These included 'more intensive' involvement of non-executive direc-tors in the 'monitoring of cash balances and inter-company dealings'. Quinn Group had also 'passed a formal board resolution that requires all decisions of a material nature that could impact on the company's regulatory position to be agreed at board level'. Quinn Insurance agreed to reconstitute its investment committee and appointed KPMG, the consultants, to carry out a review of its corporate governance.

There were a number of bombshells in Quinn Group's May 2008 report to bondholders, but the bondholders were still unaware of the sheer scale of the company proprietor's equity gamble, or that so much had been bet on Anglo Irish Bank.

The regulator and Anglo had gone to extraordinary lengths to help Quinn paper the cracks in his empire. But the fear of everyone concerned was that when trading picked up on the stock market after the summer lull, Anglo would again come under attack from the short-sellers.

This time it might not be strong enough to survive.

8. An Anglo-Irish Solution to an Anglo-Irish Problem

'I won't say I approved the plan but I didn't disapprove it. I was aware because I got the phone call. Approved? I didn't say to David, "That is a lousy plan, you can't do that."'

In early June, David Drumm flew to his old stomping ground of Boston for his annual four-week holiday. He brought his briefcase with him.

It would not be the most relaxing of holidays. Apart from meetings with Bain Capital – a multibillion-dollar venture-capital fund that he thought might be interested in taking part of Quinn's stake – he had an operation on his sinuses, which had been bothering him for months.

On 27 June the Anglo board held its monthly meeting in the five-star Fota Island hotel and golf resort, owned by the Fleming Group, a large Cork developer. It was the first board meeting for PwC partner Donal O'Connor, a new director. Drumm had approached him to join the Anglo board about three months previously. The Anglo chief executive briefed O'Connor fully on the Quinn crisis prior to his joining the board.

Anglo's key lending executives for Ireland, the UK and the United States gave presentations to the board about how tough market conditions were, but they affirmed their uniform belief that the downturn would be only temporary.

Morgan Stanley also gave a confidential presentation outlining the steps taken in an attempt to unwind the Quinn CFD position. The giant investment bank had given the problem the code name 'Maple', a reference to the supposed resemblance of the Anglo logo to a maple leaf.

Quinn was not mentioned by name in the presentation, but every board member was well aware of the identity of the investor at its centre. The Morgan Stanley advisers described the efforts made to place Quinn's shares with sovereign wealth funds, private equity and existing institutional shareholders. To date all efforts had failed.

Drumm dialled into the Fota board meeting from Boston. There was, he said, another matter that needed to be drawn to the board's attention. Three days before the Cork board meeting, Drumm had received a letter from Patrick Neary, the chief executive of the Financial Regulator, seeking a written report on the bank's exposure to Quinn.

'You will recall from previous discussions we had, when this exposure [to Quinn] was in the region of €1.3 billion to €1.5 billion, that Anglo did not wish to see any increase above this level and, in fact, had a desire to reduce the exposure,' Neary wrote. The regulator now understood that Anglo's exposure to Quinn had since risen to €1.8 billion, and he was aware that Quinn was due to draw down a further loan facility of €200 million from the bank. In the light of Quinn's existing borrowings, Neary asked Drumm if he considered 'such a large facility appropriate'.

The board then heard why the facility was deemed necessary. Profits from Quinn's core cement, insurance and glass businesses were now falling as the Irish economy moved into recession, and cash flow was tightening. Although Anglo's loans had been made not to the Quinn Group but to Sean Quinn and other members of the Quinn family, they were nonetheless secured against the family's Quinn Group shares. The Quinn Group – under the credit terms agreed with the banks from which it had direct borrowings as well as with its bondholders – had to maintain a certain ratio of cash flow relative to debt. The group's cash profit was €490 million in 2007, but it had now fallen to €432 million. As a result, its cash flow, as measured by the cash profit, was too low relative to its debt. In banking terms, Quinn was close to breaching its covenants. In a note to Anglo, the Quinn Group said that 'post June . . . we will not be in compliance'.

The Anglo board was told at Fota that the Quinn Group had sought a temporary relaxation of the terms of the loans from its lenders. Quinn Group had loan facilities in the sum of €825 million with a lending syndicate headed by Barclays, which also included AIB and Bank of Ireland. These banks agreed to a loosening of the terms, but only if there were 'no further inter-company loans or distributions'.

The Quinn Group bondholders – mainly private American investors, wealthy individuals and investment funds, who were owed €430 million – had taken a harder line. They were now pressing to commission an independent report into the family's assets and liabilities held outside the group before agreeing to waive the loan covenants.

Referring to this proposed report, the Quinn Group had written to Anglo stating the obvious: 'This point has significant disclosure issues for the Quinn family and its financiers outside the group.' In other words, any such independent report would reveal the full extent of Quinn's Anglo investment, with potentially disastrous results for both parties.

The letter to Anglo put forward an alternative proposal. Anglo would advance a further €200 million, not to the Quinn Group but to a separate company controlled by Sean Quinn. That company would then lend the money to Quinn Group, boosting its reserves and reducing its net debt.

'In now seeking additional cash from outside of the group, we will not need the waiver and will, in effect, protect the confidentiality of our dealings outside the group,' the Quinn Group wrote. 'Of the €200 million, €150 million can be retained on deposit with Anglo but cannot be subject to a lien.'

Drumm was perplexed. The bank was being asked, once more, to save Quinn's hide. Not only would the bank be increasing its exposure to Sean Quinn, but it was getting no security from the group in return.

The chief executive wanted the bank's minutes to record just what he was being pressurized into doing. If he refused the loan, the bondholders would unearth the scale of Quinn's position in the bank's shares. The threat of this disclosure, Drumm felt, left him with little or no option, and he wanted the board to be fully aware of the reasons why Anglo would be increasing its exposure to the Quinn family. It was 'very rare', FitzPatrick says, for Anglo to discuss individual clients by name, and individual loans, at a board meeting, but the nature of this loan was different. Drumm and his team wanted the board to know exactly what the loan was for.

Drumm was also tired of the Quinn issue being discussed, as he saw it, 'away from the boardroom table' – between FitzPatrick and other directors, and at the bank's 'informal' dinners before board meetings. He realized little was being written down. He was putting himself in real danger of being left to carry the can if anything went wrong. This time, the decision had to go into the board minutes. The board would be told that the purpose of the loan was to keep Quinn's suspicious bondholders at bay – and they would be asked to approve it.

FitzPatrick and the board approved the €200 million loan, but only subject to the blessing of the Financial Regulator. Approval would be sought from the highest authority in the land for a highly dubious transaction. To facilitate the cover-up of Sean Quinn's multibillion-euro gamble on Anglo shares, the country's third-largest bank would, with the sanction of the Regulator, deliberately increase its exposure to Quinn against both the bank's and the Regulator's own better judgement.

Fintan Drury did not attend the Fota board meeting. The day after the meeting, he officially resigned as a director of Anglo.

'Every time someone left the Anglo board there was always a going-away bash, but not this time,' an Anglo source said. 'Fintan left without saying goodbye.'

Drury had been chairman of the bank's risk and compliance committee, whose other members were Lar Bradshaw and Ned Sullivan. The role of this committee, according to the bank's annual report, was 'to oversee risk management and compliance', to review 'the key risks and compliance issues inherent in the business and the system of internal control necessary to manage them' and to present its findings to the board. Drury never publicly discussed the reasons for his resignation from the board, and from such an important committee, at this crucial time. Privately he told acquaintances that his term was originally up in January and any extension would be only temporary. He was replaced by Bradshaw as chair of the risk committee.

On 4 July, Drumm gave a detailed written response to Neary's query over the new €200 million Quinn loan. He chose his words carefully. 'As you know,' he began, Anglo had been working 'closely' with Quinn Group to help it meet its working capital requirements. 'We have, as you are aware, released circa €250 million of security which was held by way of a group guarantee,' Drumm wrote. 'This release was facilitated to ensure the group could meet its liquidity and solvency ratios, and to allow the auditors to sign off the accounts.' Anglo, in return, had taken a 'full personal guarantee' from the Quinn family and a 'first legal charge' over their shares in the group, according to Drumm's letter. This gave the bank 'security on €1.7 billion of equity'.

Drumm then took Neary through exactly what he was going to do. Anglo would advance a further €200 million to the Quinn Group via entities controlled by Sean Quinn. The bank believed that Quinn owed a total of €1.3 billion to its other banks, led by Barclays, and its bondholders. Anglo, Drumm said, was prepared to allow the Quinn family to borrow up to €2.3 billion, taking their total debt, group and non-group, to €3.6 billion. Anglo valued the Quinn Group at €3 billion, or €1.7 billion after allowing for existing group debt.

Drumm said Anglo was prepared to bring the bank's total lending to the Quinns to €2.3 billion based on their having a total of €2.8 billion of collateral. This was made up of property assets worth €900 million, Anglo's hold on shares in the group valued at €1.7 billion, and the return of the temporary loan of €200 million. The monies from the temporary loan, which were required to satisfy the syndicated loan and bondholders covenants, would be put on deposit and used simply to net off the total debt position. Quinn had committed to returning the money, once profitability was restored, but Anglo had no charge over the deposit.

Drumm also told Neary that Quinn had made an 'irrevocable' commitment to sell property worth €500 million and the same value in shares (including part of his Anglo stake) by the end of 2008. This would leave Anglo with a €1.1 billion exposure to the Quinn Group. Drumm said he felt confident Quinn had 'sufficient headroom' on its syndicate debt and that its 'strong cash flow' would be enough to service all its debts, including those to Anglo. 'Depending on the outcome of the share placement project, which you are aware of, we should be in a position to restructure the overall debt early in 2009,' he wrote.

It was all extremely delicate. Con Horan, the senior official in the Financial Regulator's office overseeing the deal, started during this time to attend board meetings of the Central Bank to update it on Quinn.

FitzPatrick, for his part, says he had no issue with the loan being advanced to Quinn. 'We were doing it with the full knowledge and full acceptance of the Regulator,' he says. The bank's hand was also being forced by the Quinn bondholders. 'The bondholders were in a very strong and very safe position,' he says. 'They [had] a very little amount out for the amount of cover that they got. Difficult people.'

No one on the board, according to FitzPatrick, was asking the executives whether they were convinced that Quinn would be able to repay the bank. There were some concerns at board level, however, over Quinn's planned expansion into Britain, a key part of his business plan. Board member Noel Harwerth, a former chief operating office with Citibank International, was a director of Royal & Sun Alliance, a big insurance company in Britain. She did not believe Quinn's projections.

The more immediate concern, though, FitzPatrick recalls, was getting Quinn's CFD holding 'into a safe form and out of the casino' before the markets clicked back up a gear at the end of summer.

The clock was ticking.

At the beginning of July, David Drumm sent a memo from Boston to Anglo's board saying talks with Bain Capital were going well and he was hopeful the private-equity firm would pick up some of the shareholding linked to Sean Quinn's CFDs.

A few days later, on Monday, 7 July, Drumm arrived back in Anglo's Dublin offices utterly deflated. He just could not get Bain over the line.

He told Horan that he had met Bain and was still hopeful a deal could be done, but it would take more time. Horan ordered Drumm to ensure that, whatever the solution, Anglo would not be in breach of the Financial Regulator's guidelines on large loan exposures. Under the rules, the bank could not lend any one client more than 25 per cent of its 'own funds'. This meant that Anglo was not allowed to lend Quinn the sum of money he'd need to buy up the entire 28 per cent shareholding linked to his CFDs. It needed outside help.

At 10.45 p.m. on 8 July, Drumm sent a short e-mail to Matt Moran, the bank's chief financial officer, proposing a new approach. It read: 'Matt I spoke to Willie [McAteer] about moving the game forward tomorrow with a select group of clients – he will brief you. Time for action.'

The next day Drumm asked Pat Whelan, then head of Anglo's Irish loan book, to draw up a list of the bank's richest twenty or twenty-five clients. Drumm pored over the list. Eventually he whittled it down to ten clients – ten businessmen who had made their fortune in property. (The group was particularly strong in house building and shopping centres.) The bank would ask each of the ten clients to buy 1 per cent of the bank's shares from Sean Quinn's brokers. The Quinn family would take on a further 15 per cent. Quinn could then sell his remaining 3 per cent CFD position in Anglo into the market, at a time of his own choosing, and use the proceeds to help pay down his Anglo debt.

Drumm's list was governed by two criteria: financial strength and discretion. The ten had to be trusted not to disclose their share purchase to anyone.

The idea behind this Anglo-Irish solution to an Anglo-Irish problem had been knocking about among the bank's senior executives for some time. The possibility had also been mooted at board level in June. But in that first week in July, Drumm put flesh on it and went about executing it with great speed.

He rang Horan to tell him that Anglo had decided to place some of the CFDs with a group of rich individuals. He said that the bank was going to provide a 'bridging loan' to some of these individuals to give them time to raise the cash for the share purchase by selling off assets.

Horan expressed concern about how the Quinn family was going to take ownership of the Anglo shares. Drumm told Horan that

Quinn would have to set up various holding vehicles outside Ireland in order to facilitate the transfer of the shares into the hands of his children – a process that would also be financed by Anglo.

Neither man was happy about the delay that these arrangements would unavoidably involve. Both understood the deal had to be done as quickly as possible, as they feared hedge funds could attack Anglo again at any moment.

Anglo and the Financial Regulator believed that the bank's funding of the Quinn family share purchase was meant to be only a temporary arrangement. Quinn had lined up Credit Suisse First Boston and other banks to finance the deal long term and reduce his borrowings from Anglo. Banking documents had been exchanged between Quinn and Anglo discussing how this might work.

After speaking to Horan, Drumm rang the ten clients on his list – who would become known as the 'Maple Ten' or the 'golden circle' – to sound them out. The developers were told the futures of both Anglo and Quinn were at stake, and that they would be viewed as a 'friend of the bank' if they helped out. The request was made in a very particular business context: each client had huge borrowings from Anglo and faced into uncertain economic times.

Even so, Anglo made the terms of the deal temptingly attractive. The bank was to lend each of the ten all the cash required to buy 1 per cent of the bank. Three quarters of the sums being lent would be secured only on the shares themselves. The bank would have recourse to the borrower's other assets for a sum equivalent to just 25 per of the loan. In other words, if repayments were not made, the bank would pursue the borrowers for just one quarter of the total sum they had borrowed. Normally such borrowing would have had 100 per cent recourse, but Anglo had made exceptions to this rule in the past for wealthy businessmen.

Despite the attractive terms, a number of the would-be investors were wary. These were not seasoned equity investors, and the clandestine nature of the deal made them nervous. Anglo assured them that both the Financial Regulator and Morgan Stanley were happy with the deal. That same day, 9 July, Drumm rang FitzPatrick to tell him the plan was going ahead. FitzPatrick was in the South of France, on his one and only ever visit to view the mansion he co-owned with Angela Cavendish at Cap Ferrat.

'I won't say I approved the plan but I didn't disapprove it,' Fitz-Patrick says. 'I was aware because I got the phone call. Approved? I didn't say to David, "That is a lousy plan, you can't do that."'

FitzPatrick claims he did not discuss with Drumm the names of the ten Anglo clients – 'David told me that there was no need for me to know' – or the terms on which the bank was lending them money to buy shares in the bank. 'We weren't talking about recourse at all. We were talking about whether they were of substance . . . in other words were they using people of limited resources just to get it off? But if they were using Gerry Gannon, a really high-net-worth guy [it was a different matter]. I presumed it was 100 per cent recourse . . . I also said, And by the way what happens if they make money on that? Can we use the profits to reduce their core debts? And David laughed and said, You are always the same, Sean, you are always look-ing for too much.'

Over the next twenty-four hours Anglo and Morgan Stanley hastily drew up the paperwork. It would be a complex set of trans-actions. Quinn had built up his CFD position through nine different providers; Morgan Stanley now had to orchestrate simultaneous share sales to the Quinn family and the Maple Ten. Just before the deal was due to be executed between all the different parties, Whelan rang FitzPatrick to tell him the deal was now very close.

When in early 2009 this was put to FitzPatrick by his old bank, which was preparing its own legal files on the matter, he could not remember the call and rang up Whelan to complain. 'I said, That is a load of shite, Pat. You never rang me but there is one way of finding out: get out your phone records. He said, Sean, I remember looking down the Hill of Howth. I remember it well because I was talking to you. I said, Pat, get out your phone records. He got out his phone records, and [they showed that] he did ring me. He did. He must have. I buy that. Pat is a decent guy. I believe Pat.'

Whelan told an Anglo internal investigation that he gave Fitz-Patrick some of the names of the borrowers, including Gerry Gannon. FitzPatrick says Whelan also remembers him asking: 'Are these people of substance? We are not lending money to [someone] knowing that he can't pay us back.'

FitzPatrick says he found out only after the deal had been done – when he returned to the office from the Continent – that it had been financed by Anglo with only 25 per cent recourse.

On Friday, 11 July, four of the businessmen on the Anglo list – Gerry Gannon, Seamus Ross, John McCabe and Sean Reilly, all house builders – entered Anglo headquarters on St Stephen's Green. Each was given an appointment at a different time to help ensure none would learn the identity of the others.

Gannon and Ross had been among Drumm's first clients when he started as a young lender with Anglo. Gannon was the founder of Gannon Homes and owned huge land banks in North and South Dublin. With Michael Smurfit, Gannon co-owned the K Club, which had hosted the 2006 Ryder Cup.

Longford-born Ross ran Menolly Homes, one of the country's biggest house builders. He owned Dunboyne Castle in Co. Meath and had made millions building luxury houses on the grounds of the K Club. He also owned the chic Dylan Hotel in Dublin.

John McCabe ran McCabe Builders, which he had founded in 1972, and lived on a stud farm in Meath formerly owned by Charles Haughey. He was a prolific property investor in Ireland, the UK and the United States, often with Paddy Kelly, another large Anglo client, and a major house builder in Ireland; he had also built head-quarters for Bord Gáis, the state gas company.

Sean Reilly had the lowest profile of the four. His McGarrell Reilly Group was a house builder in the commuter belt around Dublin. Reilly had ploughed his profits into office buildings, includ-ing the Cisco Building in Clontarf and the Watermarque Building in Ringsend.

Two Morgan Stanley staff met each of the four investors individu-ally. This was intended to reassure the four that the deal was above board. The commission owed by each of the Maple Ten to the blue-chip investment house would be covered by their Anglo borrowings.

Drumm discussed the transaction over the phone with Quinn that same day. (In a subsequent letter to Drumm, Quinn described the conversation as 'heated'.) He called Drumm back again and told him: 'We should all consider it over the weekend.' Quinn was unhappy that he did not know the identities of the Maple Ten and said he wanted more time to think about the deal.

Nailing down the deal with the other businessmen on Anglo's list was trickier: it was early July and all six were out of the country. Drumm rang Tony Campbell, Anglo's boss in North America, and asked him to meet Gerry Conlan and Paddy McKillen, two more of the Maple Ten, who were travelling in the States. Anglo would provide Campbell with all the paperwork, Drumm said.

Conlan was a native of Co. Kildare who had made a fortune selling his share in over 400 acres of land near Naas for €315 million to a group of Galway businessmen. He then ploughed some of the money into a private-hospital group centred around Mount Carmel, a maternity hospital in Rathfarnham, South Dublin.

Belfast-born McKillen was an international property investor who had, with FitzPatrick, put money into the Savoy Hotel deal. He owned the Jervis Street shopping centre in Dublin and had built a property empire stretching from North America to Vietnam.

Both men were intercepted on their travels and signed up for the deal.

That Saturday, Drumm and Whelan flew to Nice, where Paddy Kearney, a big client of the bank, was holidaying. Over breakfast, the bankers explained the deal and Kearney, too, signed up to it. Kearney owned shopping centres along the border in Northern Ireland and in England. He had also co-founded PBN Property with Neil Adair, a former head of Anglo's Belfast office.

Gerry McGuire – the owner of the Laurence Centre, a shopping centre in Drogheda, and the next name on the Anglo list – was also holidaying in Nice. He, too, agreed to participate in project Maple.

From Nice, the two Anglo executives flew to the Algarve, where Joe O'Reilly was on holiday. That afternoon Drumm convinced O'Reilly, the owner of the Dundrum shopping centre, to sign up.

Matt Moran rang Drumm at Faro airport, where the bankers were waiting to fly back to Dublin, to inform him that the deal had been run past the Financial Regulator and that it had raised no objections.

Morgan Stanley had rung Horan at home earlier that day to discuss the deal. Horan told them to make sure they kept 'everything right in terms of the markets'. Immediately afterwards Moran rang Horan to confirm the conversation had gone well.

Now there was only one name left. On Monday morning, Drumm met Brian O'Farrell in his Malahide office. O'Farrell was an auction-eer with O'Farrell Cleere and owned the Northside Shopping Centre, which he was hoping to knock down and rebuild at a cost of €1 bil-lion. He knew Drumm well – the two lived near each other in north Co. Dublin. He, too, agreed to invest.

The Maple Ten was now complete.

On Monday, 14 July 2008, Anglo arranged a conference call with Quinn. He had been told the previous Wednesday that a deal was close and now he expected to hear the details.

Quinn and Liam McCaffrey were on one side of the conference call; Drumm, McAteer, Whelan and Moran were on the other. Drumm told Quinn he was placing the shares with a group of clients of the bank. He declined to give their identities, citing banking con-fidentiality.

Quinn went crazy. He was furious that Drumm was withholding important information at this late stage of the game.

It is likely, too, that Quinn's resistance to crystallizing his losses on the Anglo investment had only deepened over the preceding months as other attempts to unwind his position proved unsuccessful. When, on 31 March, Anglo had drawn up the original memorandum of agreement with Quinn to place the shares, they had been trading at €8.45. They were now trading at around €4.50. A terrible situation had got considerably worse, and the cost to Quinn of sorting it out had become even greater. Quinn told Anglo to hold off from placing the shares. He would put more money on deposit with the bank to buy time so that he could think about the deal.

Quinn found it hard to stomach that he was about to lose €1 bil-lion on his Anglo position, and that the net beneficiaries, as he saw it, would be hand-picked clients of the bank. They were buying his stock at rock-bottom prices and, in his eyes, they stood to make a fortune.

Drumm was livid over Quinn's reaction. On three occasions in the last six months, the bank had intervened to bail out the businessman, aiding him after Bear Stearns collapsed, helping to get his accounts signed off by his accountants and preventing bondholders from launching an investigation into his Anglo investment. Quinn's reckless buying of Anglo shares had badly destabilized the bank.

Drumm and Quinn both stormed off the conference call, but the others continued. It was clear that Anglo was under no obligation to heed Quinn's request for more time: it had security over Quinn's shares in the Quinn Group. He was in no position to oppose the bank. Recognizing that the bank was in complete control, Liam McCaffrey agreed to send an e-mail confirming the Maple Ten deal would go ahead as planned that day.

Michael O'Sullivan, Quinn's account manager, and Whelan handled the lending side of the deal. Anglo lent the Quinn family about €650 million to take a 15 per cent direct stake in the bank and advanced the Maple Ten €451 million to take another 10 per cent. Moran and McAteer handled the treasury side with Morgan Stanley to ensure the CFD providers transferred Quinn's position smoothly into the new hands. About fifty people inside Anglo, including more than ten lending executives, knew of the secret transaction, which passed through the compliance, finance and risk departments of the bank.

With the deal finally done, the Financial Regulator was informed. There was relief all around.

FitzPatrick says he did not know the full details of how the deal was put together. 'On getting the information from David [while in Cap Ferrat in July] I immediately passed it on to the rest of the non-executive board,' he recalls. 'No one on the board, including myself, was involved in any of the architecture, were involved in talks with any of the Ten.'

FitzPatrick was personally acquainted with some of the Ten, and had known Gannon in particular for a long time, but he says neither Gannon nor any of the others consulted him before doing the deal. 'Never, never. No one rang me up. I don't know whether they were asked not to speak to me . . . David was chief executive now at this stage for the guts of four years. He was running his own show. He was clearly the boss and he was seen as the boss.'

When the deal was completed, FitzPatrick rang each director of the company individually to tell them the news. Many were on holiday. None of the board members raised any questions about how the deal had been done, he says. 'They were all thrilled. Everyone was delighted because it would appear to be the end of a saga which was convulsing or annoying us or irritating us or really killing us for nine months.'

The deal – which involved the bank providing about €1.5 billion in loans to clear up the Quinn mess – did not come up at the bank's next board meeting, FitzPatrick says. 'We never actually discussed it, hard and all as that is to believe. It was a problem that the board was dealing with for a long time and suddenly there was light at the end of the tunnel that this was going to be dealt with.'

No one on Anglo's board, FitzPatrick says, asked to see the bank's legal advice on the transaction. 'You are dealing with a group of guys in which you had complete trust. There were no doubts,' he says. 'There was no worry and no concern. We were dealing with these people on a daily basis. There was no sense that they weren't telling us the truth. There was no sense that we needed to check it all up. If someone said they had legal advice you said that is very good news.'

(It is not quite true that 'there was no worry and no concern'. On 10 July Anglo director Gary McGann e-mailed Drumm seeking reassurances that the bank was fully protected if news of the Maple Ten transactions leaked out. Just before 7 p.m. that day Drumm told McGann: 'Thanks for the support Gary . . . The entire transaction has been explained to our regulator, is the subject of legal advice and is being handled by Morgan Stanley who must pass their own compliance regime.')

FitzPatrick says: 'In hindsight I kill myself. I should have brought it up. We should have had some session on the whole thing – let's look at that whole thing again and say what happened with that, what are we doing, how is it being done, are we happy with that.'

In normal times, FitzPatrick pleads, this might have happened; but these were not normal times. Anglo had to move on from the Quinn share debacle quickly, he says, and concentrate on holding on to deposits as investors lost confidence in the bank.

In any case, FitzPatrick says, he had no sense at the time that there was anything 'dodgy' about the Maple Ten deal. Anglo had taken advice on it from its lawyers, Matheson Ormsby Prentice, and from Morgan Stanley. 'We had [also] got clearance from the Irish Stock Exchange,' he says. (Anglo director Anne Heraty was on the board of the Exchange. A source close to the Irish Stock Exchange confirmed that it knew about the deal and allowed it go through because the Financial Regulator told them to allow it.)

'If you take all of that and all of the legals, the Irish Stock Exchange, the Financial Regulator and the Central Bank were all aware of it . . . There was no sense of, Oh Jesus Christ this is a bit dodgy . . .' he says. 'No one on the board felt that there was something irregular here or something that needs to be sort of hushed up.'

Each of the Maple Ten was free to sell his shares when he wanted. Each pursued a different strategy. Sean Reilly sold almost all his shares early on, for example, while others held on.

When details of the placement were announced publicly on 15 July 2008, the statement told only half the story: Quinn and his family were unwinding a CFD position in the bank and would, in the process, buy a direct stake of 15 per cent of the bank. The fact that Quinn had actually held 28 per cent of the bank through CFDs was not disclosed, nor was the existence of the Maple Ten.

Media estimates of Quinn's losses were pitched at the time at €1 billion, based on his controlling 15 per cent of the bank through CFDs. In truth, as his actual exposure was almost twice that figure, so too were his losses.

'In recent years, we have been highly impressed with Anglo's ability to outperform the banking sector in terms of profit growth and we are confident this trend can be maintained over the longer term notwithstanding the current difficulties being experienced in international banking,' Quinn said in a statement.

A day later, in a letter to Drumm marked 'Private and Confidential', Sean Quinn threatened to sue Anglo Irish Bank over the Maple Ten deal.

'I am very aware and appreciative of your support over the past year during a difficult period for us,' Quinn wrote. 'However, I am not sure that we were treated fairly during this period which represented a five-year low in the Anglo share price.

'We were in effect forced to sell the shares regardless of market price on the downside. There seemed to be a degree of panic driving the process which I feel did not reflect a properly considered action plan. Despite our requests we were given no visibility on who the purchasers were.'

The Quinn share saga did not end there. Drumm became suspicious of the planned Credit Suisse First Boston refinancing of the loan advanced to the Quinn family to convert CFDs to shares. Its margin, he believed, looked low and he asked for an assurance from Quinn that Credit Suisse would not lend any of his shares to hedge funds to short Anglo's stock.

Quinn could not give him this assurance. Drumm was enraged that Anglo might again have to face attacks from short-sellers. The stand-off led to a delay in the refinancing, during which Anglo's share price kept falling; eventually the refinancing drifted away with it.

On 12 August, Drumm e-mailed Horan asking him to contact him urgently. Horan was on holiday and did not ring back until a few days later. Drumm told him that the planned Credit Suisse First Boston refinancing was falling apart. Horan told Drumm to ring his boss, Neary, as he himself was on holiday and could not deal with the issue.

On 18 August, Drumm and McAteer met with Neary to discuss the demise of the Credit Suisse First Boston refinancing. Horan returned from his holiday at the end of August.

On 9 September, Neary and Horan met with Drumm, FitzPatrick and Ned Sullivan, who was on the bank's board audit committee. The meeting took place inside Anglo's headquarters – the first time the regulators travelled to the bank rather than the other way around. Neary would later evocatively describe the meeting as a 'What the hell now?' moment.

Quinn's problems, Drumm said, were getting worse. His business empire was under huge strain and would crack if the bank did not lend him more money. Drumm and Quinn had agreed a plan whereby the businessman would sell off assets to reduce the bank's debt, but this would take time to implement.

Drumm asked to be allowed, in the short term, to advance a new loan to Quinn that would breach the Financial Regulator's guidelines on lending to individual clients. Neary, however, put his foot down. He was adamant there would be no more lending to Quinn.

'It was a very strange meeting,' FitzPatrick recalls. 'It was all over the place. I was staggered at what was going on. Neary said to David at some stage, Make sure you do your homework properly on the Quinn loans – in other words make sure they are properly structured.'

The meeting ended inconclusively, FitzPatrick says. The Quinn family's borrowings from Anglo hit €2.8 billion in the final months of 2008, arguably breaching the regulatory barrier; but Anglo treated the borrowings of Quinn's children, who had several hundred million euros of loans each, as separate from those of their father.

In October – by which time the liabilities of Anglo and five other Irish banks had been guaranteed by the Irish state in an effort to restore confidence in the sector – the Financial Regulator fined Quinn Insurance €3.25 million, and Sean Quinn was personally fined €200,000 for 'breaches of the regulatory requirements'. It was the largest fine ever handed out by the Irish financial regulatory authorities. The breaches related to Quinn's failure to notify the regulator of the €288 million he borrowed from the Quinn Group to cover his Anglo share-trading losses.

In the wake of the ruling, Quinn made a grudging act of contrition. 'While I accept that I made mistakes, I feel that the levels of fines do not reflect the fact that there was no risk to policyholders or the taxpayer but are a result of the pressures existing in the current environment. However we will pay the fines and move on.'

Horan later told the team carrying out a market-abuse investigation into the affair that the Department of Finance knew in broad strokes that Anglo was trying to place shares controlled by Sean Quinn in 2008 long before the controversial deal emerged into the public domain in January 2009. Horan claimed that the department knew of the transaction through its membership of the Domestic Standing Group, set up to oversee the financial stability of the state. This committee, which met at least once a month during the crisis, was made up of Neary, Hurley and either David Doyle or Kevin Cardiff, the two most senior civil servants in the department.

It is true that at the time the Financial Regulator did not know the identities of the Maple Ten or the terms on which they were borrowing from Anglo – but that was because it did not ask. There was nothing to stop the Regulator finding out all the information it needed prior to allowing the deal to go ahead or indeed in the months afterwards. It failed to do so – and its later claims that it was misled by Anglo on this matter are not justified.

The Department of Finance admits that Cowen, as minister, knew of the Quinn 'overhang' of shares in 2008. 'The details of this were a matter for the institution itself and, as appropriate, the Financial Regulator,' it says.

Patrick Honohan, who was appointed Central Bank governor in September 2009, would later say in a detailed report into Ireland's financial collapse that the Quinn CFD affair was 'a major preoccupation' of the regulatory authorities at a time of huge turbulence in the financial markets.

Their attentions should have been elsewhere.

9. Drinks with McCreevy, Dinner with Cowen

'I sort of said, Where are the guys in Goldman Sachs going with this? We were trying to make sure that we were going to get a fair crack of the whip from them.'

It was late August 2008 when Sean FitzPatrick walked through the revolving doors of the Shelbourne Hotel, a few doors east of Anglo headquarters on St Stephen's Green.

Normally a hive of activity for the city's business community, the Shelbourne was seasonally quiet. The grand old hotel had been bought for €140 million in 2004 by five businessmen led by the developer Bernard McNamara. Financed by Anglo, over three years the new owners spent €125 million expanding and redecorating the landmark property – money they later admitted they would never see again. It was one of the most grandiose, and foolhardy, investments of the boom.

Inside the hotel, at the famous Horseshoe Bar, sat Charlie McCreevy, FitzPatrick's friend from his days training as an accountant with Craig Gardner. McCreevy greeted his old friend warmly. The Kildare man had come a long, long way from his days jousting with FitzPatrick over the J.C. Carr audit. After fifteen years as a backbench Fianna Fáil TD, he had been appointed to Albert Reynolds's cabinet in 1992. Upon the party's return to power in 1997, Bertie Ahern appointed him minister for finance, and over the next seven years he drove the low-tax fiscal policy that was widely credited at the time with fuelling Ireland's economic boom.

Appointed European internal markets commissioner in 2004, after Ahern came to view him as too divisive in the Finance brief, McCreevy landed in Brussels as a champion of the free market. In an early speech given in April 2005 he set out his vision as commissioner. 'Whatever initiatives we take, the cost of regulation has to be reduced.

As finance minister in Ireland I saw what great entrepreneurial energies that a "light touch" regulatory system can unleash.

'Twenty-five years ago, we were the sick man of Europe. Today we are among the richest countries in Europe . . . Economic freedom through low taxes, open borders, good corporate governance and light-touch regulation have been absolutely indispensable to the scale of the success we have seen.'

McCreevy divided opinion in Brussels just as sharply as he had in Dublin. In the late summer of 2008 – by which time the shortcomings of light-touch regulation had become painfully evident – he was central to Europe's response to the global financial crisis.

That August evening in the Shelbourne, the EU commissioner and the Anglo chairman discussed the unfolding events. McCreevy was still an influential figure within Fianna Fáil and along the corridors of the Department of Finance, but FitzPatrick insists he did not ask McCreevy to lobby the government on Anglo's behalf – and that he had never sought help from McCreevy when he was minister for finance. 'I never went to [McCreevy] ever, when he was in government or when he was minister for finance. Ever. I was never down in the Galway races [where Fianna Fáil held an annual fundraising event]. It wasn't because I was trying not to be seen down there. I wasn't interested in either races or that whole scene.'

The men did discuss the credit crunch and the dramatic slowdown in the Irish economy. The crisis facing the banking sector was showing no sign of abating. Central banks globally were pumping billions into the financial system in the form of emergency liquidity assistance to improve the flow of funds. But nervousness was reaching new levels. Now thoughts were moving beyond the question of liquidity: the solvency of some of the world's biggest financial institutions was in doubt.

Within Anglo, however, there was no sense of panic about the bank's solvency position. That August, management undertook a review of the bank's loan book and classified just 0.6 per cent of loans as non-performing. (This figure, well into a property downturn, was identical to the figure for 2004.) Another 2.6 per cent of the book was classified as being on a 'watch' list, meaning the bank was managing it closely. Those figures did not suggest any threat to the bank's survival.

McCreevy and FitzPatrick agreed these were extraordinary times, but there was no sense that Ireland was about to go back to being one of the sick men of Europe.

The commissioner was not the only politician that FitzPatrick met that summer. At the end of July the banker had played a round of golf with the Taoiseach, Brian Cowen. Cowen was just three months in the top job.

In his tenure as minister for finance, from September 2004 to May 2008, he had failed completely to introduce measures to dampen down Ireland's property bubble or its banks.

On Monday, 28 July, according to a copy of FitzPatrick's Anglo diary, he was with Cowen from 10 a.m. to 5 p.m. (Cowen's official diary, released under the Freedom of Information Act, is blank for the same day.) The Taoiseach played a full eighteen holes of golf with the banker on Druid's Heath, a spectacular course at the foot of the Wicklow mountains. After the round the banker and the Taoiseach went for an unscheduled dinner in the golf resort's hotel. What did they discuss? 'The world, Ireland, the economy. I am not going to go into that now with you,' FitzPatrick says, adding, '[It was] absolutely nothing to do with Sean Quinn or with Anglo Irish Bank or anything like that.' It is hard to believe that FitzPatrick and Cowen did not discuss the specifics of Anglo's troubles, but FitzPatrick insists this was the case.

Uncharacteristically, FitzPatrick refuses to be drawn further on the day he spent with Ireland's leader at a most critical time in the history both of Anglo and the country.

The response of the Irish state to the global financial crisis mirrored that of Anglo and the other Irish banks. At every stage the nature of the threat was misunderstood and its scale underestimated; and the existence of a wholly home-grown problem – the bubble in Irish property prices – was not recognized.

On 23 July 2007, with the credit crunch starting to take hold, a meeting of the Domestic Standing Group – comprising senior officials from the Central Bank, the Financial Regulator and the Department of Finance – concluded that the threat posed by the global tightening of credit was real but 'exaggerated', and that there was no need for 'undue haste' in policy responses. In the last three months of that year, following the crisis at Northern Rock, the Financial Regulator called in senior executives from all of Ireland's banks to make presentations on their exposures to big property developers. Tom Browne, then Anglo's chief operating officer, met with the Regulator on behalf of Anglo to discuss how much the bank had lent to its largest clients. The meeting took less than a day and Browne reported back to the bank that it was a cordial affair.

As the crisis worsened in domestic and international property markets, Patrick Neary dispatched inspection teams into five Irish banks in early December to assess their exposure to their top five property-developer clients. The operation was known as the 'five-by-five'. The results were extraordinary. In one unnamed bank, there was no comprehensive review of group exposure to the clients on an annual basis, and no formal annual review of clients' audited financial statements or cash flow. The bank's valuations of property, often running to hundreds of millions of euro, were based solely on clients' own estimates. A number of banks were unable to obtain a net-worth statement from one very large property developer, with total borrowings of more than €1 billion, because the developer was 'unwilling to disclose such details in writing'. Three other developer clients provided statements of their net worth that had not been certified by a third party. Another bank included €100 million of working capital loans when calculating the net worth of a developer client: the bank had, in other words, counted its own money as part of the client's wealth. And one bank simply took the word of a developer regarding the level of his indebtedness to other banks.

The five-by-five inspection was outlined in gruesome detail two and a half years later in a report on the banking crisis by Patrick Honohan, who became governor of the Central Bank in September 2009. Honohan said that the high-level inspection detected 'deeply flawed processes' within the banks and should have caused 'great alarm'. The 'obvious lesson' from the five-by-five was that loan appraisals were 'totally inadequate'. Personal guarantees – as pioneered in Ireland by FitzPatrick, and then used widely as security by a number of Irish banks – could not be relied upon.

Honohan characterized the reaction of the authorities to the inspection results as 'relaxed'. Despite 'a catalogue of banking deficiencies', the post-inspection meetings on the five-by-fives lasted only 'twenty to thirty minutes'. This was soft-touch, not light-touch, regulation.

The authorities were also assuring themselves that Ireland's hothouse property market was not a threat to the stability of the banking system. The Financial Stability Report is the key annual health check of the financial system by the Central Bank and Financial Services Regulatory Authority. The report produced in November 2007 predicted a 'soft landing' for the Irish property market. In his September 2009 report, Honohan would say that the findings of the 2007 'Financial Stability Report', 'a major tool of fiscal stability policy', was not based on any quantitative calculations or analysis. It included a highly selective reading of the evidence and appears to have been, Honohan said, 'a triumph of hope over reality'.

On 24 January 2008 a confidential paper was circulated within the Department of Finance, addressing the stability of Ireland's financial institutions. It recognized that Irish banks could be seen as overexposed to property and might struggle to fund themselves if the crisis deepened, but it also trotted out the usual reassurances about the safety of the Irish banking system.

On 8 February a PowerPoint demonstration within the Department of Finance gave an overview of 'Financial Stability and Resolution Issues'. For the first time, the possibility of a state guarantee of banks' deposits and liabilities was aired. The thinking at this stage was very much against a state guarantee of bank liabilities, however: 'As a matter of public policy, to protect the interests of taxpayers, any requirement to provide open-ended/legally-binding state guarantees which would expose the Exchequer to the risk of very significant costs [is] not regarded as part of the toolkit for successful crisis management and resolution.' The presentation did not rule out a guarantee altogether if the situation deteriorated to the point where one was needed 'to maintain confidence in the overall financial system'.

On 8 March the department acknowledged internally for the first time that the failure of a small bank 'could trigger systemic failures'. At this stage the department's fears centred primarily around Irish Nationwide Building Society.

Irish Nationwide was a mutual, owned by its members and in theory run for their benefit, but it did not act like one. It called itself a building society, but under Michael Fingleton, its chief executive, at the height of the bubble it wrote four times as many commercial mortgages as residential mortgages. It offered developers loans to cover 90 per cent of the cost of buying land and often took success fees and stakes in ventures. It was a hedge fund posing as a building society.

For two weeks every year, of course, Irish Nationwide was also a banker to Sean FitzPatrick, when it warehoused his loans from Anglo. In February 2008 KPMG, the building society's auditor, explicitly warned Fingleton about the reputational risk associated with this arrangement.

There was also official wariness about Anglo. On 21 May 2008 Department of Finance officials met with Michael Somers, chief executive of the National Treasury Management Agency, the body that managed Ireland's sovereign borrowing. The meeting records: 'The NTMA has placed some deposits with the main banks.' However, as a means of easing funding worries, the NTMA intervention was not greatly useful to Anglo. Somers deposited some €300 million with both AIB and Bank of Ireland, but he later said he was 'hesitant' about placing any more than €40 million with Anglo – the bank that probably had the most urgent need for the liquidity.

In a series of interviews and talks, Somers later outlined his deep reservations about the bank. 'Looking at Anglo, we took a view that the business model was odd – it wasn't an outfit with a whole load of branches but they were raising an awful lot of money and they were lending an awful lot of money and they seemed to be paying over the odds for what they raised and charging over the odds for what they lent,' he told RTÉ in May 2010.

'It was just an institution we were unsure of,' Somers told the MacGill Summer School in July 2010. 'You just get a gut feeling. Did I share this information with anybody else? I certainly did not.'

Somers – whose brother Bernard Somers was a close friend of Fitz-Patrick – said that had he expressed any doubts about Anglo, he 'would have been blown out of the water', so well regarded was the bank.

During the summer of 2008 Drumm, still spooked by the spring-time run on deposits, held two meetings with Rabo Ireland to discuss merging the two entities. Rabo Ireland's Dutch parent company, Rabobank, had a triple-A credit rating and was ranked the fourth-safest bank in the world by *Global Finance* magazine. The chink in Rabo's armour was its Irish subsidiary, ACC, which had lent exces-sively to Irish property developers. Drumm proposed taking over Rabo's Irish problem developers, over a third of whom had already stopped making repayments; in return, Rabo would offer Anglo the safe haven of its triple-A rating for its deposits.

Rabo senior management in Utrecht refused to entertain the pro-posal. The bank had no intention of immersing itself any deeper into the mire of the Irish property market. Instead, Rabo ordered its ACC executives to pursue developers aggressively for repayment and to wind down all of its property-related business as soon as possible.

The Irish banks took a different approach.

Mutual support between Irish institutions – known as the 'Green Jersey' agenda – was being encouraged at the very highest of levels. The operation of this agenda would later become an integral part of Garda investigations into the banking collapse. Denis Casey, chief executive of Irish Life & Permanent, would state in an affidavit sub-mitted to gardaí that he attended a meeting on 13 March 2008 with the Central Bank governor, John Hurley, and the chief executive of the Financial Regulator, Patrick Neary. Bear Stearns was collapsing and Irish banks were struggling to raise funds on the wholesale money markets. This was particularly problematic for IL&P, which had a small deposit book and thus was heavily reliant on the whole-sale market. Four days prior to the meeting, Standard and Poor's, the ratings agency, had placed IL&P on 'negative outlook'.

'There was a flowing conversation about the deterioration in global funding markets and about how the risks were increasing as the crisis continued with no resolution in sight,' Casey recalled in his affidavit.

The *Daily Telegraph* had recently run an article headlined 'Irish banks may need life support as property prices crash'. The article quoted Professor Morgan Kelly, the UCD economist who was gaining a reputation as a painfully accurate forecaster of developments in the Irish property market and banking sector. 'We have a domestic recession now colliding with a global recession,' Kelly told the newspaper. 'It is the state of the banking system that will determine how terrible this will be, and frankly that is looking very shaky. We are going to see banks on life-support with very big bailouts.'

Neary and Hurley, the two most senior officials responsible for Irish banking, were determined that this should not be allowed to happen. According to Casey's statement, 'They spoke of Irish institutions needing to "don the green jersey" and "circle the wagons" to provide each other with mutual in-market support at a time of unprecedented turmoil in global financial markets in order to maintain confidence in the system and protect financial stability.' Casey added that Neary and Hurley 'indicated that similar conversations would be taking place with the CEOs of other financial institutions'.

Around this time, Drumm passed on much the same message to his Anglo colleagues: Neary had asked him to examine ways of 'pooling resources' between Irish banks. No specific mechanisms were put in place, but both Casey and Drumm left their respective meetings with the regulators in no doubt that the state wished them to help each other where possible.

Anglo would be the first bank to the test the strength of the Green Jersey. Its half-yearly financial statement was due on 31 March. The St Patrick's Day Massacre had caused a run on the bank's customer deposits that Anglo needed to build back up again.

Banks have two main categories of deposit: 'inter-bank' and 'customer'. The latter category comprises deposits by non-bank companies, large corporations and insurance companies, as well as those of ordinary customers. Customer deposits are said to be relatively 'sticky' – i.e. stable – and are therefore more sought after than inter-bank deposits. In spring 2008 Anglo could have plugged the funding gap caused by the flight of deposits by accessing the inter-bank market, but the bank also needed to boost its customer-deposits figure, because the markets might punish a bank for being weak in that area. The level of customer deposits would be one of the first numbers to be scrutinized by analysts in the half-year figures.

IL&P was uniquely positioned, among Irish banks, to help Anglo. The group included a deposit-taking mortgage bank, Permanent TSB; but it also included a life-assurance company, Irish Life. A deposit from Irish Life would be classified not as 'inter-bank' but as 'customer' – the category where Anglo needed help. The two institutions were not direct competitors to Anglo, and this facilitated cooperation.

At 11 a.m. on 31 March, the last day of Anglo's half-year, Anglo's Isle of Man division transferred €1 billion to IL&P group treasury. An hour earlier IL&P had placed €750 million with Irish Life, its assurance wing. Just before 4 p.m. that afternoon Irish Life transferred €750 million to Anglo in three tranches of €250 million each. The transactions resulted in a net outflow of €250 million from Anglo, but the crucial customer-deposits figure was upped by €750 million.

At its results announcement in May, Anglo coolly reported that customer deposits had grown by 22 per cent, or €5.6 billion, to €54.5 billion, for the half-year ending 31 March. It did not refer to IL&P's helping hand.

Much later, Anglo's lawyers Matheson Ormsby Prentice told the bank that 'There is no evidence that the March transaction was advised to the Financial Regulator [by Anglo] before it took place.' Equally, MOP concluded, 'There is no evidence that the Financial Regulator raised any "red flag" with regard to the transaction.'

A dangerous precedent had been set. Anglo had pulled the wool over investors' eyes by artificially boosting its customer deposits without apparently seeking the approval of the Financial Regulator. The Financial Regulator had failed to spot what was going on. It was a bad miss the watchdog would come to regret.

Brian Cowen, then minister for finance, was aware of the theory, if not the practical details, of the Green Jersey agenda. In a confidential briefing note on 7 May 2008 William Beausang, a senior civil servant in the Department of Finance, told Cowen in a memo: 'The Central Bank is liaising with the major domestic banks at CEO level to explore the options that may be available for mutual support between the Irish banks in a crisis situation and to respond to any problem in small institutions in a collaborative fashion.'

As the end of June approached, IL&P – whose financial year was the calendar year – faced its own half-year-end balance-sheet problems. Permanent TSB had only a small deposit book, and financed its huge mortgage business on the now locked-down wholesale money markets. To achieve liquidity, it was able to use its residential mortgage book as collateral to draw down funds from the European Central Bank. The markets frowned on the use of this facility: ECB funds were short term and 'emergency' in nature, and thus carried a stigma. A high reliance on ECB funding would damage confidence in the institution. On 21 April, Michael Manley, a senior civil servant in the Department of Finance, had prepared a note for Cowen on the subject: 'The Irish banks continue to have adequate collateral to access ECB funding, but the CBFSAI [Central Bank and Financial Services Authority of Ireland] are concerned that extensive recourse to ECB funding could be perceived as a negative signal in the market place.'

The following day Manley met with the Central Bank and the Financial Regulator and prepared a ministerial briefing note that detailed how ECB funding of Permanent TSB has risen from 12 per cent of total funding at the end of December to 22 per cent of funding on 22 April. The Central Bank and Financial Regulator 'outlined the implications of increased reliance on ECB funding'.

On 26 June, just before the publication of the group's half-year accounts, IL&P entered into a so-called 'repurchase agreement' under which it received €2.9 billion in cash from Anglo, and in return gave Anglo security to the value of €3.4 billion. The transaction successfully reduced the bank's reliance on emergency ECB funding for just long enough for the snapshot of its balance sheet to be taken. On 3 July the repurchase agreement matured and IL&P duly repaid the €2.9 billion to Anglo. The arrangement was entirely legal, but its sole purpose was to allow IL&P to paint itself in a better light.

By 26 August 2008 Cowen and Lenihan were back at their desks after the summer holidays. Over the summer, contingency measures had been put in place to counter any future problems in the banking sector. The Department of Finance drafted a 'heads of bill' for a state guarantee of distressed credit institutions. Groundwork was also done to prepare for the possible nationalization of one or more institutions. For all that, a briefing document drafted for Lenihan on 3 September by his department played down the crisis, stating Irish banks were in 'relatively robust financial health'. The 'maintenance of confidence' was key, the civil servants told the minister.

Within twenty-four hours, that confidence was to be severely shaken. Moody's, the international credit agency, downgraded Irish Nationwide bonds sharply and put the bank on 'negative watch'. In a handwritten note, William Beausang told Lenihan: 'This is not good news . . . there is a clear potential for future difficulties.'

Worse was to come. On Friday, 5 September, at 6.15 p.m., Reuters ran a story claiming Irish Nationwide was in talks with its lenders to 'avoid insolvency'. The story did not refer to a source, but it was detailed and included the name of a London accountant, Neville Kahn of Deloitte, who had been lined up as a possible administrator. Kahn declined to comment when contacted.

The Reuters story enraged Fingleton, who immediately threatened legal action. By 10.45 p.m. Reuters had backed down and retracted the story.

That night Brian Cowen appeared on the *Late Late Show* on RTÉ television. 'The deceleration is happening much faster than anyone ever expected,' he told the show's presenter, Pat Kenny. 'We must take whatever steps are necessary now so that we can get back to the good times as soon as possible.

'We are not going to tinker around with the market. There is a correction taking place in the domestic housing market. There is also a credit squeeze taking place and people cannot get access to credit. That is the issue.'

Although officially the Reuters story was depicted as a false alarm, the Moody's downgrade put the authorities on high alert about Irish Nationwide. Michael Walsh, the chairman of Irish Nationwide, and Fingleton were told by the Central Bank that the building society might have to be taken over by Bank of Ireland or AIB. Both AIB and Bank of Ireland, however, refused point blank to go near the troubled building society.

As a result, according to FitzPatrick, the Financial Regulator asked Anglo to step in. 'What happened was Pat Neary had rung David Drumm with a view to us looking at the possibility of taking out [i.e. acquiring] Irish Nationwide,' FitzPatrick says. 'David Drumm had asked me to progress that with the minister [Lenihan], which I did.'

Neary told Drumm that the Financial Regulator had already sounded out AIB and Bank of Ireland with a view to supporting Irish Nationwide, but they had refused. FitzPatrick reckoned Anglo should grasp the opportunity. 'I said . . . this could be a great chance for us of actually getting the government to back us,' he recalls. Anglo would take over Irish Nationwide loan books, including its residential mortgages, and this would provide Anglo with access to ECB funding.

Walsh was also pushing behind the scenes for a deal. 'I don't know if Michael Walsh had been in touch with me before that but he certainly got in touch with me then. I put him in touch with David and they spoke,' FitzPatrick says. 'Michael Walsh saw us as the obvious people to do it because we had a better knowledge of their loan book than anybody else and we wouldn't be as scared of it and therefore wouldn't write off as much and more importantly we would be able to handle it. On the other hand, the negative was that you were going to actually get a concentration of borrowers. For instance, Sean Mulryan was a big one of ours [and] a big one of his.'

Fingleton was not in the loop, according to FitzPatrick. 'This was done behind Fingleton's back,' he says. 'There was tension between Michael [Fingleton] and Michael Walsh.'

FitzPatrick says: 'We more or less said we are prepared – for Ireland, and that might sound strange now – to actually take on that book, but what we want is a funding guarantee. And we want a loan guarantee from the Central Bank that they would underwrite any losses. We would look after it and we would be in a good position to run it down over a period of time because of our knowledge [of the loan book].

'We didn't see it as an opportunity to create more profitability but we did see it as an opportunity to eventually paint a picture of ourselves in the eyes of the new world of aiding and abetting the state with a weak institution.'

Anglo also hoped a merger might convince the markets the bank was stronger than it appeared. 'The advantage was this: here was a [building society] that was falling and who did the Irish government give it to? Not another bank that was going to fall but a bank who they think a lot of. That was what was in it for us. It would state that we were beyond it. We were saying that if Irish Nationwide fell, someone has got to pick it up. Because if it falls, then someone else will fall.'

Drumm asked FitzPatrick to meet with Lenihan to put the merger to the Department of Finance. One evening in early September the Anglo chairman slipped into the Department of Finance.

FitzPatrick met Lenihan in his private office on Merrion Street. The two men had never met before. FitzPatrick sat down in a soft chair in the minister's office with just a coffee table separating him from Lenihan and Kevin Cardiff, the senior civil servant in charge of banking. Cardiff took notes. David Doyle, secretary-general of the Department of Finance, came in and out.

'Basically what they were talking about was Anglo,' FitzPatrick recalls. 'It was a lead-on to the whole issue of Irish Nationwide. I spoke to him about that. But I didn't really speak to him. He was taking phone calls. He was getting up and going out. He was very, what's the word . . . distracted. He just didn't focus in. It wasn't a good meeting.'

FitzPatrick had thought Lenihan would be keen on the idea he was proposing, as he believed it had the backing of Neary, but 'he wasn't really interested. I never grabbed his attention.'

The likeliest explanation for Lenihan's lack of interest is that he knew that merging Irish Nationwide with Anglo would not have solved anything. Indeed, though Lenihan never acknowledged it subsequently (and may not have recognized it at the time), both institutions were close to going bust.

FitzPatrick says he was not quizzed at the meeting about how Anglo was doing. For his own part, he says, he did not recognize that the bank he had built was in terminal decline. 'I didn't have a concern about Anglo Irish Bank at that stage myself,' he recalls. 'I wasn't really, really . . . concerned about the solvency of the bank. I never dreamt of that.'

(Shane Ross, in his 2009 book *The Bankers*, quotes Doyle asking FitzPatrick at this meeting how things were with the 'Sandman', a reference to Sean Quinn, but FitzPatrick has no recollection of this.)

FitzPatrick gave the minister a printed presentation about Anglo, based on outdated figures from the start of the year. He says the minister did not even look at it. FitzPatrick left the meeting frustrated but not downcast. The situation was manageable, he felt. Neither Lenihan nor his civil servants had expressed any concerns about the quality of Anglo's loan book. Solvency was still not seen as an issue. 'Not alone the department but no one in the bank was [worrying about insolvency]. Let me put it to you this way: if I was going into the department about the funding of the bank and I thought we had a loan book that was really dodgy, then you would be taking a different stance. You would be looking to be saved because that was going to kill you.

'It was seen as a wholly temporary situation where the world availability of credit had gone AWOL. [We thought it was] mainly caused by the American situation. It was only a temporary situation and we needed to see ourselves through that. Bad debts was not an issue.'

FitzPatrick told Drumm the meeting had not gone well, and asked him to meet with Cardiff later to try to convince him of the merits of a merger with Irish Nationwide. Walsh pressed the case as well. But the Department of Finance, which by now was calling the shots on the future shape of Irish banking, did not bite. When the story of the INBS–Anglo merger talks was broken by the *Irish Times*, Fingleton angrily denied that any discussion had taken place; Lenihan would also publicly deny any knowledge of an approach having been made.

Over the following two weeks, six months of pent-up fear and anxiety in the US banking sector would burst open, with devastating consequences. On 7 September the US government took control of Fannie Mae and Freddie Mac, two corporations established after the

Great Depression to fund the US mortgage market. On the weekend of 13–14 September, amid fears that Lehman Brothers, the giant US bank, was about to go bankrupt, an urgent meeting was called between the Central Bank, the Financial Regulator, the NTMA and the Department of Finance. The greatest concern related to Irish Nationwide. Goldman Sachs, the investment bank that only two years earlier had tried to sell the society, was appointed to advise the state on what to do.

FitzPatrick was worried that should the review be extremely negative about the society's property loans, officials might think that things were as bad or worse inside Anglo. FitzPatrick rang Peter Sutherland, whom he knew from his days in UCD. Sutherland was a former Irish European commissioner who was then chairman of Goldman Sachs International.

'I rang him during the crisis in September at the behest of David Drumm,' FitzPatrick recalls. 'I sort of said, Where are the guys in Goldman Sachs going with this [review of Irish Nationwide]? We were trying to make sure that we were going to get a fair crack of the whip from them.'

FitzPatrick says the call, which he described as a 'soft chat', was made to reassure Sutherland – who was not directly involved in the review of Irish Nationwide – that Anglo was fundamentally sound. '[I told Sutherland] we were facing funding problems and it was not as bad as he was led to believe,' FitzPatrick recalls. 'We were sort of saying things like the state should help. The NTMA should be supportive of banks . . .'

FitzPatrick says he also called Basil Geoghegan, an Irish senior Goldman executive who had been working on Irish Nationwide. The two bankers knew each other from working together on the flotation of Aer Lingus, where FitzPatrick was a board member. FitzPatrick lobbied Geoghegan, too, to ensure that Anglo wouldn't be adversely affected by any extrapolation from Irish Nationwide's situation to Anglo's.

On Sunday, 21 September, the Department of Finance was updated by Goldman. The investment bank said there was 'real value' in the building society but warned 'liquidity [is] a big issue – at current rates [the society] reaches limits in 11 days, but [there is a] real danger of acceleration'. Contingency plans were needed in case the society had to be taken over quickly by the state.

On Monday, 15 September, Lehman Brothers, crushed under the weight of its exposure to the sub-prime market and unable to secure either state support or a rescue by another firm, filed for bankruptcy. On the same day Bank of America agreed to take over Merrill Lynch, which might otherwise have suffered the same fate as Lehman. It also emerged that American International Group, the giant insurance corporation, would need to be rescued by the US government at vast cost. The knock-on effects of Lehman's failure reverberated around the world; with liquidity scarce and trust even scarcer, the global financial system came very close to seizing up.

In Ireland, early on in the crisis, a consensus was formed that no Irish bank should be allowed to fail. This feeling grew stronger after the demise of Lehman, with its dramatic side effects: the conventional wisdom was that allowing Lehman to fail had been a mistake. In his affidavit Denis Casey would later recall that he had been told repeatedly by the Regulator in September 2008 that Anglo was 'systemically important' and could not be allowed to collapse.

A Department of Finance briefing note to the minister on 17 September stated that 'all [the banks] are under pressure, especially the smaller ones', but insisted 'Irish banks are well capitalised, highly liquid and have built up good financial buffers over a number of years.' This view – which would soon be exposed as nonsense – became something of a mantra. At the launch of the Irish operations of Australian bank Macquarie, on 19 September, Brian Cowen said the Irish financial-services sector had 'weathered developments well to date'.

The Irish public begged to differ. A scarifying discussion took place on the *Liveline* phone-in programme on RTÉ Radio One on 18 September. Callers voiced their fears that their savings were no longer safe, and the opinion was expressed that it was better to keep your money anywhere, even under the mattress, than in Irish banks. The programme's presenter, Joe Duffy, said: 'If they come out with their hands on the Bible and say "We are not in trouble", why should we believe them?' A fuming Lenihan phoned RTÉ director-general Cathal Goan to complain that the state broadcaster was scaremongering.

On Saturday, 20 September, at 11 a.m., Drumm, McAteer and Moran met with Con Horan, the prudential director at the Financial Regulator's office, and Hurley to discuss Anglo's preparations for its financial year-end and the actions it was taking to strengthen its balance sheet. Anglo told the regulators it was facing an appalling funding situation: the bank had lost €5 billion in deposits over the previous week. By the end of the month – Anglo's financial year-end – the bank feared that figure could reach €10 billion. Admitting this to the market in the year-end result statement could lead to a further run on its deposits.

The meeting was very tense. Anglo told the regulators it was going to work with IL&P ahead of its year-end, as it had been doing all that year. Horan pressed Anglo to ensure that it was satisfied that whatever it did would not mislead the market. A note by Horan from this meeting refers to his asking Anglo to submit a 'paper' outlining how this might work. Anglo never submitted the proposed paper, nor was it demanded by the authorities. Even at a time of unprecedented crisis, here was an example of the Financial Regulator trusting bankers to obey the rules rather than taking a hands-on approach to enforcing them.

It was a very busy day for the Financial Regulator. Its officials also met with all the other banks to canvass their views on potential mergers and to find out how their deposit bases were holding up. Later that day Lenihan substantially raised the ceiling of the state's deposit-guarantee scheme, from €20,000 to €100,000. The minister for finance said: 'I want it to be known that the government is confident about the strength and resilience of the Irish financial system. The government is committed to the stability of our financial system, so that money placed with an Irish credit institution would not be at risk.'

On Monday, 22 September, Drumm and FitzPatrick held a secret meeting with IL&P chief executive Denis Casey and chairwoman

Gillian Bowler to discuss a possible merger. Tentative talks about such a move had taken place earlier in the month, but now they were much more urgent, as Anglo was close to running out of cash to fund itself. The meeting was held in the Westin, a five-star hotel in Dublin city-centre.

Casey dismissed a merger out of hand. He suspected that Anglo was not as strong as it claimed to be.

According to Anglo files initialled by David Drumm and later obtained and published by the *Irish Daily Mail*, a series of crunch meetings took place between Anglo executives and the Central Bank in the wake of the Lehman collapse. Drumm states in the documents that, post-Lehman, he told the Central Bank that Anglo was losing up to €1 billion in deposits every day. 'The Central Bank were receiving twice-daily liquidity updates and I was receiving calls every day from the Financial Regulator,' Drumm claimed.

Things came to a head towards the end of September, when Drumm went to the Central Bank to beg it for emergency funding. Hurley, according to Drumm, told him he had only €4 billion readily available to cover all the country's banks.

'I will never forget how shocked I was,' Drumm wrote. 'It seemed incredulous [*sic*] that the Central Bank in its role as "lender of last resort" would come up so short. They only had less than 1% of the country's bank's assets in reserve – insufficient to even deal with one minor run on one bank.' Drumm returned to Anglo dejected. The Central Bank, which had known of the crisis for over a year, had not built up anything like a big enough war chest to help it or anyone else, he believed.

Sources close to the Central Bank, speaking to the *Irish Times*, later disputed Drumm's claim, saying the Central Bank could have provided Anglo with so-called emergency lending assistance but feared the negative impact on Irish banks' reputations of doing so.

'Leading up to the 29th of September things were real bad,' Fitz-Patrick recalls. 'I mean real bad. It got real bad treasury end and financial end, meaning our liquidity. The Central Bank might have been thinking of giving us money but they said they didn't have money to give us. They could only lend so much because they couldn't get it. We said don't be so stupid, will you not get the ECB to lend money to us?'

Minutes from a meeting between the Department of Finance, the Central Bank and the NTMA, dated 22 September 2008, show all three bodies knew of the crisis facing Anglo. The minutes, headed 'Liquidity and how to provide a war chest', state: 'Anglo already requesting seven billion facilities and want to activate a swap with the Central Bank who will not do so unless absolutely necessary.' The meeting concluded that €18 billion could be cobbled together from various sources to rescue Ireland's teetering banking sector if required.

On 23 September, with the state fast running out of options, the Department of Finance, in a 'brainstorming' session, looked at virtually every option, from merging Irish Nationwide with the EBS and Irish Life & Permanent, to pumping billions into Anglo. It also looked at the idea of a 'bad bank', parking all toxic property assets in one place and swapping government bonds in return for property loans as a means of injecting new capital into the banks. They even considered merging AIB and Bank of Ireland, to create a single national champion.

On the same day that the government brainstormed, FitzPatrick went into the market and purchased Anglo shares worth almost €1.1 million, believing them to be 'good value' at €3.92. His good friend Lar Bradshaw, a non-executive director, bought shares worth €196,000.

'We sort of said, Jesus Christ, look at what is happening,' FitzPatrick recalls. 'The share price is coming down, it is a very good buy. It is an announcement of our confidence. It is a traditional way of directors turning around to the public and saying we believe in the bank.'

The announcement of confidence by FitzPatrick and Bradshaw did not have the desired effect, and officials now felt they had to respond to concerns relating not only to Anglo's liquidity but to its solvency. On 25 September, Neary insisted that 'there is no evidence to suggest Anglo is insolvent on a going-concern basis – it is simply unable to continue on the current basis from a liquidity point of view.' Irish Nationwide was in a 'similar' position, he said.

The Department of Finance, however, estimated 'on some assumptions' the losses facing Nationwide and Anglo to be €2 billion and €8.5 billion respectively. This was the first official (though not public) acknowledgement that both institutions faced something more fundamental than just a funding problem.

Globally, the carnage continued. Perhaps the most telling foreign development during these late-September days was at Fortis, the Belgian bank. On Friday, 26 September, the bank was unable to raise the €15 billion to €20 billion in overnight funds it needed to meet its obligations. It subsequently started to lose institutional and retail deposits. The bank accessed €5 billion from the ECB in emergency funding and was part-nationalized, with the Dutch, Belgian and Luxembourg governments investing €11.2 billion to take a 49.9 per cent stake in the group.

Though Fortis was active in the Irish market, through a joint venture with An Post, it was not the main item on the agenda as officials gathered at the Central Bank on Sunday, 28 September. Nor was Anglo. The feeling was that Anglo would be able to survive the coming week. The officials instead focused on the massive funding issues facing Depfa Bank, a German bank that was based for tax purposes in the International Financial Service Centre in Dublin and regulated by the Central Bank.

Monday morning dawned to more panic. Dexia, a French–Belgian bank, suffered a massive fall in its share price, prompting talk of yet another nationalization. Wachovia, America's sixth-largest bank, was sold to Citigroup. And it became clear that the US Congress would vote against the first draft of a key plank in the American government's response to the unfolding banking crisis, the Troubled Asset Relief Program.

From early morning Anglo's share price plummeted. The main question now was how much longer the bank could continue to meet its repayment obligations.

'Everything just happened in a flash,' FitzPatrick says. 'Because money was going in and money was going out. We were getting good money in and other money was going out. If anyone wanted to get the money out, then we said, Yeah, of course, we will get it straight away. We will give it to you now. We were always going to be able to draw down bank lines to make sure that we had the money as I understood. But David then was sort of saying to me at this stage, This is getting very, very tight now. We are in trouble.'

10. Saving Anglo

'I could see his eyes bulging at me and he said, Are you going to resign? I said, What? No. I was after coming out after what I was thinking was a good interview and he was furious.'

Shortly after lunchtime on Monday, 29 September, FitzPatrick and Drumm left Anglo headquarters for a crisis meeting with Brian Goggin, the chief executive of Bank of Ireland, and Richard Burrows, its chairman. Anglo had requested the meeting only that morning because its funding position was now critical.

The meeting took place in Bank of Ireland's Baggot Street headquarters – a building FitzPatrick partly owned. The two Anglo bosses drove the short distance, entered the building through the car park and were discreetly shown up to the boardroom.

'[We wanted] to get them to buy us, or to get them to lend us some of their residential mortgage loan book, which we could use to raise new money from the European Central Bank, or to put money with us. They were saying, We are all having difficulties,' FitzPatrick recalls.

It was not the first time Goggin and FitzPatrick had discussed a potential link-up between rival banks. A mutual acquaintance, Donal Geaney, sat on the board of the Bank of Ireland. In 2005 Geaney had arranged a dinner between the two men to talk about a potential merger of the two institutions.

FitzPatrick says he believes that there was a feeling at Bank of Ireland board level that a merger should be explored. Anglo's share price was soaring, turning the heads of even the seasoned directors of Bank of Ireland, traditionally Ireland's most conservative lender.

Bank of Ireland was viewed by stock-market analysts as falling behind its rivals. Its asset-management arm and a joint venture with Britain's Royal Mail were failing to deliver the kind of spectacular profits being made by Anglo, AIB and Irish Nationwide. Goggin, then only a year in the top job, was under pressure to grow profits.

Taking over Anglo would have given Bank of Ireland a huge property-development book and made it the biggest bank in the country.

The discussions never became serious, which suggests that Bank of Ireland was not overly anxious to take over its smaller rival. Anglo, for its own part, was growing fast and felt no strong need to do a deal.

Now, in a profoundly transformed situation, Bank of Ireland turned down Anglo's proposals. After looking hard at Anglo's figures, it formed the view that the bank could collapse at any moment.

FitzPatrick and Drumm returned to St Stephen's Green. FitzPatrick rang Dermot Gleeson, the former attorney general, who was chairman of AIB. 'I asked him to meet with me. He would not meet with me. He was too busy. There were lots of things going on, lots of things going on. He was under pressure as well.

'I said, Look, we are facing great difficulties. I need to talk to you and I need to talk to you urgently. He wouldn't meet.

'Gleeson was very uptight. Obviously bothered . . . He was more or less saying we are all in difficulties here . . . The whole market has dried up. The international money market, it is just gone . . . So lookit, Sean, we all have our problems so you are on your own. So that was that.'

Anglo's share price, which on Friday stood at €4.28, fell to €2.30 at the closing bell on Monday. Despite the precarious state of the bank, and the desperate visits to Bank of Ireland and calls to AIB, FitzPatrick met his old school friend Jackie O'Driscoll for dinner that night. 'I knew there was problems with commercial deposits moving because we were talking about that . . . But it all happened very quickly. Don't forget it had happened back in March and it was beaten down. I didn't sort of see it as the end of the world. I didn't.

'I wasn't running the bank . . . What could I do? If I was going to be forceful then I would have to be right in the middle of absolutely everything. And driving the whole thing. And, if you like, pushing David aside, but David wasn't welcoming me into this. You know that was the way it was. David was the chief executive and I wasn't going to undermine him with his own colleagues and everything like that. I didn't try to muscle in on it.'

The news was now spreading among senior decision-makers in the state that Anglo was hours from going bust. There was a widespread belief that if Anglo fell, the entire Irish banking system might follow.

After 6 p.m. Cowen and Lenihan, and their respective secretaries-general Dermot McCarthy and David Doyle, met at the Department of the Taoiseach. Hurley and Neary soon joined them, along with two senior Finance officials, Kevin Cardiff and William Beausang. Paul Gallagher, the attorney general, also called in a little later.

Documents released to the Public Accounts Committee in 2010 reveal both the sequence of events and how badly informed every-body at the meeting was ahead of the biggest economic call in the history of the state.

The government simply had no idea of the scale of the black hole inside Anglo and the Irish banking sector generally. Only the previous day, PwC, advising the government on the crisis, had estimated that Anglo, Irish Nationwide and Irish Life & Permanent had a collective €5 billion in bad debts in a 'stressed case' scenario. Losses on Anglo, PwC, advised, could be as much as €1.5 billion – very big, but not a mortal threat to the economy.

(At the time of writing, Anglo's losses – relating almost entirely to loans already executed by September 2008 – were estimated to be €40 billion.)

At 6.43 p.m. that evening Kevin Cardiff received an e-mail from Merrill Lynch. Attached was its report – commissioned by the Department of Finance just two days earlier – outlining the state's options. Anglo had 'exhausted all possible sources of liquidity', Merrill said. The report ruled out letting Anglo fail, as this would lead to a 'fire sale' of its assets; this in turn would force other banks to make massive write-downs, wiping out their capital bases. Letting Anglo go to the wall, it concluded, would be 'very damaging' to the entire Irish banking system, which it described as 'broadly sound'.

Merrill did not make a definitive recommendation but looked at a range of options, from an 'immediate liquidity provision' of €5 billion for the entire Irish banking system to nationalizing the two most troubled banks, Anglo and Irish Nationwide. The longest portion of the sixteen pages of advice it gave the government related to how to introduce a secured lending scheme for the banks, under which commercial property could be exchanged for government bonds or cash. This would give Anglo access to the liquidity it so badly needed to keep trading.

The Merrill Lynch report contained just seven sentences relating to the option of introducing a blanket guarantee of the liabilities of the six Irish banks. The advantage of this approach, the investment bank said, was that it would halt the run on deposits and even attract back fresh overseas deposits to replace the deposits lost in recent months. However, such a guarantee – which Merrill Lynch estimated could involve liabilities to a value in excess of €500 billion – 'would almost certainly negatively impact the state's sovereign credit rating and raise issues as to its credibility. The wider market will be aware that Ireland could not afford to cover the full amount if required.'

At 8.40 p.m. Cardiff received a second e-mail, this time from PwC. The consultants said Anglo had borrowed €900 million from the Central Bank, was out of reserves and had to repay 'over €2 billion' to an unnamed party the next day.

Lenihan had that day approved the Central Bank support for Anglo; the letter was eventually made public in the 2009 annual report of the Comptroller and Auditor General, the state-spending watchdog.

(In terms of funding PwC also said that on 27 September, €1.9 billion, or 35 per cent, of Anglo's corporate deposits were 'under the control of Irish Life Assurance'.)

While members of the government and senior civil servants met that evening, AIB and Bank of Ireland were clamouring to hold an urgent meeting with the government.

About 9.30 p.m. AIB chairman Gleeson and chief executive Eugene Sheehy, and Bank of Ireland's Burrows and Goggin, arrived at the Department of Finance. They were forced to kick their heels for two hours while the government and its officials conferred on what to do. Finally the bankers were let in as the clock approached midnight.

They, too, told the Department of Finance that Anglo was running out of funds, and that the bank would soon be unable to meet immediate claims for payment. A billion-euro deposit lodged by a German bank, they said, was due to mature in the morning. Anglo could not access funds to meet the repayment.

('I had no idea was there any particular trigger or was there any particular issue that we could not pay out the next day or two,' Fitz-Patrick says. 'That could have been there but I still don't know to this day whether that existed or not.')

It was clear that Anglo could not survive another day. AIB and Bank of Ireland said that Anglo's failure to meet its obligations would lead to an immediate outflow of funds from the country's other banks. It was a threat to the entire system. The two banks pressed for the state to guarantee all the liabilities of the country's banks, to nationalize Anglo and possibly Irish Nationwide, and to change the management of Anglo. They feared a domino effect if Anglo was allowed to survive outside state control, as it would certainly collapse.

FitzPatrick believes that the officials in the Department of Finance accepted the arguments of the two biggest banks that his bank was bust and needed to be taken into state control. 'There was a huge push by the Department of Finance to have us nationalized,' he says. 'Guys were gunning for us to be nationalized.'

According to a highly detailed account of that night by the *Sunday Business Post*, 'Cowen's response was, "We're not fucking nationalising Anglo."'

In the early hours of 30 September it was agreed that the government would guarantee the liabilities of the six Irish banks: AIB, Bank of Ireland, Anglo, Irish Life & Permanent, EBS and Irish Nationwide. It was an extraordinary measure brought about by extraordinary times. Out of the menu of options outlined by Merrill Lynch, Cowen and his government went with the option of a state guarantee, despite its adviser's clear warning that if it had to be honoured, it could threaten the state itself.

It was a blanket guarantee of all deposits and the vast bulk of the entire banking system's other liabilities, including most of its debt. The total sum involved was around €440 billion, some €60 billion less than Merrill Lynch's hasty estimate, but still more than twice the country's GNP. Every taxpayer and citizen in the country was now on the hook for every last penny owed to depositors and bondholders by six unstable institutions.

On the night of 30 September both Cowen and Lenihan defended their decision to the Dáil. 'There is understandable concern that the Exchequer is potentially significantly exposed by this measure,' Lenihan said. 'I want to reassure the House and the Irish people that this is not the case. The risk of any potential financial exposure from this decision is significantly mitigated by a very substantial buffer made up of the [banks'] equity and other risk capital.'

The total assets of the six Irish financial institutions concerned, Lenihan claimed, exceeded their guaranteed liabilities by approximately €80 billion. 'By any measure there is, therefore, a very significant buffer before there is any question of the guarantee being called upon,' he maintained.

FitzPatrick says he had no input into the decision by the government to guarantee the banks. 'No. No. Absolutely zilch. I had no idea whatsoever. None.' He had recently spent an entire day with the Taoiseach; he had influential friends in Charlie McCreevy, Peter Sutherland and Fintan Drury; but instead of trying to influence the course of events he had had dinner in the home of his old school friend Jackie O'Driscoll in Bray and gone to bed at 11 p.m. A contact within the Central Bank rang him at 5.30 a.m. to tell him what had happened, and that it would be reported on the news at 7. No one from his own bank rang him to report the events of that morning, FitzPatrick says. It was only later in the day that he discussed the guarantee with Drumm and the board.

'We spoke during the day about the relief of all that. It wasn't that the guarantee was a relief. It was that the government had stepped in behind the banks . . . Everyone was happy that that was going to be it. Suddenly we woke up the next day and it was a brand new day.'

The idea of some sort of state guarantee of the liabilities of the Irish banking sector had been advocated by influential figures from various quarters. Writing in the *Irish Times* on 17 September, the solicitor and property developer Noel Smyth, a major client of Anglo, outlined his plan for a guarantee of deposits. 'If the government was to persuade the Central Bank to guarantee all deposits in Irish banks operating under a banking licence from the Central Bank in the state, the effect would ensure that depositors considering investing in Ireland would know they had a state guarantee and that the banks would always ensure their money was repaid,' Smyth wrote.

Smyth asserted that 'None of our banks in Ireland are in the remotest area of trouble or of any concern', and he advocated the deposit guarantee as a means of restoring confidence in a fundamentally sound system; but even he did not advocate a guarantee of anything more than the banks' deposits.

David McWilliams, the popular economist, published three articles that endorsed the idea of a guarantee: on 21 September in the *Sunday Business Post*; on 24 September in the *Irish Independent*; and finally on 28 September in the *Sunday Business Post*. In his final article McWilliams went all out and suggested a blanket guarantee covering both depositors and bondholders. 'The only option is to guarantee 100 per cent of all depositors/creditors in the Irish banking system,' he wrote. 'This guarantee does not extend to shareholders, who will have to live with the losses they have suffered. However, it applies to everyone else. If the minister [Lenihan] does this, he will not only staunch any funds outflow, he will show leadership and be seen as someone who is coming up with a solution that can be copied all over the world.' McWilliams argued that this would buy enough time for the banks to sort out bad debts associated with excessive property lending. He would later claim – in *Follow the Money*, his 2009 book on the Irish economy – that he played a key role in convincing Lenihan to introduce a blanket guarantee. (Lenihan played down the significance of McWilliams's intervention, telling RTÉ in November 2009: 'There were many other people sharing ideas at that particular time, not just David . . . I don't think he has a unique patent on the government decision to give the guarantee, but he was arguing for that course of action.')

Once the guarantee was agreed in Government Buildings in the early hours of 30 September, the chairmen and chief executives from AIB and Bank of Ireland were called back to a second meeting. It was decided that the two leading banks would each make available to Anglo a short-term credit facility of up to €5 billion each, guaranteed by the government. The Central Bank would also make available up to €3 billion through an asset-swap facility, whereby Anglo would pledge certain loans in return for funds. Some €1 billion of the facility would be made available the very next morning.

It wasn't needed. With the state now standing as guarantor, funds flowed back into all the Irish institutions, including Anglo. It had gone from being viewed as one of the riskiest banks in Europe for deposits to one of the safest. The share price bounced.

The unilateral introduction of the guarantee enraged other European governments, most notably Britain's, which feared that it would attract funds into Ireland to the detriment of the UK's struggling banks, and that British banks with operations here would be at a disadvantage. The European Commission said that the guarantee would be investigated. Ireland's commissioner, McCreevy, defended the guarantee, saying that governments 'don't have the luxury of waiting forever and a day to make up their minds about critical matters'.

A few days after the momentous events of 29–30 September, a researcher from the Marian Finucane show on RTÉ radio rang FitzPatrick to ask if he would go on the programme that Saturday.

'I said no,' he recalls. 'David [Drumm] was in the room with me and he said: Why would you not go on? It will be great, you would be better than me. You are better known than me and so on.'

About an hour later Billy Murphy, Anglo's public-relations adviser, rang FitzPatrick. The RTÉ radio show had also called him to see if FitzPatrick would go on.

FitzPatrick decided to accept the invitation. Initially he thought he would be part of a panel to discuss the day's newspapers, but as the weekend approached he was informed that he would be interviewed solo.

FitzPatrick knew Finucane: he had helped to raise money for a charity she founded. 'I knew her but I wouldn't have been friendly with her,' he says.

On the day before the interview, he met with Murphy to go through what he should say. 'Basically it was: be humble. Humility, every chance I could get at,' FitzPatrick recalls.

Just after 11 a.m. on Saturday, 4 October 2008, Sean FitzPatrick entered the radio studio and sat across from Finucane. He listened to the news headlines as he waited for his interview to begin. They were particularly grim.

'A special pre-budget cabinet meeting is being held at Government Buildings this morning. It comes as the latest Exchequer figures show a deficit of €9.4 billion and the need to borrow €11 and a half billion euro . . .'

FitzPatrick began nervously but soon hit his stride, putting in a typically bravura performance. The crisis, he told Finucane, was a 'once-in-a-century occasion'. He denied Anglo had lent money excessively and claimed that property developers accounted for 'less than 20 per cent of our books'.

'Anglo Irish Bank has made mistakes because we are in the business of risk and I'll admit that. Have we been reckless? No. I don't believe that.

'I think that the world has changed since last Monday. As a chairman of a bank, we are going to have to take into account the views of the taxpayer in a way that we have never done before. We are in a whole new paradigm for the boardrooms of Irish banks.

'We were all on the brink. It was very close . . . It was a matter of days, I would have thought – that is why the government acted so decisively and so boldly. I am saying thank you unashamedly because we owe our lives to the government and what they did,' he said.

FitzPatrick asserted that 'it was not just one bank, it was all of the banks' and that the Irish banks 'had spoken with each other'. This gave the impression that Anglo had been talking to its rivals as a peer. The truth, however, was that while every Irish bank was in trouble, only Anglo was on the brink of total collapse that night.

'This was not a shameful position to be in, Marian. This was a reality . . . It was a dangerous place but it wasn't a shameful position because it was not the creation of Irish banks.

'If the Irish banking system had collapsed there would have been chaos and the real economy would have suffered . . . We would have been in uncharted territory and anything could have happened.

'We were concerned as all the banks were . . . If Anglo were down in isolation you would worry more but all of the banks were down that day in Ireland.'

FitzPatrick admitted that he had feared an 'Armageddon' without the guarantee. 'I believe the decision made last Monday is probably the most important decision made, in an economic point of view, since the foundation of the state.'

FitzPatrick declined Finucane's invitation to apologize to the Irish taxpayer for having to bail out the banks. 'It would be very easy for me to say sorry,' he said. 'The cause of our problems was global, so I can't say sorry with any degree of sincerity and decency, but I do say thank you.'

Wearing a pink shirt and dark suit, he walked out into the car park of RTÉ. A journalist ran up to him. 'I could see his eyes bulging at me and he said, Are you going to resign? I said, What? No. I was after coming out after what I was thinking was a good interview and he was furious . . . He was very aggressive. He had a photographer just going bang, bang, bang . . . I had never seen such outright hostility, even from a person I had hit, from rugby matches, from anything at any level whatsoever. They followed me right to the car. I am wondering what is going on. I got into the car, closed the door, and pulled off and that was it.'

Calls flooded in to FitzPatrick's phone. Drumm was 'thrilled', Fitz-Patrick recalls, at his performance.

Pat Molloy, the former chief executive of Bank of Ireland, also rang him. 'He said to me he'd heard it and he just wanted to say full marks to me. He thought I had got guts to go on,' FitzPatrick said.

Mick Bailey, one of Anglo's earliest developer clients, who with his brother Tom made a €25 million settlement with the Revenue Commissioners in 2000, also called, as did other developer clients of the bank.

FitzPatrick said that they were all 'very positive' and believed 'Anglo had taken too much shite.'

The more politically astute Gary McGann, however, was not pleased. 'Gary didn't like that kind of stuff [doing interviews]. He was negative about the very fact I went on.'

The Finucane interview led to some critical comment in the following days, but it was relatively tame. It was only over the following weeks and months, as Anglo's crisis intensified and clips from the interview were replayed, that public anger deepened. FitzPatrick's refusal to apologize, in particular, played a very important role in making him the face of Irish banking and of the national crisis the banks had precipitated.

In retrospect, FitzPatrick says: 'I told what I believed was the truth. I told it all very clearly. I did not see it as an issue particular to Anglo Irish Bank but to every bank in the world. I saw there was a big, big issue and it was a once-in-a-hundred-year tsunami. That was what it was. Now we were going to have the guarantee. I didn't know whether that was going to work but I thought it was brilliant. I wanted to thank the government.

'It was fantastic what the government [had] done. They have to be congratulated. We realize everyone is a stakeholder now. We appreciate that and we have to live up to our responsibility. A whole new beginning and everything like that. She said, Well, the story out there was that you guys were the ones who brought it all down. I said, Don't be ridiculous, this was a world thing. Do you not understand? It was just pulling it down. No one could get any money.

'The thing that offended most people apparently was, would you not apologize? If I didn't steal tuppence from you, then I can't apologize even though things have gone very badly for me and for you. I did not do it so therefore how can I apologize? But I am very grateful for your support now. That was what I was saying. Joyce [his sister] was listening to it and she said really that was a very good answer but no one really went through it in any great detail.'

Later on the same Saturday, FitzPatrick drove to Greystones to give a speech at the Charlesland Golf Club. He had agreed to speak as a favour to George Jones, a local Fine Gael councillor. Sean Mulryan and Sean Dunne were also on the original bill to speak, but they both, perhaps wisely, never turned up. The title of the event was innocuous: 'The relationship between the Local Authorities and the Business Sector'.

'It was something to do with civic week in Greystones or something like that,' FitzPatrick recalls. After talking about the events of the week leading up to the guarantee, the Anglo chairman turned to the subject of the budget being prepared by Lenihan. He proposed that the government should scrap universal state pensions and child benefit.

'That was the first thing in the newspapers on Monday. People were writing in to me saying how dare you. I didn't mean it. The context was, lookit, if it was me earning this income, why should I get a state pension?' he said.

FitzPatrick says he stands by both his remarks in the Finucane interview and the Greystones speech even today. 'Nothing has come back to haunt me in that I believe everything I said. I can't think of anything I said on the Marian Finucane show that I would be embarrassed about, although I mightn't like hearing it again. I still believe that state pensions shouldn't be paid to people who can afford to live without them. I still believe kids' allowances should not be paid to people who can afford to live without them.'

Later that weekend FitzPatrick received one more phone call. It was from Richard Burrows, the chairman of Bank of Ireland. According to FitzPatrick, 'He said, Sean, I heard you on the Marian Finucane show and the board here are very upset about it. I said, Oh, because I didn't refer to Bank of Ireland at all. He said, No, Sean, what you were saying was that this was an international thing and it was common to all banks and yet we were asked to put €10 billion aside for you guys on the night of the guarantee. I said, That may well be true but this is the first I have ever heard of that. He said, Well, not alone that, Sean, it actually took a number of hours – I couldn't tell government there and then and it had to go through our credit committee. I said, Well, I did not know anything of this. And then of course the guarantee came and it wasn't required. I sort of said, Jesus Christ, I did not know anything about that, which I didn't.'

A few days later FitzPatrick got a letter from AIB chairman Glee-son expressing feelings very similar to Burrows's.

Dear Sean,

I was out of the country at the weekend. On my return on Sunday I was shocked and angry to read a transcript of your interview with Marian Finucane. In the interview, you significantly misrepresented the following matters:

(a) The events of Monday
(b) The liquidity position of AIB
(c) The nature of your communication with me

You conveyed an impression that all of the banks were in the same situation on Monday last and denied that it was Anglo alone who had an acute liquidity problem, which it would be unable to fix on Tuesday.

The truth is that on Monday night AIB was asked by the Governor of the Central Bank of Ireland (in the presence of the Taoiseach and others) to provide emergency funding to solve Anglo's liquidity problem, not just on Tuesday, but for every succeeding day until the end of the week.

AIB acceded to the request and arranged to provide Anglo with €5 billion in liquidity until the weekend. The reason AIB was able to do this, was because it had liquidity in excess of its own requirements available on Monday, not just for Monday night but for the rest of the week and beyond; Anglo was not going to be able to balance its books without assistance.

It is frankly outrageous for you to indicate that AIB's liquidity was good for only a matter of days. It is entirely inaccurate for you to say 'this was not caused by any one bank' when the truth is it was Anglo alone which required to be saved on Monday.

As to our communications, as you know the only communications between us in the last few months, was that you rang me on Monday asking for a meeting between the CEO and Chairman of Anglo and AIB, which I declined, indicating that we were very busy and that there was nothing we could do for you; at that stage you suggested that we should go together to the Minister and I declined that invitation also and left you with my genuine best wishes in the situation you found yourself.

Your interview conveys an impression of a different sort of contact between us. While that is not perhaps a major point, what is undoubtedly significant is that you feel entitled to share an (in my view inaccurate) account of our communications, in public without any prior consultation with me.

The reason I am writing to you now rather than speaking to you is that I am not any longer prepared to risk you sharing confidential telephone conversations with a chat show in which AIB's position on critical issues is significantly misrepresented.

Finally, given the way you have chosen to misrepresent AIB's liquidity position in such a reckless way, and imply that you were privy to it (which you were not), you need to know that I reserve the right to put the record straight on each of the foregoing issues at a time and manner of my choosing and at any time from today onwards.

Yours Sincerely,
Dermot Gleeson

FitzPatrick rang Gleeson after reading the letter. He says he told Gleeson that he had had 'no idea' that AIB had agreed to contribute to an emergency fund to rescue Anglo. FitzPatrick says that Gleeson was sceptical but eventually accepted his explanation.

FitzPatrick today is not exactly repentant at having given the impression that the Irish banks were all in the same boat. 'Do you not think it was a little bit naive for your man to turn around and say, Not alone have we got money for Monday but we also have for the rest of the week and beyond? Pretty revealing. When I spoke to him on the Monday, he wouldn't speak to me. Not because he didn't love me or anything like that but because he was up to his fucking eyes.'

Anglo phone transcripts for 1 October 2008 note a query from an employee at the Financial Regulator's office about a series of transactions involving Anglo Irish Bank and Irish Life & Permanent between 25 and 29 September. The official was told by a member of Anglo's treasury team that the transactions had been undertaken in order to 'manipulate our balance sheet'.

'What we have done is boosted our customer funding number . . . so when our snapshot is produced at the beginning of December, it looks as good as possible, it's not a real number,' the Anglo executive said.

After a further innocuous query, the member of the Regulator's staff concluded: 'OK, that's grand, right, I think that's everything.'

The transactions in question broadly replicated the deposit swap between Anglo and IL&P of six months earlier, just before Anglo's half-year-end. The main difference was that Anglo's funding position had gone from bad to catastrophic in the intervening period, and the September transactions were accordingly on a much bigger scale.

On 24 September Drumm and Anglo finance director Willie McAteer had met with Neary in his office to discuss the bank's 'critical funding position'. McAteer recalled in an internal Anglo report that he had told the regulator that the bank 'will be managing the balance sheet at year-end'.

Neary's reply has gone down in Irish banking folklore: 'Fair play to you, Willie.'

Even in normal times, billions of euro flow through the financial system in the run-up to banks' reporting dates. If bank A has a line of credit with Bank B, then the line might be called in at a crucial moment to puff up the balance-sheet profile.

In the six months prior to September 2008, Anglo had been more active than ever before in the practice. Anglo's treasury team was fighting hard all year to keep its funding position intact and as time went on they were being forced to go to ever greater lengths to do so. It completed what its legal advisers called 'balance-sheet management' transactions with Lehman Brothers, the Royal Bank of Scotland, ABN AMRO and AIG.

Anglo's year-end fell on 30 September – a moment when it was haemorrhaging deposits and on the brink of going bust. Even the Green Jersey would only stretch so far. Moving billions of euro from one bank to another at a time of national crisis and great uncertainty was fraught with risk.

Irish Life & Permanent could not simply put billions on deposit with Anglo. That would have represented a serious and unacceptable risk to IL&P shareholders at a time when IL&P had its own liquidity problems – and when Anglo's solvency was very much in question. The gambit resorted to in March would have to be trotted out again.

On 25 September Anglo Isle of Man placed £978 million (€1.2 billion) with IL&P group treasury; after a short delay the money arrived with IL&P the following day.

On 26 September IL&P group treasury moved £978 million to Irish Life, its life-assurance company, in three tranches.

On 29 September Anglo's Dublin office sent €2 billion over to Irish Life & Permanent group treasury; Anglo had now placed a total of €3.2 billion with IL&P over the course of four days.

IL&P then sent €2 billion from group treasury into Irish Life, which then sent €3.2 billion, the total amount it had received, back to Anglo. Again, as Anglo had received the money from an insurance company, and not from IL&P's other arm, Permanent TSB, it could book the money as a customer deposit.

It was, like the March deposit swaps, pure artifice – but on a much larger scale. There was no risk to IL&P, and, as there was no net gain in the criss-crossing of funds, the arrangement did not boost the liquidity of either institution.

On 29 September, Anglo clamoured for more support, but Casey was adamant no more funds were to be advanced.

'Each of these requests were declined by IL&P on my direction, as Anglo Irish Bank was not in a position to provide collateral for the proposed additional support,' Casey said in his June 2010 affidavit submitted to the gardaí. The collateral was important from Casey's point of view, as it ensured that IL&P was not put at risk. Nobody was prepared to trust Anglo.

The government guarantee introduced in the early hours of 30 September changed all that. With the guarantee only hours old, it was agreed that Anglo would send €4 billion more over to IL&P, which in turn sent €4 billion to Anglo via Irish Life. Using the by-now familiar circular mechanism, Anglo then got €4 billion of customer deposits back from Irish Life. In total, €7.2 billion had been transferred in each direction, a truly enormous sum. The Irish Life money neatly plugged the balance-sheet gap caused by the post-Lehman exodus of customer deposits from Anglo.

The safety net of the government guarantee allowed Anglo to begin to rebuild its balance sheet. Within three days of the guarantee, funds flowed back into Anglo. The IL&P arrangement was no longer needed and it was reduced by €6 billion.

FitzPatrick says that neither he nor any member of the board was informed of the IL&P transaction at the time. 'I wasn't like that. That is not the way I work. I know now, looking back on it, it looks very obvious: Why wouldn't you have looked at it [Anglo's funding position] closer than that?'

As chairman, he says, 'you would only see a balance sheet from one month to the next when you are doing your monthly accounts. There were no great problems with the balance sheets. I don't think we did results for August because we were preparing for September. So the last set of accounts I would have seen would have been July.'

FitzPatrick knew Anglo's funding was in serious trouble. It did not occur to him, he says, to ask how big the hole ultimately was in its deposit base, or how it had somehow been filled come results time.

On 23 October, Anglo met with its auditors Ernst & Young to discuss its end-of-year accounts. As Vincent Bergin from E&Y prepared to leave the building, he was called into the office of Colin Golden, Anglo's head of finance. Golden had a number of items relating to the accounts jotted down a piece of paper. One of them was IL&P.

An Anglo note of this meeting records the following: 'discussed IL&P transaction'; 'gave context – tough environment, strong relationship with IL&P'; 'placement with IL&P bank, deposit from customer'; 'regulator aware'; '[Bergin] said he believed it was "technically sound".'

Bergin afterwards told his colleagues in the E&Y audit team about the issue. However, he would later state that he was not told at that time exactly how the circular mechanism had been structured and as a result never approved it.

By the end of October the issue of the IL&P transaction had come to the attention of the Department of Finance. It had been described in some detail, if somewhat buried, in a report on Anglo compiled for the government by PwC, which called it a 'boosting' of Anglo's balance sheet; but no concerns were raised about its legality. 'We believe there is no legal right of set-off,' PwC said. This was an important point: in PwC's view, Irish Life & Permanent could not set off its deposits with Anglo against the deposits it took from Anglo. If there was no right of set-off, the transactions could be viewed as entirely separate. The only problem, unknown to PwC or Ernst & Young at the time, is that IL&P did not share this view of the transactions. It firmly believed that there was a right of set-off. Anglo was seeing apples, where IL&P saw oranges. If there was a right of set-off, then Anglo would have to 'net off' the two deposits and could not achieve the desired boost to its corporate deposits.

The National Treasury Management Agency spotted the massive flow of funds between the two institutions in the PwC report and flagged it up with Kevin Cardiff, then deputy secretary-general of the Department of Finance.

Cardiff recalled to an Oireachtas committee in May 2010 that the NTMA asked him if he had seen 'the figure of €7 billion, as it looked a little strange'. 'The Department would have been aware of it later in October [2008], at which time we brought it to the attention of the Financial Regulator ... On that day or within a day or two I telephoned the office of the Financial Regulator to ask if it had seen the figure on page 118 [of the PwC report].'

Mary Burke, head of the Financial Regulator's banking division, was asked to investigate. In an e-mail on 24 October she updated Neary and Horan on what she had found out: 'Anglo maintains that Ernst & Young, their auditors, have just reviewed it and seem satisfied that it meets accounting rules ... Anglo advised that they understood that the Financial Regulator was aware of the transaction, referring to yourselves.'

Burke also noted that Peter Fitzpatrick, finance director of Irish Life & Permanent, 'positioned this transaction as a response to the governor's suggestions that Irish banks should help each other out'.

An internal IL&P note by Peter Fitzpatrick, dated the same day, backs up Burke's report: 'We believed that we were supporting the system [in a way] that had been encouraged by the Financial Regulator and by the Central Bank in the course of a number of meetings which we had with both of these parties. In relation to the Central Bank, I stated that John Hurley had pressed us to support the system.'

On 3 November, according to Anglo records, the bank met again with E&Y to discuss the PwC report. The Anglo records of the meeting claim that the bank 'deliberately' pointed out the reference to the IL&P transaction but E&Y 'expressed no opinion'.

On 18 November senior Anglo executives led by McAteer discussed the transaction with the board's audit committee. The committee's chairman, Gary McGann, and committee member Donal O'Connor both attended the meeting, the latter by conference call from Australia, where it was after midnight. O'Connor, a chartered accountant, was the director most capable of understanding the transaction. At one stage he said the transaction 'sounded' like window-dressing. This was not per se illegal but it was certainly something O'Connor, as an accountant, might want to know more about. O'Connor was reassured down the phone line by the bank's financial team that it was normal 'balance-sheet management' that had been approved by the Financial Regulator. McGann later told investigators that he did not understand the exact nature of the transaction at that time and that he, too, was told it was legal.

The 2008 year-end snapshot presented its own particular problems for Sean FitzPatrick.

As far back as the summer of 2007 FitzPatrick had become concerned about the extent of his enormous private borrowings with Anglo.

'I remember sort of saying to [a named employee of the bank] I had better get it refinanced, and she said, Yeah, it is probably better because it can't be right, you know,' he recalls.

In the autumn of 2007 Bank of Ireland sent FitzPatrick a letter offering to take €70 million of his loans away from Anglo, but the parties could not agree terms. 'We were fighting over part of the security,' FitzPatrick recalls. He was also unhappy with the rate of interest they were proposing to charge him.

He succeeded in refinancing between €30 million and €35 million of his Anglo loans in late 2007 and early 2008. All of his investments with Quinlan Private were refinanced, for example, with First Active. These included his stake in the Four Seasons Hotel in Prague; his share in Maximilianhöfe, the retail and office development in

Munich; and his shareholding in Jurys Inn, the budget hotel chain. FitzPatrick also did other refinancing deals with other banks.

Come September 2008, there was little prospect that FitzPatrick's loans would be accommodated with Irish Nationwide as per the normal warehousing arrangement. Irish Nationwide was by then under too much intense scrutiny to get away with it. Most of his investments had fallen sharply in value and there was no chance of having his loans refinanced elsewhere.

The loans would stay in Anglo. The bank's 2008 annual accounts, due to be published the following February, would, for the first time, reveal the true scale of FitzPatrick's borrowings with the bank. FitzPatrick had got his loans down from about €129 million, but even after the partial refinancing of his investments his Anglo borrowing still stood at €87 million.

FitzPatrick was not the only Anglo director facing year-end debt problems. Willie McAteer, Anglo's finance director and chief risk officer, owed Bank of Ireland €8.25 million, money he had borrowed over the years to take up share options in Anglo.

The loans were secured only on his Anglo shares. As the value of the shares plummeted in September 2008, Bank of Ireland demanded that he repay the loan. McAteer told the bank he was unable to do so at such short notice. Bank of Ireland told McAteer that in that case it had no choice then but to sell his Anglo shares, which it held as security, into the market.

This was as much a problem for Anglo as it was for McAteer. Under Stock Exchange rules, all company directors have to tell the market if they sell shares in their own company. Even at the best of times, a finance director selling shares in his own bank just days before its year-end would worry any investor. In the febrile atmosphere of September 2008, it could easily have prompted a run on the stock and tipped a fragile Anglo over the edge.

Facing this grim scenario, on 29 September Anglo lent McAteer €8.25 million to pay off Bank of Ireland. An ad hoc credit committee, consisting of a number of senior staff in the bank, signed off on the loan.

Ad hoc credit committees were not without precedent in Anglo. Big developers sometimes waited inside the bank while urgent loans were signed off by such informal committees. Later, the loans – having already been disbursed – were formally rubber-stamped at credit committee.

At the time McAteer's loan was granted, the value of his Anglo shares was still greater than the value of the loan. Anglo appeared to lend to McAteer on preferential terms, taking security only on the shares, with no further recourse to the executive's other assets. This was the same deal he had enjoyed with Bank of Ireland; but what was unusual about Anglo's offer was that it was done when the price of McAteer's Anglo shares was in absolute freefall.

Anglo, however, would later claim that the generous arrangement was down to a mix-up. Anglo regularly lent money without any recourse except to the underlying asset, and the bank later claimed it had mistakenly used a standard non-recourse template to do the deal. When this was discovered, in January 2010, McAteer duly signed a new form giving the bank full recourse to his assets.

FitzPatrick says he knew nothing about the loan to McAteer. 'I was not involved in the decision to grant Willie the loan,' he says. 'I had no idea that it was done until well after 30 September. It was sometime in November when David said to me, Do you realize that Bank of Ireland were going to move on the loan to Willie? I said, What do you mean? . . . I never knew of the non-recourse.' FitzPatrick says McAteer did not tell him at the time about his problems with Bank of Ireland, but they discussed the affair later. '[McAteer] was sort of saying, Well, I didn't have a choice. I had to take down the loan. The loan was forced on me by the good name of the bank. I had to preserve it.'

Preserving the good name of the bank would become an increasingly difficult task in the months ahead.

11. Stepping Down

'She said, Da, you couldn't go to jail? You can't be arrested? . . .
I said, Ah no, Sarah, for God's sake.'

At board level, the most pressing issue of all in the run-up to the preparation of Anglo's year-end accounts in September 2008 was the health of its loan book. It was abundantly clear that Ireland's property boom was well and truly over.

In June 2008 Merrill Lynch launched a new piece of research that aimed to track the asset quality of the Irish banks. All the indicators in the first edition were negative. From a peak in March 2007, house prices had fallen 14 per cent. The Central Bank reported a severe tightening of lending standards and that loan growth had halved. Construction activity was down 18 per cent and FÁS, the state training agency, predicted 65,000 job losses in the sector.

Market realities dawned slowly on Anglo's developer clients. They blamed the dramatic fall-off in the number of property transactions, and falling prices, on the tightening of credit.

This was a convenient excuse. The truth was that, right across the property market, there were signs of a devastating over-supply. In the three years to the end of 2008, just under 220,000 new houses were built in Ireland. The natural demand for housing in the country, based on population statistics, is about 30,000 units per year.

Ireland boasted 1.9 million square metres of shopping-centre floor space and 1.3 million square metres of retail-park floor space built or under construction, or a total of 3.2 million square metres of non-high-street floor space. That compared with less than 500,000 square metres of shopping space at the end of 1999 or just 850,000 square metres of shopping space at the end of 2004. Ireland, heading into a recession, was over-shopped.

Economist Dr John McCartney concluded in an article for the

Economic and Social Research Institute that the Dublin office market was 'overbuilt'. At the end of July 2008 less than 20 per cent of the 428,000 square metres of office space under construction was reserved for a tenant. In other words, 80 per cent of it was speculative.

Bank of Ireland's response to the evidence of a bursting property bubble, in September 2008, was to reduce by half the value of development land held as security. Thinking at Anglo, however, was not so advanced. A group of Anglo board members, led by Lar Bradshaw, had grown sceptical of the management view of problem loans. Bradshaw suspected by the summer of 2008 that Anglo must have more bad debts on its books than it was declaring, and he increasingly raised questions about this at board level. Drumm insisted his team had its numbers right.

FitzPatrick asked Bradshaw and Donal O'Connor, a former managing partner of PwC, to carry out an independent review of the loan book in September. The chairman wanted to be sure that the provisions for bad debts were large enough before signing off the annual accounts.

O'Connor and Bradshaw met seven of Anglo's most senior lenders over a number of days. They reviewed the bank's twenty biggest loans in Ireland, including facilities issued to Derek Quinlan, Bernard McNamara and Sean Quinn, and looked at 82 per cent of the bank's Irish loan book in total. They concluded the 'extreme-case potential loss' was €797 million on loans of €43 billion. This was practically the same as the executives' view. When Anglo's two independent directors also took into consideration a potential €200 million loss on loans advanced to Sean Quinn, they put the figure for that year's estimated losses at €1 billion.

The directors were 'pretty comfortable' that 67 per cent of Anglo's Irish loan book was 'performing'. While a third of the book was not performing (i.e. not meeting all their interest and repayments schedules) this was seen as only a temporary situation brought on by the credit crunch. O'Connor and Bradshaw reviewed 'stressed' or worst-case valuations for forty-five loans on development land and five investment property cases and concluded that the Anglo executives' provisions for possible losses on these loans were 'accurate'.

In a presentation made after the review, O'Connor and Bradshaw concluded: 'While we could argue at the margin on a few conclusions, the book is well provided for in [an] "extreme case" scenario.' O'Connor and Bradshaw added, 'clearly management [is] "all over" notable or watch cases'.

Just over a week after the announcement of the Irish guarantee, the British authorities moved to protect the country's banking system by pumping £50 billion of capital into its banks on top of extending liquidity support. They recognized that the issue of solvency, and not just liquidity, was now top of the banking agenda internationally.

In Ireland, by contrast, there was no talk at the time of recapitalizing the banks. Right up to the announcement of the guarantee, and in the weeks that followed, the Financial Regulator and the Central Bank insisted that the only problem facing Irish banks was access to funding.

On 2 October 2008, in an infamous RTÉ *Prime Time* interview, Patrick Neary, the chief executive of the Financial Regulator, stuck to the line that the issue for the Irish banks was one of liquidity and not capital. 'By any estimation, the Irish banks are so well capitalized compared to any banks anywhere across Europe that I am confident that they can absorb any loans or any impairments that will emerge in the ordinary course of business over the foreseeable future,' he said.

The government guarantee was a lifeline for the Irish banking sector, and deposits flowed back into Anglo after it was announced, but there was still extreme nervousness in the wholesale money markets. Anglo had the highest credit risk of any Irish bank, when measured using credit default swaps, bond-insurance instruments studied closely by the international markets. The cost of insuring Anglo bonds against default was almost 80 per cent higher than the equivalent cost for AIB bonds.

The insolvency of Iceland's two largest banks, Glitnir and Kaupthing, in early October pushed that country close to bankruptcy. Ireland's difficulties were not yet on that scale, but the lesson of Iceland – that a small country could be brought low by an out-of-control banking sector – was not lost on observers of Ireland.

On Monday, 3 November, Willie McAteer, Anglo's finance director, received a call from Oliver Whelan, head of funding and debt management at the National Treasury Management Agency. Ireland was trying to raise €4 billion with a new treasury bond and the NTMA was struggling to get international support.

Whelan decided to call on the Irish banks to ensure the bond issue did not fail. He told McAteer that AIB and Bank of Ireland had already agreed to purchase Irish bonds – in other words, to lend money to the state. McAteer asked Whelan to give him one hour, as he would have to get Drumm's approval. Drumm told McAteer to go ahead and subscribe for the maximum amount allowable: €500 million. He probably calculated that he had little choice. The state had just rescued the Irish banking sector; Anglo could hardly turn the NTMA down now that its support was needed. Besides, the transaction would be 'funding neutral' for Anglo, as it could simply take the NTMA bonds and swap them for cash with the European Central Bank.

The NTMA in its 2008 annual report would describe its November bond as 'strongly oversubscribed, reflecting continued investor confidence in Irish government debt'. However, based on figures later given in its annual report, it is clear that about €1.5 billion of the €4 billion bond issue was taken up by Irish banks. Anglo, at €500 million, put up the biggest portion. The Irish banks' involvement was six times the size of their collective subscription for the previous bond issued in April. Even at this early stage, there were signs of the contagion effect of the banking guarantee on the ability of the state to fund itself.

The guarantee did little to soothe fears of investors about the solvency of Irish banks. Irish bank shares continued to slide. Investors picked on the banks one by one, like bullies in a schoolyard. In the forty-eight hours to the close of trading on Friday, 7 November, for example, Bank of Ireland lost 30 per cent of its value and for a few hours was valued at about €1.5 billion less than Anglo.

The relentless pressure on Irish bank shares was rooted in the widely held belief that the institutions needed more equity capital. On 19 November, Cowen told the Dáil that 'all options' were being considered to save Ireland's banks. Cowen said Lenihan had recently met with the governor of the Central Bank, the Financial Regulator and PwC to discuss the accountancy firm's reports for the state on the banks' capital and loan positions.

As he spoke, shares in both Anglo and Bank of Ireland were trading below €1.00. Cowen said the report could not be published because it was 'commercially sensitive', but that it showed the lenders were in excess of their regulatory capital requirements on 30 September, the day the guarantee was announced. He insisted the report showed that under stressed scenarios capital levels would remain above regulatory levels up to 2011. Cowen admitted, however, that 'international market expectations' on the levels of capital held by banks had altered. 'Meeting these expectations may be challenging, with consequences for the sector and the wider economy.'

Anglo meanwhile hired Morgan Stanley to help it raise capital, and indicated that it would seek to raise up to €1 billion to boost its capital 'buffers'. The bank also hired PwC to work on 'Project Vista': a top-secret plan to prepare it for a quick sale if a buyer could be found.

Behind closed doors, Brian Lenihan was hearing an altogether bleaker analysis of the black hole emerging inside Anglo Irish Bank and the entire Irish banking sector. This analysis came not from civil servants in the Department of Finance or from bank regulators, but from some of the biggest venture-capital funds in the world, which had landed in Dublin to see if they could make money from Ireland's banking crisis.

Representatives from multibillion-dollar funds including Apax, Blackstone, Texas Pacific Group and Kohlberg Kravis Roberts were all billeted in Dublin's finest hotels. Their interest was primarily in Bank of Ireland, the best-managed of the Irish banks, but sources say the private-equity players also discussed the state of the other Irish banks.

Mallabraca, an Irish consortium assembled in the summer of 2008 by financiers Nick Corcoran, Nigel McDermott and Bryan Turley, was among the first to contact Lenihan. The consortium assembled a heavy-hitting team of investors, including the New York financier

J.C. Flowers and the Carlyle Group, whose negotiating team was led by Olivier Sarkozy, the half-brother of French President Nicolas Sarkozy. Mallabraca also courted Middle East sovereign-wealth funds. It set up operations at the Merrion Hotel, directly across the road from the Department of Finance.

Each of the private equity firms that rolled into the Department of Finance predicted the same thing: multibillion-euro losses on property-related loans across all of the Irish banks' books. Their analysis of bank losses, although still well short of what would ulti-mately emerge, was far more negative than that put forward by PwC, Neary or the Central Bank.

Lenihan asked a number of private-equity consortiums to look at investing in Anglo. None liked what they saw, and the feedback Lenihan received was grim. Anglo would need at least €5 billion immediately in new capital, not the €1 billion the bank had set out to raise. Some cautioned that it could ultimately be far, far more. The sums were greatly in excess of the bank's own predictions or the esti-mates of any of the government's advisers.

The private-equity groups baulked at taking on the risk without a massive new state guarantee – not of Anglo's liabilities, which were already covered, but of the value of its assets. If they were to get involved, a number of them insisted, the government would have to pick up the bill for up to 90 per cent of any future loan losses. To write an open-ended cheque to support a private-equity takeover of Anglo would be a non-runner politically. When this was explained to one consortium, Lenihan was bluntly told that he would have no other choice but to nationalize Anglo before Christmas.

Internationally there was concern about the eventual cost to the Irish state of recapitalizing the banks. The *Daily Telegraph* quoted Michael Klawitter, a strategist at Dresdner Kleinwort, who said the cost of insuring Irish sovereign debt through credit default swaps had surged. 'The markets have begun to see a risk to the solvency of the Irish government,' he said. 'They are questioning whether it has the financial muscle to back up the guarantees.'

On 25 November the Department of Finance approved Anglo's issuing of a €1.5 billion bond under the government guarantee scheme. Against all the negative views from private equity, and the question marks about its year-end balance sheet, Anglo management was talking up the bank's prospects.

Behind the scenes, though, provision was being made for the growing likelihood that Anglo would not be able to survive as an independent entity. Executives began to contemplate the fate of the Maple Ten in the event that the bank should find itself under new ownership. They had already seen their Anglo shares lose almost all of their value. A change in ownership could leave the ten business-men badly exposed, as any new owner would consider them simply as debtors and not as friends who had done their bit to rescue the bank.

Around 13 October, Anglo executives met to discuss how to pro-tect the Ten. The original loan letter read: 'Recourse to the borrower will be limited to 25 per cent of the balance outstanding.' On foot of the executives' meeting, a new letter was prepared for the clients' files which stated: 'Recourse to the borrower will be limited to 25% of the balance outstanding or to the value of the shares on expiry of the facility.' The latter clause was new, and was intended to allow the Maple Ten to claim, in the event that the bank was taken over out-right and its shares became valueless, that they were entitled to walk away from their debts entirely. Copies of the letter were to be placed on file to be ready for use if required. Due to what executives termed a 'clerical error', however, the letter was posted to the clients.

Later the bank rectified the situation by getting the Maple Ten to agree to ignore the letter. Although the terms of the loans were not ultimately amended, the drafting of the revised loan letter was a clear case in which Anglo executives left their non-executive board out of the loop and appeared to act more in the interests of their clients than of the bank.

On 3 December, Anglo Irish Bank held a press conference in Herit-age House to announce its figures for the financial year ending 30 September.

The bank's annual results presentation was usually an informal and relaxed affair where the bank would be upbeat about how it had exceeded market expectations with more record profits, continue to be conservative on potential loan losses and talk up its loan 'pipeline'.

This year would be very different. As Anglo's accounting year ended in September rather than December, it held the dubious honour of being the first bank in Ireland or the UK to report full-year results since the collapse of Lehman Brothers.

FitzPatrick did not attend the press or analyst meetings: he had stopped doing so not long after he stepped down as chief executive. In his opening remarks, Drumm described the events of the previous year as the 'most extraordinary financial upheaval' in the bank's history. He said that Anglo's pre-tax profits were down 37 per cent to €784 million in the year to 30 September, after setting aside €500 million to cover future losses on loans, mostly to developers.

Drumm described the €500 million provision as 'quite a whopping provision to take, but it's recognizing the world we are in'. McAteer described the provision as 'a demonstration of prudence'. The bank expected to write off no more than 11 per cent of its €8.9 billion Irish development loan book − a figure that would be reached, McAteer emphasized, only in a 'very distressed' situation. The maximum Anglo would lose on its development loan book, McAteer said, was €2.76 billion over three years. Based on the profits it would earn from its good loans, the bank would make profits equivalent to 2008 levels. Should losses turn out to be double the worst-case figure, Drumm added, Anglo would still break even.

Drumm admitted the bank had been under huge pressure in the run-up to the state guarantee. In September the bank had lost €4 billion in large corporate deposits, he said, but things had improved since the guarantee. (Drumm made no explicit mention of Irish Life & Permanent's last-ditch boost to Anglo's corporate-deposits base, without which his bank would have had to announce corporate-deposit losses of €11.2 billion.) He added that Anglo was not considering merging with any other bank or doing a deal with private equity to bring in fresh capital. The requirement for capital ratios in Europe was rising, but Anglo was going it alone. Drumm also announced a pay cut for executives, a pay freeze for ordinary staff and the scrapping of all bonuses, and he predicted there would be 'no daylight until 2011'.

Analysts were sceptical of Anglo's figures, and some of them would soon become downright suspicious. The previous March the bank had said that its exposure to property development was 15 per cent of its loan book, or €10.4 billion. It now revealed that, in total, a bit over 23 per cent, or €16.9 billion, of its €73 billion loan book was exposed to property development. The bank said it had 'reclassified' a number of loans and included rolled-up interest in its calculation. It was also lending more working capital to developers to allow them to finish projects.

Anglo had downplayed its exposure to the property market, and the market reaction was savage. The bank's shares plummeted 29 per cent to 67 cents, their lowest level in eleven years; its stock-market value now stood at €509 million, down from a peak of €13.6 billion. Janus Capital, an American investment fund and the bank's second-largest single shareholder, dumped more than 1 per cent of the stock the day after the results. Its largest shareholder, Invesco, also sold stock.

Soon after the release of the bank results, Willie McAteer flew to America on his standard two-week, fourteen-city tour of the US and Canada to present the results and strategy to large institutional investors. On 10 December he flew home unexpectedly, cutting the tour short. A day later Anglo's shares hit 28 cents.

Any hope that Anglo would be able to raise capital independently from the markets was now rapidly disappearing. A proposal was made that government should underwrite a rights issue – in other words, the company would go to its shareholders to raise money, and if there was a shortfall, government would step in and buy the shares. Any new offer of shares would have to be placed at a steep discount to the prevailing market price – an extremely difficult situation, given that the share price was approaching nil. The markets could no longer be convinced to give one penny more to the bank, and the Irish taxpayer was emerging as its sole source of capital. The government was making it known that, if it was to rescue Anglo or any other bank, it would demand a change in management.

Change was already on the way. As part of the state bank guarantee, the government was entitled to elect two new 'public interest' directors to the board of each of the six covered financial institutions. The day after Anglo announced its results, it emerged that Anglo's state-appointed directors would be Alan Dukes, the former Fine Gael leader, and Frank Daly, the former head of the Revenue Commissioners.

After a political career during which he had served as minister in four different departments, Dukes worked as a public-affairs consultant from 2003 with Wilson Hartnell, the public-relations firm that acted for the Quinn Group. He tetchily dismissed the suggestion that his Wilson Hartnell work created a conflict of interest with his new role at Anglo, stating categorically he had never worked on its Quinn account.

It was a political masterstroke on Lenihan's part to appoint Dukes, distancing his own political party from Ireland's most toxic bank – and a bank that had lent so heavily to Fianna Fáil-supporting developers during the boom.

Daly was a career civil servant who had joined the Office of the Revenue Commissioners in 1963 and rose to become its chairman in 2002. Before his retirement in March 2008, Daly had clawed back billions of euro for the state held in offshore bank accounts and mechanisms for tax-evasion.

Dukes and Daly would now take centre-stage at Anglo board meetings.

The sands were shifting, and Sean FitzPatrick knew it. His enormous loans from Anglo would not sit well with this new regime. The borrowings had already attracted attention within political circles.

On 10 December, Brian Lenihan rang Financial Regulator Patrick Neary demanding to know more about FitzPatrick's loans and how they had escaped the regulator's attention. (Lenihan claimed he spotted the loans himself while looking at Anglo's draft annual report.)

One person close to the bank said that FitzPatrick spent much of that week trying to engage with Drumm on how his loans would be treated in the published version of the accounts. Directors' loans are traditionally reported as part of a combined figure in the annual accounts, rather than being broken down and listed by individual director. There was no onus to disclose FitzPatrick's specific figure, but even to include his huge exposure in the collective figure would send the overall number spiralling. In the new Anglo, with public-interest directors on board, there would be no avoiding a full disclosure.

On Saturday, 13 December, FitzPatrick asked his three closest friends on the board, past and present – Gary McGann, Donal O'Connor and Fintan Drury – to meet him in the office of Smurfit Kappa, the packaging company FitzPatrick chaired, in Clonskeagh, south Co. Dublin, before going to lunch in Ashton's, a pub nearby. It was a convenient location for all four men.

FitzPatrick told his friends he was going to step down the following week. 'The decision was made to go on the Saturday,' FitzPatrick recalls. 'It was coming all the time. There was no particular one moment. Let me put it this way: Gary never said, By the way, Sean, are you looking at your position? Donal never said it and Fintan never said it. I would have been saying, I think I have got to go.

'Basically I felt I had to go because I knew the bank was going to be under more and more pressure in relation to the financials, in relation particularly to the funding. My sense was that they didn't need me as an added distraction on that and therefore I should go.'

FitzPatrick said he took the decision himself to step down and nobody told him to go. In reality, with Anglo's share price close to zero, the bank's funding falling apart, nationalization on the horizon and a state presence on the board, it was probably only a matter of time before he would be sacked.

Over the very same weekend, the government announced that it was preparing to face up to the gaping capital needs of the Irish banks by pumping up to €10 billion into them. The capital was to be invested on the basis of a 'case-by-case analysis', Lenihan said, according to the level of impairments on the loan books of all the Irish financial institutions as estimated by PwC. There were no specifics as to how much would be invested in each bank.

The following Monday morning FitzPatrick told Drumm of his plans to resign. FitzPatrick next set up a meeting with Dukes and

Daly, and asked Ned Sullivan, Anglo's senior independent director, to attend.

'That was the first time I told them about various things, including about the loans. I could see the reaction on their faces was negative,' FitzPatrick recalls. 'I was quite keen to tell [the government directors] . . . I wanted no surprises for them. I didn't want them to hear it from anyone else, the Department [of Finance] or anyone else. I wanted them to hear it from me about the board, what the board was paid, what their bonuses were, and that is why I had Ned with me from the remuneration committee.'

FitzPatrick recalls that he also gave Dukes and Daly a list of all the bank's loans to directors. 'They made a comment about one or two guys . . . They made a comment about Tom Browne and I think they made a comment about Gary [McGann],' he says.

Browne owed the bank €14 million, McGann owed €11 million and Drumm owed €8 million. Unlike FitzPatrick's, all these loans had always been included in the bank's annual report to shareholders. It was FitzPatrick's loans, worth some €87 million and hitherto secret, which made the biggest impact on the new directors. 'I turned around and it was the first time, they were going like this [taken aback] and I went, Jesus Christ, look at that reaction. I said, I will tell the guys in Finance. They said, Yeah. That was it.'

On Tuesday, 17 December, FitzPatrick attended the annual Christmas party for Anglo pensioners in Heritage House on St Stephen's Green. After exchanging greetings with former colleagues, he slipped away from the festivities. He went to an upstairs room and rang his board colleagues on a conference call. 'I was by myself . . . [I] would have said, Lookit, gentlemen, I have decided that I want to resign from the bank, and thank you very much for all your support in the period, and I really enjoyed my time here.'

The call over, FitzPatrick was alone. He could hear the party of a hundred people going on below, oblivious to what had just transpired a few floors above them.

'It wasn't at all emotional,' he said. 'I left fairly quickly after that. No one knew.'

The next day would be his final day at the bank. It started with a meeting in the Department of Finance. Kevin Cardiff and Anne Nolan, senior officials in the department, were present, along with Padraig O'Riordan, managing partner of Arthur Cox and the state's legal adviser on banking. Donal O'Connor and Ned Sullivan accompanied FitzPatrick.

'I said: I am going to resign. They said they were sorry to see it happen and wished me the best of luck.'

Later that morning FitzPatrick held a teleconference to formally announce his resignation to the board. The minutes of FitzPatrick's final board meeting note that his resignation was 'accepted with regret' and record the department's 'disappointment' regarding the director's loans issue. O'Connor was duly appointed chairman with the backing of the Department of Finance. After O'Connor took over, FitzPatrick left the teleconference.

The meeting continued through more painful business. According to the minutes, the department told Anglo that 'further questions remained to be answered at a later point' about FitzPatrick's loans and it 'enquired as to any regulatory or legal breaches which may have incurred'. The civil servants also queried whether FitzPatrick would be able to repay the loans.

The department questioned a payment of €934,000 to Drumm to compensate him for a €5 million cap on executive pensions introduced by the government in 2006. The department also asked that Anglo set out its plans 'should management's capital-raising efforts not succeed'. The idea that government would underwrite the planned rights issue was now officially dead in the water.

According to the minutes of the meeting, Drumm then told the board that 'in light of recent events and in the absence of explicit government support, the credibility of management was significantly undermined'. Consequently, he felt he had no alternative but to tender his resignation.

The board told Drumm it would be 'very detrimental' to the bank's efforts to raise fresh capital if he resigned. It instructed him to draft a term sheet for government support and separately push forward with a new capital-raising from investors. Reluctantly he agreed.

After he left the board meeting, FitzPatrick met with Billy Murphy, his trusted public-relations adviser, to draft his resignation letter. Murphy led Drury Communications, which he had co-founded with one-time Anglo director Fintan Drury in 1988.

As FitzPatrick prepared to compose his resignation letter, something unexpected happened. 'I remember Donal O'Connor coming in to me and saying Lar [Bradshaw] has got to resign as well.' One of the loans that FitzPatrick warehoused with Irish Nationwide was his joint loan with Bradshaw to invest in the Nigerian oil well. FitzPatrick told O'Connor that Bradshaw had had no idea the loans left the Anglo books at year-end.

'No one had added two and two, and thought, Oh Jesus, I have refinanced part of Lar's borrowings,' FitzPatrick says. 'It never dawned on me at all.'

Despite FitzPatrick's protestations, Bradshaw stood down.

In his resignation letter FitzPatrick addressed the issue of his loans from Anglo: 'The transfer of the loans between banks did not in any way breach banking or legal regulations. However, it is clear to me, on reflection, that it was inappropriate and unacceptable from a transparency point of view.

'I am fully responsible for my own decisions and actions and I regret that I had adopted this approach. I have always pursued high standards in my personal and professional life and I failed to meet those standards in this instance.'

In response to FitzPatrick's resignation Lenihan issued a statement in which he repeated his commitment to underwrite the capital needs of Anglo Irish Bank 'on appropriate terms' and to ensure its 'long-term strength and viability as a bank of systemic importance to Ireland'.

In his final hour in the bank's St Stephen's Green headquarters, FitzPatrick watched the RTÉ nine o'clock news. Peter Murray, the former chairman of the bank and a friend, sat beside him.

Eileen Dunne, the RTÉ presenter, began the report. 'We begin with some breaking news. Leading Irish businessman Sean FitzPatrick, the chairman of Anglo Irish Bank, has resigned tonight in a controversy over directors' loans. In a statement a short time ago Mr FitzPatrick said his resignation related to an €87 million loan he had from the bank . . .'

FitzPatrick watched the rest of the news and then left the building. He retrieved his car from Anglo's underground car park and drove through the Christmas-shopping traffic to his home in Greystones.

At the time, FitzPatrick recalls, he believed his resignation would be 'a one-day wonder. I thought it might be over by two or three days later.'

The next day Triona FitzPatrick heard Shane Ross, the independent senator and journalist, discussing the affair on RTÉ radio with presenter Pat Kenny. FitzPatrick's indignant recollection of this, over a year later, indicates that he had little understanding of how the public and the media would react to his loans scandal. 'They talked about concealment,' he says. 'This was concealed from people. I said, God, yeah, but it wasn't really concealed, sure the Central Bank knew about it. It wasn't as if the loans weren't in existence. They were in existence. They never went out of existence. They just went out of the bank at the end of the year. Are you trying to tell me that people actually have been misled? And that was the next step then, that it was concealment to mislead people, that people would feel better about the bank not knowing that I had the big loans.

'I was sort of, just, Jesus Christ, I never thought about that at all. That's not right at all and it couldn't be seen as that.'

While FitzPatrick, in his interviews with Tom Lyons, explained the initial rationale for warehousing his loans at Irish Nationwide in terms of an accounting concern relating to his involvement with property syndicates, it is impossible not to see 'concealment' as being the main reason for the warehousing in later years. Not every loan he hid on Irish Nationwide's balance sheet was related to syndicate investments, and the degree of misrepresentation involved in hiding the loans clearly exceeded the potential confusion that might have arisen from the syndicate-loan figures.

After resigning as chairman of Anglo, FitzPatrick also stood down from all his other board positions: as chairman of Smurfit Kappa, as a director of the credit-check company Experian, the food company

Greencore, the investment fund Gartmore, and as a state-appointed director of Aer Lingus.

The day after FitzPatrick quit Anglo, Drumm too resigned. He had waited twenty-four hours at the behest of his board, but he knew the Department of Finance was no longer prepared to allow him to remain in charge. 'It is appropriate for me to step down today, given last evening's announcement in relation to the resignation of Sean FitzPatrick,' he said in a short statement.

Political reaction to FitzPatrick's resignation was hostile. 'In relation to Mr FitzPatrick's loans, I think this is unacceptable behaviour,' Lenihan told RTÉ in an interview on 22 December. 'The position taken by Mr FitzPatrick is that there was nothing illegal involved, but if there was nothing illegal involved it was grossly unethical because it involved the concealment of essential information from the shareholders of the company and from the auditors.'

The loans scandal at Anglo snapped the last thread of shareholder confidence in the bank. On the Monday of Lenihan's interview, Invesco Group dumped 12 million shares. Anglo's largest shareholder effectively bailed out.

The government moved swiftly to recapitalize Anglo. A sum of €1.5 billion would be invested in the bank, by way of preference shares, to make the bank, in Lenihan's words, 'indestructible'. The new shares would give the state control of over 75 per cent of the voting rights in the bank. A meeting was called for mid January to secure shareholder approval.

Lenihan said that the 'misbehaviour of management meant that, even with a state guarantee, there was uncertainty about the viability of the bank'. There was no hope of launching a rights issue, whether underwritten by government or not. Government had no choice but to step in. But it baulked at taking full control. 'Were we to go the nationalization route, we would be affirming that we have no confidence in the bank as a bank to survive,' Lenihan said.

Just after New Year's Day 2009, FitzPatrick flew to South Africa. He stayed in the President Hotel in Cape Town with his family, played golf and tried to relax. 'I went away in early January to South Africa.

I was down there with Triona and with Sarah. Sarah was watching the internet and keeping cool with me,' he recalls.

There was plenty of news back home to catch up on. On 7 January, Willie McAteer resigned, completing the clear-out at the very top of the bank. Anglo said it would now split his role as finance director and chief risk officer into two. Matt Moran was appointed finance director designate and the bank would seek to hire an outsider to oversee risk.

Two days later Patrick Neary, whose performance as chief executive of the Financial Regulator was by this point universally discredited, announced that he was bringing forward his retirement date. An inquiry into the Regulator's knowledge of FitzPatrick's loans was the final straw. It showed that the scale of FitzPatrick's borrowings had been made clear in quarterly reports submitted by Anglo to the Regulator's office for the previous seven years. It also found that Irish Nationwide had alerted the Regulator's office in early 2008 to the loans; that an official in the Regulator's office had asked McAteer if warehousing FitzPatrick's loans was legal; and that McAteer, having received legal advice, assured the official that it was. Incredibly, the Regulator took no further action.

Neary said in his resignation statement that he personally was unaware of the loans until Lenihan raised them with him in December. 'So far as I am concerned, I was not advised of any such matters in early 2008 and there has been no oral, written or e-mail escalation of these issues to me or to the authority over the period until the matter was raised with me by the minister on 10 December 2008,' he said.

Neary's defence was ignorance, a breakdown in communication. He retired with a €630,000 golden handshake and a €143,000-a-year state pension.

As FitzPatrick relaxed in South Africa, new Anglo chairman Donal O'Connor was preparing for the extraordinary general meeting that had been called for 16 January to approve the government's €1.5 billion capital injection into the bank. He was understandably nervous, and rehearsed his answers repeatedly with his public-relations advisers and bank executives in the week before the meeting. O'Connor worked hard on his apology to shareholders. He was keen to explain precisely what had transpired with FitzPatrick's loans and to reassure shareholders that Anglo still had a future.

At some point during the preparations, Anglo's treasury team urgently contacted O'Connor. A credit-rating agency was asking searching questions about the bank's deposit book. In particular it wanted to know more about its dealings with Irish Life & Permanent. O'Connor – who had observed in November that the transactions 'sounded' like window-dressing – had sought to find out more about the issue after he became chairman of the bank.

The circular treasury deal was discussed at a meeting between Anglo and Ernst & Young on Sunday, 21 December. Anglo notes from the meeting record that the IL&P transaction came up 'in context of media attention on SPF [Sean P. FitzPatrick] loans'.

On 13 January O'Connor received a report back on the transactions from Anglo's treasury division. When he saw the IL&P deal outlined clearly on paper, he realized that the transaction might be construed not as 'normal' balance-sheet management but as something much more serious: a potential fraud. The rumour now was that Standard & Poor's was about to downgrade the bank's credit rating because it believed the transaction was merely an artifice. The downgrade by the powerful ratings agency would be one revelation too far for a bank with a by-now brittle reputation.

Ernst & Young were called into the Financial Regulator's office for questioning on the IL&P transaction on 15 January. Neither Neary nor Horan attended the meeting. Bernard Sheridan, then head of consumer protection codes department, led the meeting on behalf of the Regulator. Vincent Bergin led the meeting on behalf of E&Y.

Bergin admitted E&Y had signed off initially on Anglo's accounts on 2 December 2008. His 'rationale', according to the note of the meeting made by staff of the Regulator, was that the transaction had happened and therefore had to be accounted for. 'VB [Vincent Bergin] explained that E&Y were told by Anglo that the Financial Regulator was aware of the transaction, which they considered to be significant in the context of the disclosure of the transaction in the accounts, but it was not relevant in the accounting for the transaction. He also noted that it was contained within PwC's report to the Financial Regulator. Accordingly, he deducted that the Financial Regulator was aware of the transaction, however, he acknowledged that he did not check directly with the Financial Regulator.'

Bergin indicated that he wanted to emphasize that 'he was not happy now with the transaction and that no licensed bank should be engaging in transactions of this nature'.

He would not comment, the notes of the meeting say, on 'his happiness when he first became aware of the transaction'.

'In relation to market abuse and any obligation to report to us, VB stated that they were aware that Anglo had got legal advice that there was no issue. However, he admitted that he had not seen the letter.'

Sheridan indicated that the Financial Regulator wrote to Anglo on this issue on 11 December 2008 in the context of the Market Abuse and Transparency Directive. It also asked to see the legal advice Anglo had received on the transaction. 'E&Y were not aware that the Financial Regulator had written to Anglo in this regard.'

Sheridan told Bergin the Financial Regulator was 'keen' to find out more from E&Y both about the affair and the accountants' handling of it.

Anglo, financially weakened and already reliant on state support, could not bear another scandal.

Government ministers were called to a cabinet meeting later that afternoon. Cowen was in Japan on a trade mission and sat down at midnight Tokyo time to chair the meeting over the phone to Dublin. The decision was made to fully nationalize Anglo. At 4 p.m. Dublin time O'Connor was called to the Department of Finance and told that the government was formerly withdrawing its offer of €1.5 billion in state funds to bail out the bank.

Returning from the meeting, a shocked O'Connor informed board members of the government decision around teatime. It was clear the bank could no longer fund itself without state support and could not resist nationalization. The entire board – with the exception of the public-interest directors and O'Connor, who had joined the board only seven months before and had the backing of the government – would have to resign. Following the cabinet meeting,

Lenihan contacted Neelie Kroes, the EU competition commissioner, and informed her of the nationalization decision.

The Department of Finance convened a press conference for 8 p.m. 'The funding position of the bank has weakened and unacceptable practices that took place within it have caused serious reputational damage to the bank at a time when overall market sentiment towards it was negative,' a department statement said. 'Accordingly, the government believes that the recapitalisation is not now the appropriate and effective means to secure its continued viability. Therefore the government must move to the final and decisive step of public ownership.' The statement described Anglo as being 'of systemic importance to Ireland'.

It was a carefully crafted statement. The only 'unacceptable practice' publicly known at the time was FitzPatrick's loans. The IL&P and Maple Ten transactions were still only known about behind closed doors.

FitzPatrick learned of the nationalization by a circuitous route. On 15 January the *Irish Times* published a report stating that Declan Quilligan, head of the bank's UK operations, was poised to be named the bank's new chief executive.

'I texted him to congratulate him,' FitzPatrick recalls. 'He thanked me and said that he was just after hearing that the place was going to be nationalized.'

FitzPatrick was shocked. 'Absolutely there was no sense of that coming. I did know that there was a lobby at the end of September to nationalize it. I knew people were fighting for it and I knew people were fighting against it. . . I think the Department of Finance was for nationalization. I think one or two of the directors of the Financial Regulator and the Central Bank were against it.'

FitzPatrick did not speak to Quilligan, who was close to Drumm, but instead rang Gary McGann for an update. 'Gary said to me, I think it is being nationalized because they are using you and the Irish Life thing as well as the final straw,' he recalls.

The extraordinary general meeting of Anglo Irish Bank shareholders was due to take place the following day, 16 January. Anglo considered postponing the meeting to give O'Connor longer to prepare under the changed circumstances. Citigroup and Merrill Lynch, the latter now owned by Bank of America, reported huge losses that same week, and shares in Barclays were also plummeting on concerns it might need more capital; O'Connor concluded that it was better to avoid adding to the general sense of panic by calling off the meeting without a full explanation.

More than 800 shareholders assembled for the meeting beneath the lights of the domed Round Room in Dublin's Mansion House. They knew their investment in the bank was now worthless.

O'Connor's slide presentation focused on FitzPatrick's loans. Slides showed that FitzPatrick had loans worth €87 million outstanding at the end of September, and then tracked the value of the former chief executive and chairman's loans over the years. In 2007 FitzPatrick had disclosed loans worth just €7 million when in fact he had borrowings of €129 million from the bank. O'Connor said the annual warehousing of the loans at Irish Nationwide had escaped attention within the bank because there had been 'no specific process to monitor it'. When he admitted that the bank's auditors, Ernst & Young, were not aware of the FitzPatrick loans, O'Connor was booed by the audience.

FitzPatrick flew in from from Cape Town the following morning, landing in London en route to Dublin. 'At Heathrow Sarah and myself had to collect our gear because we weren't flying the whole way through on Aer Lingus, so we had to go down to Terminal 1 and check in. And as we were checking in Sarah said, Do you mind if I go over and get a paper? And I said, Not at all, Sarah. Sarah went over to look at the papers.'

She came back and they both went to a special X-ray area to check in their golf clubs.

'I looked at her,' FitzPatrick recalls. 'I said, Are you all right, Sarah? She said, I am grand. I knew there was something wrong so I started walking with her. She said, Da, you couldn't go to jail? You can't be arrested? I said, Ah, Sarah. She said that was what it says in the paper. Tears then. I said, Ah no, Sarah, for God's sake. You know yourself. I would have told you if I had been arrested or if some policeman had been on to me. And she said, But it says in the paper . . . I said, Ah, don't mind the journalists.'

Coming out of arrivals in Dublin airport, FitzPatrick half expected a pack of journalists to be waiting for him. '[A named colleague] had rung me. He said, Do you have to come home? If I were you I wouldn't come home to this fucking kip. This fucking place . . . I said, Don't be ridiculous. He said, I am serious, it's terrible. I just didn't believe him.'

There was no pack waiting at the airport, but FitzPatrick rang a neighbour in Greystones who worked as a porter in Anglo and who told him that reporters were waiting at the house. 'He was very loyal to me, and very good to me in the bank, just a really decent guy. He would have been getting the house ready, putting the fire on for us, and he would have seen the media outside the house.'

As he got closer to his home FitzPatrick rang his friend again. 'He said to me, Oh no, they are all gone now. So I said, Fair enough. The cars were gone. But in fact they had hidden in the gate directly opposite our one . . . The next thing, as we were driving up to turn left into the house, about five people ran out. I said to Triona, Just put the boot down [on the accelerator]. So she did and we drove up to the golf club . . . [The photographers] went bang, bang, bang. It was quite dark and [Triona] is driving a BMW, a big car . . . So she drove on and we just drove on to the golf club, only about 150 yards up the road. The guys didn't come up and follow.'

After a few hours FitzPatrick asked his neighbour, the Anglo porter, to collect his family and bring them back to his house; 'I stayed hidden up in the golf club with the BMW with all the gear in it. Leinster were playing Wasps that day in the Heineken Cup and I am saying – I am mad keen on rugby – I want to watch this match rather than be sitting here in a bar on a cold Saturday afternoon. So I got out of the car and I walked through a back garden into my house so no one saw me.'

The former chairman of Anglo climbed over a hedge at the back of his house. 'I watched the match and that was it. The [journalists] were outside and we said we would call the police – maybe that day or maybe a different day, I think it was that day – and the police came up but the guys were gone. Then the press were there the next day as well.'

Within one month of the Anglo nationalization, details of the IL&P transaction became public through a *Sunday Business Post* report and then a detailed RTÉ broadcast. Chairwoman Gillian Bowler and chief executive Denis Casey were called to a meeting with Lenihan and Kevin Cardiff on 12 February.

The following day, two IL&P executives – finance director Peter Fitzpatrick and head of group treasury David Gantly – both resigned. (Casey offered his resignation as well, but the board of IL&P refused to accept it; later, under pressure from Lenihan, the board accepted the resignation.)

In a statement Bowler said that it was clear the only motivation of David Gantly and Peter Fitzpatrick had been to support the policy objectives of the Financial Regulator and the Central Bank. IL&P, she stressed, had 'correctly accounted' for the arrangement in its books. However, she said, the manner in which specific support was advanced to Anglo Irish Bank during 2008 had been wrong.

That night, as the story dominated the media, O'Connor rang Bowler a number of times. Anglo wanted to lift the lid on the extent of the Central Bank's and Financial Regulator's knowledge of the transaction.

Casey, in his later affidavit for the gardaí, said Bowler made a handwritten note on a draft press release prepared by Anglo that read: 'DOC [Donal O'Connor] would like more openness about active support from Regulator and CB [Central Bank] but Department don't want this.' Casey gave a photocopy of this note in his evidence to the gardaí. Bowler has declined to comment on Casey's claim.

Buried in Anglo's statement on the matter were two significant claims. 'We wish to clarify that the inter-bank placements with IL&P were not cash collateral for deposits from Irish Life Assurance plc and no set-off arrangements existed.' This stressed, counter to IL&P's view, that the transactions were real, as risks were taken and money actually moved between the two banks.

It also said: 'The bank confirms that all transactions have been appropriately recorded in its books and records and financial statements and in its daily, weekly and monthly regulatory returns.'

The Central Bank and Financial Services Regulatory Authority issued a stinging riposte. They stated that they had indeed 'encouraged Irish banks to work together where necessary so as to continue to use normal inter-bank funding arrangements for liquidity purposes', but that they 'utterly' rejected 'any suggestion that this would have constituted encouragement of the type of circular transactions that have been referred to in recent reports and statements concerning Anglo Irish Bank and Irish Life & Permanent. Circular transactions, unlike normal inter-bank lending, do not provide liquidity to financial institutions. The Authority views the various issues that emerged in relation to the transactions involving these institutions as completely unacceptable.'

The statement did not address why the 'unacceptable' transaction was allowed to remain secret for so long, or why Anglo was allowed to present a set of financial figures to the market, even after it was nationalized, with such 'unacceptable' deposits still on its books.

Casey's 2010 affidavit included a withering assessment of the state regulators' failings in this matter: 'The Department of Finance, the Financial Regulator and the Central Bank were aware of the September 2008 transaction in advance of Anglo Irish Bank publishing its 2008 results; however, it now appears that no effective intervention was made at the time by any of these agencies to scrutinize or influence the manner in which Anglo reported that transaction.' From Casey's point of view, the Regulator's light-touch approach had failed to ensure that Anglo accounted for the transaction accurately, as IL&P had, and this was the true cause of the scandal.

E&Y was by now very anxious to discover what exactly had taken place. On 17 February, Bergin told Matt Moran in an e-mail that he was 'increasingly concerned'. He demanded documentary evidence or tape transcripts from Anglo to prove that the deal had been conducted legally. Until he got this evidence, he told Moran, he would be 'very uncomfortable'.

The IL&P revelations tripped a switch in popular and political opinion. The mood of the general public was now beyond anger. Noel Dempsey, the minister who previously appointed FitzPatrick to the Dublin Docklands Development Authority, said those involved in wrongdoing at Anglo were guilty of 'economic treason'. John Gormley, the leader of the Green Party and minister for the environment, said, 'In the US we have seen white-collar criminals being led out in handcuffs. I want to see the same regime in this country and I believe we will get such a regime here.' Anglo and its former chairman were now an international story. 'Irish stand united in hatred of banker Sean FitzPatrick' ran a headline in *USA Today*. Lenihan told the *Financial Times* on 17 March that he planned to clamp down on 'crony capitalism' and the excesses of Irish banking. 'There is a problem in all small countries with too many incestuous relationships,' he said. The Anglo revelations emerged at a time when the Irish economy was in a dramatic tailspin. Lenihan's snap October 2008 budget had included a 1 per cent income levy and a controversial commitment to means-testing medical cards for old-age pensioners. By the end of December the budget shortfall for 2008 was a worrying €8 billion. It was becoming increasingly likely that a spring budget, containing even more painful measures, was on the way.

FitzPatrick, following the emergence of his secret loans and his high-profile interview with Finucane, became the face of Ireland's banking collapse – and, by extension, of the economic downturn. 'I was shocked,' he says. 'I kept getting more and more shocked as the days went by and the pressure came on. I was hugely shocked. I had no sense . . . I had no sense of the – what's the word – the bitterness, and the coldness and the anger and the whole sense of betrayal of this.

'Fuck this, this is disgraceful, look at this guy FitzPatrick, one of the architects or one of the starters of this whole economy, look at what he has fucking done. He has fucked us all. No sense of that at all. I had no sense of that at all, absolutely none.'

The Office of the Director of Corporate Enforcement, the country's corporate watchdog, announced that it would investigate Anglo in early January. On 24 February, gardaí staged a 'raid' on the bank. It was in fact a highly choreographed visit, organized with Anglo's cooperation; bank staff reserved car parking for the gardaí. Pictures were beamed around the world.

Throughout this period, FitzPatrick remained silent. 'I got in touch with a lawyer, Laurence Shields,' he recalls. 'He was absolutely unrelenting: in no circumstances say anything . . . Even then, I felt it couldn't go on forever.'

The feverish media attention and public anger would be a strain, but for FitzPatrick there was much worse to come.

12. Bankrupt

'I said, Listen, come here. This is the one chance that I and
the bank have of getting out.'

Denis O'Brien's private jet, nicknamed the Silver Chicken, left Dublin airport on a bright March day in 2009 bound for Nigeria. On board the Gulfstream were the telecoms billionaire, his good friend Sean FitzPatrick and FitzPatrick's colleague Lar Bradshaw.

The purpose of the visit was purely business. With FitzPatrick's shares in Anglo Irish Bank now worthless, his investment in an obscure Nigerian oil well was now crucial to the former banker's hopes of repaying his debts and avoiding bankruptcy. O'Brien had lent his jet and his support in order to soothe the anxieties of the Nigerian businessmen who had been following FitzPatrick's tribulations in Ireland with increasing alarm and were losing faith in his ability to keep funding the well.

It was a big favour for FitzPatrick to ask. O'Brien, ever loyal to his friends, had accepted without hesitation. FitzPatrick backed O'Brien at the start of his career when few bankers were prepared to take a risk on him. O'Brien was now returning the favour. He had shown his support for FitzPatrick the previous month when he gave a speech at a lunch in a South Dublin golf club. 'Sean FitzPatrick has been a friend of mine for quite a number of years,' O'Brien told the gathering. 'He has made mistakes but he continues to be my friend.

'Anglo Irish backed people when others wouldn't. It backed me when I wanted to start a radio station [98FM] and nobody else would. Anglo Irish has been blamed for absolutely everything that has gone wrong in Irish banking. That is both wrong and unfair.'

Stepping out of the jet on to Nigerian soil, FitzPatrick must have looked far from the disgraced banker his African partners had read about on the internet. At his side was his old friend O'Brien, who had just been named by *Forbes* as the 305th richest man in the world, with a fortune of $2.2 billion. This was the FitzPatrick of old, confident and ready for business.

Chief among FitzPatrick's Nigerian partners was Victor Ombu, a former vice-admiral in the Nigerian navy who had been 'retired' by the then president Olusegun Obasanjo in 2001 for undisclosed 'security reasons'. Now in his sixties, Ombu knew both the riches and the dangers of the business. In his navy days he had led a crackdown on pirates and local people who attacked oil depots in the Niger delta, costing international oil firms an estimated $4 billion in lost revenues in 2000 alone.

Along with a group of business partners that included a number of ex-military men and the grandson of a former senior politician, Ombu had secured the licence for a well in the delta. In recognition of his work in securing the licence, he had been made chairman of Movido Oil and Exploration, the company set up to exploit the acreage.

As he was driven from the airport to a hotel in Lagos, FitzPatrick knew that his share in the Movido well was now his largest financial asset. He believed there could be close to $1 billion of oil trapped fifty metres below the pirate-ridden sea. If the oil were extracted, then his share of the proceeds would be more than enough to repay his substantial borrowings.

The previous summer Movido had changed tack in its exploitation strategy. Rather than extracting the oil and then plugging into an oil company's pipeline, Movido set up an Express Production System, or EPS, on top of its oil find. The plan was to collect the oil, convey it in giant tankers and then sell it on to the major oil companies.

'Risky,' FitzPatrick acknowledges. 'Pirates. All that type of stuff. OK? However, our people were very tight to the locals in the area that we were in. They were locals from there. And they reckoned that they could handle that and we believed they could.'

The previous autumn, while attending a dinner with management of Smurfit Kappa, FitzPatrick had received a phone call from his secretary, who informed him that Ombu had phoned to say 'Congratulations: we now have oil.'

However, it soon emerged that the rate at which the oil was pumping did not make it viable for production. 'We needed it to come out at around about 3,000 barrels a day,' FitzPatrick says. '[It was only] about 1,250, maximum. What we were trying to ensure was that it was sustainable at about 3,000 barrels a day.'

The Irish shareholders, not entirely trusting the data they were receiving from their Nigerian partners, hired an international team of experts to appraise the well. The experts concluded that the well's pipes needed to be cleaned; the cost of doing this was about $6 million.

FitzPatrick needed to buy some time while he tried to work out what to do; he hoped he might even be able to convince Anglo to support him. This was the situation in March 2009 when he and Denis O'Brien flew to Lagos aboard the Silver Chicken.

FitzPatrick recalls that O'Brien told him, 'I will go in there . . . I am a multibillionaire. They can Google me. I look the part.'

Upon arrival at the hotel, O'Brien went to bed. FitzPatrick and Bradshaw, meanwhile, 'worked with the local Nigerians to make a presentation for Denis. They had to make a presentation to Denis so we might get money from Denis.'

The presentation, held the next day in a meeting room in a luxury hotel in Lagos, went well. The day after, FitzPatrick, Bradshaw and O'Brien flew back to Dublin.

The game was now back on, but FitzPatrick would need the support of his old bank – a bank from which he had resigned in disgrace, and which had now been nationalized.

Denis O'Brien was not the only friend prepared to stand by Fitz-Patrick after his resignation.

In December 2008 Bernard Somers, one of Ireland's foremost corporate restructuring experts, dropped a letter in to FitzPatrick's home in Greystones. According to FitzPatrick, the letter contained reminiscences of their business relationship, which dated back a quarter-century. In the letter, FitzPatrick says, Somers 'invited me to give him a call in the New Year, in January 2009, which I did'.

FitzPatrick's finances were in ruins, and Somers could be a valuable ally. The founder of Somers Associates, the company doctor had an impressive record, advising some of the country's top businessmen and companies on developing strategy and restructuring debts. A former director of the Central Bank, Somers had also served on the boards of AIB, Independent News & Media, the country's biggest media group, and DCC, an industrial conglomerate. He had an entrepreneurial streak, backing a string of technology and telecom entrepreneurs, and had invested in the Anglo-funded acquisition of Champion Sports, a retail chain.

It had been Somers who alerted FitzPatrick when the Clegg scandal was about to break in the British newspapers.

'Bernard has helped me in every way,' FitzPatrick says. 'He has been very good counsel. He is very low-key, very calm, very measured and very balanced. He has not just helped me with the financials. He has been helping me to negotiate. He has been a giant for me, very supportive, very solid and very dependable.

'He has taken flak over it but he has also taken some credit for it as well. Why he has done it? You are going to have to ask him that. I am incredibly grateful for what he has done for me. I know my family is as well.'

With Somers's assistance, FitzPatrick started to untangle his maze of investments and chip away at the mountain of debt. It was a complicated and delicate exercise. 'We said, Right, what we need to do is talk to the bank, and the bank was anxious to talk to us as well.' The bank had long held a charge over FitzPatrick's Anglo shares; with the shares now worthless, the bank was short of security.

All of FitzPatrick's borrowing was done through a 'family facility', i.e. in the names of his wife and children as well as himself. There was a maze of cross-guarantees as a result between himself and members of his family on borrowings. Many of his assets were held jointly with his wife. 'There was no such thing as my individual loans, because every loan I had, my wife was party to. That was the way we did it,' FitzPatrick says.

Down the years, to avoid inheritance tax, FitzPatrick had bought properties in his children's names. The children did not have sufficient income to be granted the loans by themselves, so FitzPatrick became guarantor. As the bank began to unravel FitzPatrick's messy borrowings, it agreed to drop the family's cross-guarantees, making FitzPatrick the sole borrower for most of his loans from Anglo.

'I didn't look for my pension to be put into Triona's name,' Fitz-Patrick says. 'I didn't look to try to protect our home. Why? Because I didn't see any issues in terms of bankruptcy or not being able to pay the debt at that stage.'

In return for releasing the family guarantees, Anglo took a new charge against the deposit account that had originally secured the Nigerian borrowings by way of a back-to-back loan. The deposit was now to be included as part of the security of FitzPatrick's more conventional borrowings.

Anglo had lent FitzPatrick and Bradshaw about $40 million for the Nigerian venture, according to FitzPatrick, secured largely on cash the two men held on deposit with the bank. The two men and their fellow Irish investors had used a Gibraltar-based limited company as the vehicle for borrowing the money. Anglo now realized that the deal was far from ideal from a debt-recovery point of view. FitzPatrick's Anglo deposit, which had originally been security for the Nigeria loan, was now standing as security for his other borrowings. The bank held a charge against the Gibraltar company, which it could call in. But it did not have any security against the physical asset itself – the oil well in the Nigerian delta. If Movida sold the oil well, there was no guarantee that the bank would get its money back; however, if the well started to earn revenue, there was equally no guarantee that the money would come the bank's way. So the bank sought to take a charge directly against the oil well.

This was not a simple task. A dispute had arisen between Fitz-Patrick and his Nigerian partners over his legal ownership of a stake in the well. The Nigerians, FitzPatrick believes, were trying to take advantage of his financial weakness by looking for ways to push him out of the deal. The problem took months to resolve and it was only in the second half of 2009 that Anglo managed to get its charge.

In the meantime FitzPatrick tried to appease the bank by selling anything he could to raise more money. He sold the easiest assets first. Over the years he had invested €16 million in AIB and Bank of Ireland shares; now he cashed them in for a fraction of their peak value.

Other share portfolios, held with the country's biggest stock-brokers, were also cashed in – returning more money to his bank, and crystallizing substantial losses. 'I was caught very badly in terms of equities. I mean really badly. If Anglo hadn't [collapsed] I would have got out. I mean, all I would have needed for Anglo shares to come right was about €7.00.'

FitzPatrick's holding in bank shares went beyond Anglo and AIB; he also lost big on British banks, including Lloyds and HSBC. 'I thought they were safe,' he says. 'When people talk about ruin and the losses, I am one of the biggest victims of it. I have to say that very carefully because people would pillory me. They would say, Well, they have lost so much money. I have lost money as well. My commitment was there in pounds, shillings and pence.'

With the anchor of his wealth, the banking shares, now gone, FitzPatrick was financially adrift. He managed to repay Anglo about €20 million, but this was nowhere near enough.

FitzPatrick had property investments in his own name or with others in Ireland, Britain, Germany, France, Hungary, the Czech Republic and South Africa. At the start of 2009 he had been optimistic property prices would stabilize in Ireland and perhaps even rebound in other countries. He was hopeful he would be able to raise millions by selling his more mature property investments. Not all his property punts were in negative equity.

It proved impossible to sell these properties – including the Cap Ferrat house, which was put on the market with an asking price over €20 million – in a market that continued to fall. Not only was FitzPatrick watching his assets lose value; some of his syndicate investments were actually sucking in more cash. As the value of the underlying properties fell, banks insisted that syndicate investors put more cash into the debt-driven deals. When FitzPatrick failed to pay-up his share in these cash calls, his ownership interest was diluted down further.

Another expensive venture was FitzPatrick's backing of Barry O'Callaghan, the young banker who had so impressed him with a vision for a global education company called Education Media and Publishing Group. When EMPG was forced to restructure its multibillion-dollar debts at the start of 2010, FitzPatrick, along with other Irish equity investors, saw his entire investment wiped out. 'I lost €5.5 million. Clean. Gone out the door,' he says.

An investment in an Asian hedge fund managed by Goldman Sachs fell in value from $2 million to $1.1 million. From a $3 million investment in a casino in Macau, bought through a Merrill Lynch property fund, FitzPatrick got back only $168,000. The misery went on and on. Only a handful of his dozens of diverse investments, such as his investment in the Hospital Corporation of America, were in the black.

In the summer of 2009 FitzPatrick went to a birthday party for John Gallagher. Held at one of London's top hotels, it was a brief reminder of the good old days. Gallagher was nicknamed 'the smartest man in the room' by the some of the Irish media for his shrewd sidestepping of the bust. He had engineered an estimated profit of more than €1 billion when the Jurys Doyle Hotel Group – founded by his wife's father, the legendary hotelier P.V. Doyle – was sold during the boom.

FitzPatrick had invested in the Quinlan Private consortium that bought the Jurys business. The investment was now in trouble and QP was asking investors to stump up more cash or else see their stakes diluted.

At the party FitzPatrick bumped into Donal O'Connor. His old friend and successor as chairman of Anglo was coordinating internal investigations into FitzPatrick's affairs. It was an awkward meeting. The two men went back a long way, but now they had nothing to say to each other. 'I spoke to him but I didn't speak to him for longer than two minutes,' FitzPatrick recalls. 'It was just hello, howya, because I didn't want to have him compromised in any way because he was chairman of the bank.'

O'Connor did inherit a fine mess. The infamous 2008 annual accounts were presented in February 2009. The bottom line for the bank was, incredibly, the same as that presented by David Drumm and FitzPatrick the previous autumn, despite the fact that the accounts had been reaudited after the bank was nationalized.

Anglo still presented a profit of €800 million and had a net worth of

€4.5 billion. Its deposits were still boosted by billions from IL&P, but this, the bank noted, was being 'reviewed' by external consultants.

Drumm would later query these figures in an interview with the *Sunday Independent* in October 2010. 'The government has to decide which poison it wants to take. Did it agree with our accounts in 2008? I presume it did because it signed them. Or did they sign the accounts knowing that those accounts were misleading? You have to choose one,' he said.

O'Connor's contrite note to shareholders was, however, a long way from the Anglo of old. 'I acknowledge again the sense of hurt, outrage and disappointment that people feel towards the bank following disclosures regarding loans to the former chairman and other matters,' O'Connor said in a letter introducing the company's annual report. 'Anglo was determined to emerge from its current difficulties as a strong and viable finance house that taxpayers could be proud of.' His statement promised stakeholders that Anglo would address issues 'as transparently as we can'.

O'Connor had hoped to say a lot more. He wrote a secret memo setting out his concerns on the bank's liquidity that was co-signed by John Bowe, Anglo group treasurer. In the memo O'Connor said the Department of Finance told him not to be 'too negative' in his letter to shareholders.

Bowe had told the Central Bank only a few days before that Anglo's funding was already 'very weak', and the outlook was 'more negative'. AIB and Bank of Ireland had placed €4 billion on deposit with Anglo and were 'resistant' to putting any more into the struggling bank. 'On the basis of no additional accommodation [from the two banks] the requirement now increases to €7.5 billion and will not improve until progress can be made,' Bowe said.

The Central Bank told Anglo that it did not have a mechanism to support liquidity outside emergency liquidity assistance and that it would have to go to the European Central Bank if more support was required. Tony Grimes, the director-general of the Central Bank, advised Anglo to tell the Department of Finance about the situation. The minutes record that Grimes later told O'Connor that Anglo 'should not look to make any disclosure' to ratings agencies or the wider market if it was using emergency liquidity assistance.

O'Connor, the memo states, told the department that he and his board, including Alan Dukes, a former finance minister, were 'very anxious' that the chairman's statement should be an example of 'telling it as it is'. The department told O'Connor he 'should not refer to [the] emergency funding' that Anglo needed to survive. Instead, the department drafted a less 'negative' version of reality, which O'Connor then signed.

The scale of the crisis inside Anglo was deliberately downplayed for fear of its impact not only on the bank, but on the Irish banking system and the state's ability to raise money internationally to fund itself.

Soon after the publication of the annual results, there was more detail on the scale of the problems within Anglo. PwC, in a report entitled 'Project Atlas', revealed that fifteen developers owed the bank more than €500 million each. The report collated the findings of three studies carried out in the final quarter of 2008.

PwC said Anglo had 'very large exposures' to a small number of customers, which would 'likely lead to significant losses for individual developers and, in turn, the bank'.

Exposure to the rapidly declining residential and commercial property market was now the biggest risk to the entire Irish financial system. Anglo stood at the forefront. Bond investors were wary about the levels of toxic property loans on Irish bank balance sheets. Without access to funding, Ireland would face a credit lockdown.

In April 2009, and coinciding with an emergency budget, the government announced it would establish the National Asset Management Agency to acquire property loans from five Irish banks: Bank of Ireland, Allied Irish Banks, Anglo, Irish Nationwide and the EBS. By acquiring the loans at a price short of their original book value but in excess of their depressed current value, the agency would cleanse the banks' balance sheets and give them some much-needed liquidity.

NAMA was perceived as another bailout for the banks. Its launch coincided with harsh medicine for voters, including a massive hike in income levies and the abolition of a Christmas bonus for social-welfare recipients.

In its half-year results at the end of May, Anglo announced loan losses of €4.1 billion, creating the largest loss ever recorded in Irish corporate history. The bank said the rapid deterioration in global economic conditions and a significant reduction in property values had eroded the net worth of its borrowers, particularly in Ireland.

Anglo said that the level of 'past due' and 'impaired' loans rose to €23.6 billion in March from €2.5 billion in September. The bank wrote off €300 million of the outstanding debt of the Maple Ten investors who had helped to unwind Sean Quinn's position in the bank. The bank wrote off €31 million in relation to loans to directors, but stressed that it would seek full repayment of the debts.

O'Connor warned that further losses of €2.6 billion were likely in the full year and, in a 'worst-case scenario', yet another €3.5 billion could be lost. He held out the prospect of total loan losses of €11 billion; this was considered staggering at the time, but it has in fact turned out to be an underestimate.

The government immediately moved to inject €4 billion into Anglo, its first capital commitment to the institution. 'In my view, it is a disgrace that this bank evolved into the institution it did,' Lenihan said, announcing the recapitalization.

Anglo also announced that it was entering into talks with some of its bondholders about a buyback of the bonds. The bank offered to pay between 27 and 55 per cent of the original value of some of its bonds, which had been trading at levels below this. One of Anglo's bondholders was its former boss: during the summer of 2008 FitzPatrick had invested about €4.5 million in Anglo subordinated bonds. 'I had bought because I thought it was a good way of showing that I was supportive of Anglo,' FitzPatrick says.

When Anglo bought back the issue at a discount in the second half of 2009, FitzPatrick got back less than half of what he had paid for the bonds; the money went directly towards reducing his debt to the bank.

On 16 August 2009 Brian Lenihan appointed Mike Aynsley, an Australian banker, as the new chief executive of Anglo Irish Bank. Donal O'Connor, who had acted as chairman of the bank while a new chief executive was being recruited, then stepped down to be replaced by Dukes.

Aynsley was an experienced banker and, pointedly, an outsider. He had previously worked for the Asian Development Bank, based in Manila; Security Pacific, now part of Bank of America; Hoare Govett, the stockbroker; and National Australia Bank. He brought with him Tom Hunersen, a straight-talking New Yorker who had previously worked with him in NAB.

Hunersen had also worked for Bank of Ireland in America under the Irish bank's then boss Mike Soden. He briefly left banking and for a spell ran an on-line snowboarding game company and a make-your-own-meal franchise in New York. Hunersen's immediate task was to act as trouble-shooter for the accounts of the bank's biggest problem clients, including Sean Quinn and former directors FitzPatrick, Drumm, Tom Browne and Willie McAteer.

With the new regime in place, Anglo's stance on FitzPatrick's borrowings hardened. The bank called for a meeting with its former chairman at Bernard Somers's offices on Dublin's Upper Mount Street in November 2009.

'Hunersen came in and pulled everything,' FitzPatrick said. 'They pulled the loan on us. He said, We shouldn't be in this type of business, I don't like the structure at all.

'Bernard Somers said it was the most brutal meeting he was ever at in his life. There was no damnation or criticism or anything like that. It was just very professional, very cold.'

According to FitzPatrick, Hunersen said that he wanted the oil loan paid back by the following month, and advised him to sell his interest in the project. 'But I was saying, You are not going to get value for it. We can't sell it. They said, Oh no, sell it, and we will give you names of guys who will have a look at the whole thing. Hunersen said, We should not be in this. This is an exotic loan. We don't have the expertise to run this . . . I said, Listen, come here. This is the one chance that I and the bank have of getting out. Don't pull it ahead of time. Why would we have given you security and closed out your security only three months ago if then you were going to pull the loan? We would have said fuck off.'

FitzPatrick argued that the increased security had been given on the understanding that the loan could be repaid over three years.

Hunersen insisted that the loan facility was repayable on demand. 'We said, Of course, all the loans were on demand but we expected you to continue on and now you are not.'

Under huge pressure to sell, FitzPatrick talked to the Nigerians, who intimated that they might be prepared to buy out his stake. 'We were offered money towards the end of December '09. We were offered $20 million plus the loan [$40 million] repaid. I said, No, thank you. Because we were looking for more. We would have taken it, but that was what we were advised to do. Don't accept the first offer because they are going to come back with some other issues. We believed they were going to get it done.'

Instead, the Nigerians took the offer off the table. There was no prospect of a deal. Repayment of the loan was due by the end of December, but Anglo pushed the deadline back. Attempts to sell the interest to other Irish oil explorers, including Aidan Heavey's Tullow Oil and veteran explorer John Teeling, failed.

Amid the frenetic negotiations on the Nigeria well in late 2009, FitzPatrick became a grandfather for the first time. He travelled to Fiji towards the end of that year, where his son Jonathan and his Australian wife lived, to visit the new arrival. Being able to walk around without anyone knowing him recharged his batteries. He would need every ounce of energy for the months ahead.

In the New Year, Anglo started to turn the screw again. 'Everything had to be done by December, then January 1, then March 10. It was always pressure. We said, Lads, the more pressure you put on us the less credible we are to sell,' he recalls.

A final deadline was set for 10 March 2010, when the bank wanted a repayment schedule for all his debts. FitzPatrick knew he could never repay all his debts unless the bank supported him with his oil well – which it had said it would not do. If the schedule was not forthcoming, he knew, the bank would issue a demand for the repayment of the full amount due and the game would be over.

The deadline day came and passed without any communication between the two sides. The bank then issued its demand for repayment. At 3 p.m. the following day, in the Commercial Court, a branch of the High Court, Anglo lodged a legal action against its former chief executive and chairman for the recovery of €70 million. Lenihan said that Anglo management would pursue the FitzPatrick debt to 'the ends of the earth'.

The opportunity to be seen to be going after FitzPatrick without mercy was a small political godsend. The unemployment rate had almost trebled, to 13.1 per cent.

Brian Cowen, in Washington for the traditional St Patrick's Day celebration, gave an interview to CNN's Wolf Blitzer. 'You are not happy with the economy right now,' Blitzer said. 'Just a little while ago there was a great success story in Ireland but things have gone south.'

'Yeah, I mean, we are a small open economy, we have been affected very much by the world downturn,' Cowen replied.

'Who is to blame for that?' Blitzer asked.

'Well, I mean, all of us can look to . . . could anyone have foreseen Lehman Brothers and all the impact it had?' Cowen said.

'That had a huge impact on Ireland?'

'Huge.'

'So it was external, the problems that you are facing now, or was there some internal problems that you can blame yourself?'

'Both external and internal. On the internal front we had a property bubble in the domestic-housing market. But we don't have the problem of toxic paper in our banking system. We have distressed assets in the property and development portfolios of banks but we have a solution to that which we are going to announce in the next couple of weeks.'

The solution Cowen referred to was the National Asset Management Agency, or NAMA. After months of planning, and political opposition, the agency was about to get up and running. Cowen would now have to convince a sceptical Irish public that the government was on the way to cleaning up Irish banking.

FitzPatrick's arrest on the day after St Patrick's Day was swiftly followed by the arrest of Willie McAteer at his home in Rathgar, a South Dublin suburb, on 24 March. He was taken for questioning to Irishtown Garda station. The fifty-nine-year-old Donegal-born banker was held for thirty-two hours; like FitzPatrick, he opted to sleep in a cell overnight before questioning was resumed the following morning. As with FitzPatrick, the questioning focused almost entirely on Anglo's deposit arrangement with Irish Life & Permanent.

After he was released without charge, the *Sunday Times* reported that McAteer could not remember the details of meetings with IL&P, the Financial Regulator and the Central Bank over eighteen months previously. McAteer was reported by John Mooney, *Sunday Times* security correspondent, as telling detectives he wished to help them but was hampered by 'failing memory'. That same week the Garda Bureau of Fraud Investigation e-mailed David Drumm to request a meeting to discuss their inquiries. Drumm was now living in Boston with his family.

The day after McAteer's arrest, Mike Aynsley, Anglo's new chief executive, gave an interview to the *Irish Times*. The government, he said, would have to inject an additional €6 billion to €9 billion in new capital into Anglo to keep the bank afloat. (The government had already given Anglo €4 billion.) A liquidation, he estimated, would cost the state more than twice as much – between €27 billion and €35 billion – while running Anglo down over ten years would cost between €18 billion and €22 billion. Anglo, he said, had to be kept going; otherwise there would be an 'an incineration of taxpayers' money in horrendous terms'.

Aynsley also said he believed that the best way to proceed was to package up the best bits of the loan book into a new Anglo that would continue trading. The rest of the book would be transferred to NAMA or wound down.

The true extent of the losses facing Anglo and the state was now emerging.

On 1 April 2010 the front page of the *Daily Star* was splashed with the headline: 'They deserve to be shot'. The headline in large white text against a black background was flanked by smiling pictures of Sean FitzPatrick and Michael Fingleton. 'These two banking bastards have cost the state €25 billion between them,' the story began in thunderous fashion.

On 3 April the *Irish Daily Mirror* ran with the story: 'Seanie no-mates'. Journalists from the paper had stuck up 'Wanted' signs around the resort in Spain where FitzPatrick was holidaying with his wife. An unnamed 'well-known businessman' was quoted as saying: 'He is a scumbag . . . If he comes around here he'll end up in the harbour, that's what will happen.'

FitzPatrick was now firmly established as public enemy number one, the pantomime villain of the bust.

Another aspect of FitzPatrick's past that reared its head during the first half of 2010 was his involvement with the Dublin Docklands Development Authority.

FitzPatrick had been appointed by the government to the board of the DDDA in 1998 and served until the end of his second term in 2007. For most of that period the authority was largely seen as a success, and the involvement of the Anglo boss on its board was uncontroversial; but after the property market turned, questions were asked about FitzPatrick's role. The role of Lar Bradshaw, who had joined the Anglo board in October 2004 while still serving as DDDA chairman, also became controversial. Now that the bust had arrived questions were being asked by opposition politicians and the media about whether there was a conflict of interest in being a director of both a public-development authority and a bank.

Niamh Brennan – an academic expert in corporate governance who had also sat on the board of Ulster Bank since 2001 – wrote an article in the *Irish Times* on 20 December 2008 in the wake of Fitz-Patrick's and Bradshaw's resignations. 'In the final analysis, no laws, no rules, no regulations can prevent greedy, self-serving behaviour by company directors,' she wrote. 'All they can do is make such behaviour harder to engage in. Add to this, that greedy, self-serving people seek each other out. The old Irish phrase "*Aithníonn ciaróg ciaróg eile*" (one "beetle" recognises another) captures this aspect of corporate life beautifully.'

The following March, Brennan – who had sat on Ulster Bank's board during a period when it lent recklessly to developers, including most notoriously to Sean Dunne when he acquired the Jurys site in Ballsbridge – was appointed DDDA chairman. A year later the

DDDA and the minister for the environment, John Gormley, were embroiled in controversy over Gormley's refusal, for nearly four months, to publish a set of internal reports into goings-on at the authority. There were rumours that skulduggery involving the two former Anglo directors was being covered up; the truth was that the reports were lukewarm affairs that had been completed without the benefit of interviews with any former director, let alone FitzPatrick and Bradshaw, and that they found no wrongdoing by either man.

FitzPatrick rejects utterly the suggestion that there was anything untoward about his role at the DDDA. 'Niamh Brennan has come out and more or less said Sean FitzPatrick must have been involved in something because he was there for seven years . . .' he says. 'There is no proof of any wrongdoing because there was no wrongdoing.'

Perhaps the most controversial – and most disastrous – deal done by the DDDA in its history was its participation in the purchase of the twenty-five-acre Irish Glass Bottle site in Ringsend in 2006 for €412 million. Half the bank debt for the deal came from Anglo, with the other half supplied by AIB. According to FitzPatrick, the Irish Glass Bottle site 'was seen as a very important site because it was the widening out of the docklands and the expansion of the docklands. It was very important that the lessons we had learned from the past would be actually learned and actually put into play. One of the lessons was that if we wanted to control the development of the site it was important that we owned a lot of it or part of it . . .'

FitzPatrick notes that there was precedent for the DDDA getting involved in a major land deal. In 1998, around the time he joined its board, the DDDA had spent about £18 million buying twenty-two acres of land called the Bord Gáis site on Sir John Rogerson's Quay on the south of the Liffey. At the time the acquisition was seen as very risky, as the site was derelict and badly contaminated with toxins, but it had been turned into a profitable success. With the Irish Glass Bottle site, FitzPatrick says, the DDDA hoped to repeat the same formula.

FitzPatrick says he was aware that Sean Mulryan had looked at partnering Ballymore Properties with the DDDA in a bid for the IGB site. Mulryan was wary of the deal, as he felt Irish property prices might be peaking and he wanted to concentrate on his investments abroad. The authority's attention then turned to a former Fianna Fáil councillor and major developer from the West of Ireland: Bernard McNamara.

'I don't know exactly what happened,' FitzPatrick says, regarding McNamara's involvement. 'I never spoke to Bernard [about becoming involved]. Never. And there will be a court case about this which will have everything detailed down' – a reference to a complex legal battle that began in 2010 between McNamara and the other members of the consortium that eventually acquired the site. McNamara claims in his action that Paul Maloney, then chief executive of the DDDA, made 'representations' encouraging him to get involved in the bid, but this has been denied in court by the authority. FitzPatrick is adamant about his own position in the affair: 'My name will not appear having spoken to Paul Maloney about Bernard McNamara; having spoken to the rest of the board about Bernard McNamara and our experience of him; having spoken to Bernard McNamara about the board in the DDDA, the site, or the deal he could get. Absolutely zilch, zilch, zilch.'

There was little discussion at board level about whether McNamara was the right man for the job, as his reputation spoke for itself, FitzPatrick says. 'Bernard was an established builder and developer. He had done a lot of successful stuff. He had dealt with the docklands over the years and seemed to have a good relationship with them. No one thought he was a difficult man or anything like that . . . His signs were up all over Dublin. He was doing a lot of stuff for the government. He was doing civil engineering. He was doing development. He seemed to be doing everything.'

McNamara ran the numbers and said the figure they needed to bid was €412 million. It was an incredible sum for a twenty-five-acre brownfield site on the periphery of Dublin, but it was not generally viewed as such in the crazed climate of the time.

To get added firepower, McNamara brought in Derek Quinlan and Davy stockbrokers, who raised money from their private clients. The DDDA put €32 million of public money into the deal, taking a 26 per cent stake.

FitzPatrick says that the DDDA's executive team told the board that it had a valuation on the site which supported McNamara's bid; but a DDDA inquiry found that a 'professional valuation' had never been done. The absence of a formal valuation on the site was an alarm bell that apparently did not reach board level.

McNamara arranged financing from Anglo and AIB. Anglo took the lead, getting a draft valuation from CBRE in November 2006 that confirmed the €412 million valuation McNamara had come up with. (In January 2008 CBRE did a formal valuation that put the site at the same figure, even though by then property prices were clearly falling.)

FitzPatrick says he knew at the time that €412 million was a lot to pay for the site and that it now looks 'preposterous'. But at the time, he says, things looked very different. 'God, I mean, here was a guy [McNamara] very successful and he was putting his name to it. He was going to go. We had nothing but success with all the previous land.'

FitzPatrick – who had moved upstairs from chief executive to chairman of Anglo by the time the Irish Glass Bottle site deal was done – says he never spoke to anyone in the bank about financing the deal. 'Never, never, never, ever, ever. Never spoke to anyone,' he says.

This seems hard to believe, as the deal was the biggest one done that year in Ireland.

'I never went near anyone with that ever,' FitzPatrick insists. 'I didn't know what type of detail [Anglo was] discussing with the docklands about the interest or guarantees. I hadn't a clue.'

FitzPatrick says he made no inquiries to ensure his bank had done due diligence on whether it should fund the deal. 'I know you find it hard to believe and I accept that,' he says. 'I am not trying to be smart with you. I just never got involved in credit committees. That was part of the strength of the bank that I just was not. There was no confusion there at all. The guys did all the lending.'

Even though he was friendly with both McNamara and Quinlan, he says, he did not discuss the deal with them. 'Bernard McNamara never spoke to me. Derek Quinlan in a million years never spoke to me. Davy's never spoke to me. I never spoke to any of those. I never spoke to anyone in Anglo at all. I did not know what the deal was with Anglo doing the financing.'

FitzPatrick also says that he and Bradshaw excused themselves from the DDDA board's discussion of financing for the purchase. 'When the [board] decided who they were going to choose, myself and Lar walked out. Everyone said, Yeah, there is possible conflict here, so you guys leave the room. They had discussions about the whole deal which Anglo was offering them and what negotiations they had with the financing of it. Lar was a director of Anglo and I was chairman so therefore there was conflict there. We couldn't be on the discussion of what finances they were doing with Anglo Irish Bank to finance the site. Now, on the other hand, we were in no conflict should we buy the site or not buy the site. There was no conflict there.'

FitzPatrick says he was stunned by the collapse in value of the site, which has been taken over by the NAMA for €60 million, or just over one seventh of the purchase price. 'I am just knocked senseless by what has happened to valuations over the last year,' he says. 'Of course we should have done things differently. Here was a site that was bought for €412 million and is now valued at €60 million. Of course it was a mistake looking back on it . . . The point is were we wrong out of negligence? Because we didn't see it coming? Were we wrong because we didn't care? Why were we wrong? We were wrong because we didn't see it coming.

'It is very hard for me to look you in the face and say that was the right thing at the time because I know it is wrong now but at the time I believed it. What grounds had I to believe it? That was the price people were prepared to pay. I could try to say it was right at the time but I find that hard to say with conviction. I have to be credible with you and anyone else. That is what we believed at the time. I didn't think we were overpaying.'

FitzPatrick insists that once all the inquiries have been completed, 'it will be proven without a shadow of doubt that I had no hand or act in anything of a dubious nature down in the Dublin docklands over all of the seven years.'

After Anglo lodged its proceedings against him in March, FitzPatrick faced the real prospect of bankruptcy. Under Ireland's draconian insolvency laws, a bankrupt can take up to twelve years to clear his debts.

With no way of immediately repaying the €70 million-plus he owed to his creditors, FitzPatrick's only chance of heading off bankruptcy was to strike a deal with them under a voluntary scheme of arrangement.

Anglo Irish Bank was easily his largest creditor. But he also owed money to six other banks, including AIB and First Active; to businesses in which he had invested, including Cove Capital; and to the Revenue Commissioners.

Bernard Somers tried to structure a deal for FitzPatrick and his creditors. The scheme identified about €14 million of assets that were not subject to any security and could be sold, with the proceeds disbursed to creditors. These included €6 million in investments, his 50 per cent stake in his family home in Greystones and €1 million in cash. FitzPatrick also offered another €3 million, or his half of the pension pot of €6 million held jointly with his wife. There was a further €4 million available from assets that, if sold, would generate a surplus above the bank borrowing secured on them. He also offered his car, worth €20,000, to his creditors.

Somers scheduled a meeting of creditors at his offices for the first week of July 2010. As the meeting opened, Somers told the creditors that they should accept a private scheme of arrangement, because it would return more money than bankruptcy, and sooner. Under the scheme he was proposing, Somers estimated unsecured creditors faced a shortfall of €47 million and could expect a return of about 20 cents in the euro based on an asset pool of €12 million, with a payout within three years. In bankruptcy, he argued, creditors would get only 15 cents in the euro, and it would be four to seven years before they received a payout.

Somers told Anglo – which held the lion's share of FitzPatrick's total debt – that he proposed to negotiate a buyout of all the other bank debt at a steep discount and then hand over all of FitzPatrick's assets cleanly to the bank if it did not press for bankruptcy.

In a short speech FitzPatrick apologized to his creditors and told them that he accepted 'full responsibility for my own ruin'.

Anglo representatives said nothing at the meeting. The other banks expressed support for the scheme.

Later that day, after the meeting of creditors closed, Anglo gave its formal reply. FitzPatrick met with Hunersen and Anglo's legal team in its new executive office on Mespil Road, Dublin 4. At the meeting FitzPatrick was bluntly told the bank would not accept the proposal. Anglo was going to bankrupt him.

The bank disputed FitzPatrick's calculation of his debt to the bank, claiming it would rise if a number of so-called 'contingent liabilities' were taken into account. The contingents included FitzPatrick's being held liable for debts owed by wealthy fellow members of private-equity and property syndicates, for example. The bank also questioned whether it would ever get a penny back on the oil investment.

Regarding his pension of €6 million, the bank believed that if it was entitled to go after this, it would pursue the entire sum and not accept the 50 per cent he was offering.

FitzPatrick knew his old employer was not for turning. On Friday, 9 July 2010, he instructed his legal advisers to file for bankruptcy and pre-empt any move by the bank. The following Monday his lawyers filed the petition in court. A court-appointed official assignee would be put in charge of his financial future.

On Monday, 26 July 2010, FitzPatrick made his first court appearance as a bankrupt. The courtroom was only half full when he entered wearing a dark navy suit, a blue shirt and a tie. He calmly took his place on a wooden bench flanked by a pair of female lawyers. Within minutes of his arrival, the room was buzzing with lawyers and journalists.

As the hearing opened, Anglo claimed FitzPatrick now owed the bank up to €110 million out of total debts of €145 million and argued that with €50 million of assets, a trustee was needed to oversee such a complex bankruptcy. The figures cited by Anglo, which were much higher than those originally specified, had been inflated by personal guarantees and contingent liabilities relating to his property-syndicate and private-equity investments. Some of the contingent liabilities were unlikely to be called in. Even so, this was a huge level of indebtedness for a single individual, and at that time FitzPatrick's was easily the largest personal bankruptcy case in the history of the state.

After a short hearing, the case was adjourned until 22 September, and Judge Elizabeth Dunne reserved judgment. FitzPatrick and his lawyers slipped out of the courtroom and took a sharp right down a corridor rather than heading immediately for the exit. Walking quickly, FitzPatrick and his legal team escaped to a briefing room. There they chatted and drank tea.

Photographers and journalists monitored the courts' three exits. For two hours they waited. Just before one o'clock FitzPatrick went out a side entrance. He walked by himself through the gates past the television cameras and photographers.

Carl O'Brien, a journalist with the *Irish Times*, called after him. FitzPatrick said simply, 'No comment.' He walked into a blue four-by-four vehicle, driven by an old school pal, which had been quietly waiting in a car-parking space nearby. The car drove off.

Anglo was still unhappy. It wanted to appoint its own trustee, Kieran Wallace from KPMG, and mounted a legal challenge to the bankruptcy.

Anglo required three fifths of his creditors – in both value and number – to vote for the appointment of a trustee. The bank, in value terms, held a clear majority of his debts, but seven of the twelve creditors – including his wife, to whom he owed money on a joint property deal – voted for the retention of the court-appointed trustee, Chris Lehane, to oversee the bankruptcy. Justice Dunne refused Anglo's application to have a trustee put in charge of FitzPatrick's assets.

Court papers filed around that time revealed how far FitzPatrick's fortunes had fallen. In terms of income, he received €3,693 net of tax per month from an Irish Life annuity. However, he was also making a net loss of €3,505 per month on three properties he jointly owned and rented out. As a result, his net income was just €188 per month. At the peak of his earning power in 2003, as the groundbreaking chief executive of the barnstorming Anglo Irish bank, FitzPatrick earned the equivalent of €7,388 a day.

13. The Reckoning

'I had a duty. To whom? Investors. What was it? It was to make
more money. How do we make more money? We made it doing
what we did.'

At 7.15 a.m. on Wednesday, 29 September 2010, a cement truck was
driven into the gates outside Dáil Éireann. The truck's cement mixer
was emblazoned with slogans, including 'Toxic Bank Anglo' and '€500k
for golf' and '€1,000,0000 on golf balls' – references to the crippled
bank's legendary spending on expensive golf outings. The sight of the
lorry embedded in the gates of the national parliament was a very public
message to the politicians as they arrived for work some hours later.

The truck's driver was Joe McNamara, a forty-one-year old property developer from Poolagh, a village on Achill Island off the coast
of Mayo. McNamara had borrowed at least €3.5 million from Anglo
to build a development of twenty-two apartments in Galway city,
which he was struggling to sell. Speaking after a similar protest in
Galway the previous May, when he parked the same lorry in front of
the bank's regional offices, the father of two told the *Daily Mail*: 'I
don't do this for publicity: I do this to get it out of my system because
I'm furious about Anglo.'

'I know the guy,' Sean FitzPatrick says. After resigning from
Anglo, FitzPatrick twice volunteered for the Niall Mellon Township
Trust's house-building projects in South Africa; on one of these occasions, Joe McNamara was the leader of FitzPatrick's team. 'I think he
was an OK guy and I still think he is an OK guy.'

Clearly the pressure of his debts had got to McNamara. 'Without
question, yes,' says FitzPatrick. 'It is another manifestation of anger.'

Three weeks before McNamara's Dublin protest, it was announced
that Anglo would be wound down in an orderly fashion. The bank
would not lend a further cent.

Anglo management estimated that the final cost of bailing out the bank would be between €22 billion and €25 billion. Central Bank governor Patrick Honahan said the sum, while shocking, was 'manageable'; but others begged to differ. Standard & Poor's issued a negative assessment on Ireland in August. In a note to investors, the agency raised its estimate of the cost of burying Anglo to €35 billion. The burden being placed on a weak Exchequer by the seemingly endless banking rescue was spooking investors in Irish government bonds.

The gargantuan scale of the bailout prompted the *New York Times* on 31 August 2010 to ask in a feature article: 'Can one bank bring down a country?'

On 30 September, the day after Joe McNamara's protest, Brian Lenihan estimated that the final cost of the wind-up of Anglo alone would be between €29.3 billion and €35 billion. The scale of the losses was mind-boggling, representing a sum in excess of the Exchequer's entire tax take in 2009, more than double the entire annual health budget, a bill of €7,000 for every man, woman and child in the state.

In an interview with Tom Lyons on 17 July 2010, FitzPatrick struggled to understand the scale of the Anglo losses – which at that stage were still estimated at 'only' €22 billion. 'A guy actually explained it to me very well on the radio today. Do you know the 22 billion? That is more than the BP oil clean-up in Florida is going to cost. I thought to myself, That is a good way to explain it, the size of it, what does 22 thousand million mean? What is it to turn around and say it is all gone?'

The bulk of the bailout money was needed to cover losses suffered by Anglo on property loans transferred to NAMA. Swingeing NAMA discounts would also blow a hole in the capital reserves of Allied Irish Bank, the institution that so vigorously sought to rein in the once rampaging Anglo.

AIB set up famous 'Anglo win back teams' to try to poach back developer customers. Its determination to outgun Anglo led the bank right down the same path as its upstart rival, and indeed it had gone further by allowing its local branch managers to lend recklessly in small towns around the country.

Despite selling stakes in its prized Polish subsidiary, Bank Zachodni WBK, and announcing its intention to do same at M&T, a regional American bank, huge property losses meant that AIB would fall short of the new capital standards by some €9.7 billion. The state would pick up the tab, and AIB would also enter virtual state ownership.

Bank of Ireland, too, was partially taken over by the state. EBS, a small building society which made a disastrous late entry to the property-development game, was taken into state control and put up for sale. The government put an incredible €5.4 billion into Irish Nationwide, an institution whose entire loan book was only €12 billion.

Apart from its losses on toxic development loans transferred to NAMA, Anglo was also forced to recognize huge losses elsewhere in its loan book. Quinn Insurance entered administration in March 2010 after Matthew Elderfield, the new Financial Regulator, raised concerns that the group had overstated its reserves by €448 million. The insurance company had struggled to get over the financial strain of its owner's wild punting on Anglo CFDs. Quinn, once the richest man in the country, saw his net worth effectively reduced to zero. Anglo was forced to set aside up to €2.3 billion for future potential losses on loans advanced to Quinn. Quinn Insurance was taken from Quinn's control and put into the hands of administrators, who put it up for sale.

Mike Aynsley, the new Anglo chief executive, told a well-known banking analyst that there was a pattern in his conversations with executives who had left the bank after nationalization. 'Everybody who has left the bank comes into this office and says the same thing. They put their hands in the air and say, I did nothing wrong. Nobody seems to have done anything wrong here.'

For Aynsley and Maarten van Eden, Anglo's chief financial officer, the reasons for the bank's failure are twofold: a 60 per cent fall in commercial property values and debt extended to property developers at close to 100 per cent of the cost of the project.

Anglo's lending practices both fuelled the property bubble and left the bank horribly exposed when the bubble burst. Let's say Joe Developer borrows €30 million to buy an investment property. In a runaway market, the value of that property quickly rises by 20 per cent to €36 million. Joe's net worth has increased by €6 million. He uses that €6 million to raise a loan of €36 million from Anglo to buy another investment property or development site. His equity in that second loan is the €6 million profit he made in the first investment. Then, when property values crash – as they inevitably did, because the values were driven by the availability of credit rather than by supply and demand – the value of both properties falls, all the supposed equity is blown away, and the bank gets totally wiped out.

For Anglo's former chairman and chief executive, there is still a sense of bewilderment. It is sometimes hard to tell if his observations reflect his views in 2010 or the way he viewed things when he was in the saddle at Anglo – or both. 'I have never seen a loan that has gone bad look good in hindsight,' FitzPatrick says. 'We had a very solid bank, making very good profits, well diversified geographically, well diversified in terms of that our property lending was for investment property and some development.'

He repeats the Anglo mantra: 'When you put money into investment property it is not the person that you are lending the money to that you are expecting to repay. It is the people who are hiring in offices and in the retail stores and the medical practices and the legal practices. So therefore you have quite a diverse income base from which to get your repayments.' This view of things may have made sense when the bank was smaller, but it did not stand up to scrutiny by the end.

FitzPatrick admits that the bank's exposure to development lending – for projects that might not generate an income stream for years – was a very different matter. Anglo as a rule of thumb had tried to keep development lending below 15 per cent of its entire loan book. By 2008 it had smashed its own rule, with fully a quarter of its loan book devoted to development, but this was publicly evident only in September 2008, when the bank reclassified 10 per cent of its loan book as development.

'Development is always at a risk,' FitzPatrick says. 'There is always a risk that you don't get out of the game before the lights are turned off. When that happens, and it has happened in many cycles, then you are in trouble.'

FitzPatrick says the board felt that the bank had diversified geographically and was 'very well set, particularly in America, where we had very little [property] development, and also to a greater extent in the UK. The vulnerability was in Ireland, no question, looking back on it.'

He accepts that the bank's lending model – high loan-to-value ratios, security on property that would cease to be useful in the event it needed to be called on, and a generous definition of investor equity – created a perfect storm when property values dropped. 'Probably where we went wrong there was that we had existing property development where the prices had gone up and the supposed equity was greater and people were allowed draw down on that equity. That compounded things because they went into more development, and existing development then shot down.'

The bank did not exist inside a cocoon. It regularly sought outside views. Economist Rossa White of Davy stockbrokers, Mark FitzGerald of top estate agency Sherry FitzGerald, and Pat Gunne of CBRE, the commercial property consultants, were invited into the bank to make presentations to directors and executives. These external advisers voiced the consensus view that there was no bubble and that Ireland's property market was headed for a soft landing. Predictions for economic growth, meanwhile, were extremely bullish. The other leading stockbroking firms and estate agencies all took the same line, and it was rarely challenged in the media.

Anglo management was conscious of the bank's heavy exposure to property and the need to diversify. Former directors recall extensive discussions on the subject at board level from early 2006. 'It was not that we thought there would be a crash but we thought there might be a slowdown in Ireland,' one ex-director, who asked not to be named, recalls. 'To keep growing we knew we had to go into other markets and start lending more to businesses with cash flow.'

FitzPatrick says that a decision was taken 'around 2005/2006' to try to stop development lending in Ireland. But there was a caveat – an enormous one. 'Existing customers, if they had a very good track record, of course, we would support them,' FitzPatrick says.

The existing customers Anglo continued to support were its

biggest, heaviest hitters, whose ambitions were undimmed by any prospect of a slowdown. 'It was impossible to turn off the tap,' said a former Anglo Irish Bank senior lender. 'The bank had forward agreed funding for some developers and made exceptions for individual deals. It was supposed to slow but it didn't.'

Even as things worsened every week throughout 2008, Anglo continued to lend – €9 billion in total (of which €3 billion related to sorting out Quinn). Money kept going out the door. Rather than let developers go bust, Anglo continued to stand by its clients, giving them working capital to finish projects. Other banks acted similarly.

When Anglo was nationalized the reasons given were its corporate-governance failings. The truth was far more terrifying: Anglo was bust, and not far behind it was Ireland's entire banking system.

To counter market rumours in the spring of 2008, Anglo circulated a list of the top ten property-development deals in Ireland for the years 2005, 2006 and 2007 to a number of journalists and analysts. The biggest lenders were AIB, Bank of Scotland (Ireland) and Ulster Bank, in that order.

In the crazed environment of the last years of the boom, the list made Anglo look almost prudent. But the list was misleading. Anglo had stepped back from the very biggest new deals, but because it had been the market leader for so long its existing exposure to property was already more than enough to bring it down – and, because of its continuing support for its biggest clients, that exposure kept getting bigger. Over the three years covered by the list circulated by Anglo, the size of the bank's loan book doubled.

'We said we wouldn't do any lending to new developers, so if Tom Lyons came in we would say, Lookit, Tom, great to meet you, but we are not interested, thank you very much,' FitzPatrick says. 'But if Gerry Gannon knocked on the door, well, we were already into him. He was a huge success, huge equity, so we would give him equity releases. So if, say, he was lent €50 million to buy a site out in Greystones, say, the site was now worth €150 million.

'He would come back in to Anglo and say, Lookit, lads, this site is now worth 150 million . . . So what do you owe? You owe 50 million. He would say, Lads, you don't need that. Will you give me an equity release of 30 or 40 million? And the guys did. By giving him an equity release of 30 or 40 million he would then go out to Blackrock and see a site for 100 million. He would walk in with the 40 million he has in his back pocket from Anglo and say to Bank of Ireland or AIB or Irish Nationwide, Listen, guys, I want to go and buy this place out in Blackrock for 100 million. I have got 40; give me 60. They would give him 60, further leveraging the guy with our money. And we didn't take a charge over the site because we had security where we were, or so we thought.'

So it was a house of cards? 'Well, that is the sort of popular phrase. I am just trying to give you what happened.' The equity-release lending, he concludes, 'was actually creating the monster which brought us all down'.

In previous building downturns, Anglo had packaged up the assets of problem clients and passed them on to stronger clients to hold until they could work out the properties or sell them on. In this way, Anglo kept its level of bad debts well below those of its competitors, who tended to write off bad loans.

The problem for Anglo, in the property crash of 2008 onwards, was that this approach didn't work any more. Anglo had stored up a lot of problems in the final years of the boom by placing distressed assets with their bigger clients, who had never got round to doing anything with them. When the bigger clients got into trouble, the old problems resurfaced. There was nowhere to pass the parcel.

Traditionally FitzPatrick had put aside 1 per cent of the group's profits annually into a general 'rainy-day' provision (apart from any loan-specific provisions) in case things went wrong. When accountancy rules changed in 2005, the use of such general rainy-day provisions was no longer allowed. Every penny put aside for bad debts had to be linked to an actual loan.

Anglo's culture of personal responsibility for loans now acted against it. Lenders did not want to admit that loans had gone bad and should be written down or written off. So instead of dealing realistically with troubled assets on an annual basis, the bank simply hoped everything would be all right.

A big part of the reason why the bank felt compelled to continue to lend so heavily in Ireland was a fear of losing its big developer customers to rivals. Anglo found its clients being targeted not just by AIB but also by Bank of Scotland (Ireland) and Ulster Bank. Mark Duffy, the head of Bank of Scotland (Ireland), had previously worked with Anglo and went hard after its clients. He knew what to do to challenge Anglo: compete aggressively on fees.

Duffy also helped to create Ireland's residential-mortgage bubble by offering 100 per cent mortgages. Anglo was not directly affected by this, as it did not lend directly to homeowners, but the other banks all reacted by loosening their residential-mortgage terms, which caused gigantic problems when the bubble burst. And the residential-mortgage boom did impact on Anglo indirectly, as it pushed up the price of land.

Irish Nationwide's expansion was another pertinent factor. Michael Fingleton lent aggressively for the acquisition of development business. 'What [Fingleton] would do is he would buy land for €10 million [by lending to a developer] for [using a] 100 per cent [mortgage] and [the society] would get a share of the profit once [the developer] gets the planning,' FitzPatrick says. 'Then [the developer] would be able to go into Anglo Irish Bank and say, Lookit, this land with the planning permission is worth €25 million and he paid back the €10 million to Irish Nationwide. Irish Nationwide get out with their profit.'

Even EBS, which, unlike Irish Nationwide, continued to behave like a traditional building society for most of the boom period, tried to get into the game, setting up a new development division just before the bubble popped.

Most damaging of all, though, was the decision of AIB chief executive Eugene Sheehy to compete ruthlessly with Anglo for development business. It funded deals in towns in Ireland at prices that were comparable to those in major cities like New York or London. At the peak of the boom in 2007 AIB funded the acquisition of 3.7 acres of land in Tullamore, Co. Offaly, for an incredible €42 million.

A reckless spiral of virtually unchecked, fiercely competitive lending was allowed to run its course. EBS chief executive Fergus

Murphy called it 'name lending': every bank wanted to back the star developers, and this was Anglo's patch. 'I think the Anglo style was to follow up not so much the projects but the people who were managing them and bringing them forward,' says FitzPatrick. 'In hindsight you could say that probably we went too far.'

A clear example of how Anglo's relationship banking went too far can be found in Drogheda, Co. Louth. The bank financed two new shopping-centre developments in the same town: Gerry Barrett's Scotch Hall and Gerry McGuire's Laurence Town Centre. 'We were cutting our own throats by lending the guts of €100 million each in such a small town where there was only room for one centre,' says a former Anglo banker who asked not to be named. 'We fucked up.'

There were other mindless battles between banks. Anglo, for example, backed Noel Smyth, the solicitor, in his plans to redevelop the Square shopping centre in Tallaght. Smyth's plan had merit – the Square was a potential goldmine if it could be revamped. However, Liam Carroll, backed by British banks, fought both to stymie Smyth and to build his own rival development. It was ludicrous – the area simply could not support two shopping centres – yet the bankers let them slug it out.

In the drive to retain customers, Anglo also breached its own internal rules on so-called concentration risk. The bank's rule of thumb was that it would not allow more than 1 per cent of its total loan book to reside with any one client. However, by the end of 2008 Anglo had breached its own rules many times. Aside from the bizarre and exceptional case of Sean Quinn, six Anglo clients owed the bank more than €1 billion at the end of 2008: Joe O'Reilly (€1.8 billion); Bernard McNamara (€1.4 billion); Sean Mulryan (€1.4 billion); Treasury Holdings (€1.2 billion); Gerry Gannon (€1.06 billion); and O'Flynn Construction (€1.05 billion).

Just behind these six, Derek Quinlan and Paddy Kelly each owed the bank over €900 million, again, more than 1 per cent of the total book. In total, fifteen clients of the bank owed it more than €500 million each by the end.

Anglo did diversify. New offices were opened in New York, Chicago, Boston, Birmingham, Manchester, London, Banbury,

Leeds and Glasgow, while the overseas outposts in Vienna, Geneva, Jersey and the Isle of Man were beefed up. Back home the bank had expanded from its Dublin base with offices in Belfast, Galway, Limerick, Cork, Waterford and Sligo. Competition was fierce between branches, and clients were encouraged to get involved in projects in new frontiers such as Eastern Europe as well as in the established markets of North America and the UK. Much of this expansion overseas was funded by equity release on property assets held back home.

America represented 15 per cent of the bank's loan book at nationalization. Between 2002 and 2007 Anglo's lending went up eleven-fold there, from €836 million to €9.3 billion. In each of its new locations, the bank focused on its traditional strong suit of property – and this seriously diminished whatever benefits might have resulted from geographical diversification. What emerged from the global credit boom was a global real-estate crash. Anglo simply had no place to hide. 'This was only geographic diversification,' said an Anglo executive. 'It was always a mono-line property bank in every market. Its ass was out the window when the unexpected happened: a global real-estate crash.'

The property crash was global, but nowhere was it more dramatic than in Ireland. Despite Anglo's in-house commitment to make the UK its largest market, its home territory continued to dominate. Anglo's Irish loan book grew from €14.7 billion at the end of September 2004 to €43.6 billion by the end of 2008.

Everything was linked. By 2008, 11 per cent of Ireland's GDP was accounted for by construction firms generating windfall profits. The owners of these firms, such as Bernard McNamara, chose not to keep the money in their business or to pay down debts. Instead profits were leveraged upwards by more investment in property, thus ensuring that the balance sheets of these firms were ill-prepared for any downturn, despite a decade of boom.

The diversification that Anglo did undertake did not exactly represent a flight from risk. Close to the peak of the Irish stock market, in the final months of 2006, Anglo funded a highly leveraged management buyout of Davy stockbrokers from Bank of Ireland, with the firm valued at €340 million. Anglo had done the deal at the time because it saw it as an opportunity to diversify; instead it exposed the bank not only to the property bubble but to Ireland's stock market just before it crashed. This was not merely bad timing. Here, too, the bank's notion of diversification proved to be poorly thought out. The Irish stock market was dominated by bank shares – and the fortunes of the Irish banks were wholly linked to the state of the property market.

It also provided loans to individual investors in Barry O'Callaghan's EPMG, the educational publishing group. It advanced over €200 million to O'Callaghan personally to invest in the venture, the largest schoolbook publisher in the US. O'Callaghan's loans were secured largely on his shares in EPMG, worth an estimated $1 billion at the time the facility was agreed. Although Anglo held security over his shares, there was limited recourse to other assets. O'Callaghan, a former investment banker, would not accept full recourse, and the bank, keen to enlist the new generation of Irish business tycoons, acquiesced.

When US education budgets were cut, EPMG was forced to renegotiate its $4 billion borrowings. The equity shareholders – including FitzPatrick, who had personally invested $5 million – were wiped out.

FitzPatrick believes the availability of cheap money on the wholesale money market played a crucial role in the Irish banking downfall. The surge in lending from 2006 onwards in all Irish banks was overwhelmingly funded abroad and on the wholesale money markets. A funding gap emerged between the banking-system deposits and the banks' lending of roughly €200 billion, and this was filled by wholesale funding, where money was available from overseas investors for a relatively short term. It was easy money, and no one working in or regulating Irish banks ever seems to have imagined that it could dry up overnight, as it did in 2008.

FitzPatrick identifies Anglo's funding model, along with its ad hoc strategy of equity releases on property lending, as the biggest cause of the bank's collapse. 'You didn't have to have a big overhead base in order to access [overseas money markets],' says FitzPatrick.

'In other words, we could get €4 billion in the wholesale money markets rather than having eighty people over in the Isle of Man drawing a salary, a premises and all of the associated costs of running that just to raise €4 billion [from depositors] to lend.'

Chuck Prince, the former Citigroup chief executive, notoriously summed up about how banks got sucked into the wholesale-funding trend and simply could not stop. 'When the music stops, in terms of liquidity, things will be complicated,' Prince said in July 2007. 'But as long as the music is playing, you've got to get up and dance. We're still dancing.'

By August 2008 the music had all but stopped for Anglo and all the other Irish banks. According to FitzPatrick, 'We had €6 billion [of wholesale funding] maturing in '09, and we were under pressure in '08 . . . There was actually €14 billion to be repaid back by the end of 2011. Fourteen. Between August 2008 and September 2011 there was the guts of €14 billion to be paid back. Where were we going to get that? Just think about it. We couldn't repay them and we knew we couldn't repay them, looking out at the maturity.'

FitzPatrick says that he was not aware at the time of the scale of the funding mountains that lay ahead of the bank. 'I didn't know it. We didn't fully understand it. It wasn't belted home to the board.' (This comment about the board's lack of knowledge of the bank's precarious funding position is disputed by Anglo executives.)

In his report on the banking crisis, Patrick Honohan stated that Anglo was well on the way to insolvency before the collapse of Lehman Brothers and the funding crisis that ensued. Nobody, not even the regulators, had asked the simple question: what would happen when the music stopped?

The relationship between bankers and regulators was friendly – and, perhaps not coincidentally, they seem to have taken similar views of the banking business in Ireland during the boom years.

One arena in which the cosiness was played out was the golf course. FitzPatrick and Willie McAteer played at least three games of golf with Patrick Neary, chief executive of the Financial Regulator, between 2005 and 2006. There were also regular golf events organized for bankers and regulators by the Irish Bankers Federation. 'Pat

Neary was, to me, an OK guy,' FitzPatrick says. 'He didn't look the part. He didn't sound the part. But a decent enough guy. I never thought he was over-endowed with grey matter, but I didn't think he was an idiot either.'

FitzPatrick says they did 'not really' discuss Anglo when golfing with the regulators. 'We were very aware that they were our regulators so we wouldn't try to do anything with them,' he says. 'It was just a general chat. It was a game of golf, a meal, no drinks. Drive home.'

Did Neary ever express any concern about Anglo? 'No, no.'

It was only during 2008, when it was obvious that Ireland's banks were in crisis, that Neary started raising concerns with Anglo, according to FitzPatrick.

Neary, who had joined the Central Bank in 1971, was incapable of seeing that the banking system was heading towards disaster. He lacked the strength of character or independence to take a stand against the political and economic status quo governing the country at the time. And he lacked the resources to monitor the banks properly: only three staff were assigned to directly monitor Anglo, a tiny number for a bank of its scale and complexity.

FitzPatrick also recalls a special meeting with John Hurley, the governor of the Central Bank, after FitzPatrick retired as chief executive of Anglo. 'He gave me a little presentation,' FitzPatrick recalls. 'I forget what it was. It might have been a euro note or something. I don't know where that is now. It could be anywhere.'

FitzPatrick returned the invitation a few years later. 'I brought him up to speak at one of our lunches. He was brilliant. We couldn't shut him up.'

The lunch was an upbeat affair. Attendees recall Hurley happily mingling with Anglo's top bankers. His speech to the bankers raised little or no concern about the bank. The view expressed by Hurley was that the Irish property market would have a gradual slowdown.

The relationship between poacher and gamekeeper was much too familiar. The Irish banks can never be excused for their profligacy, but the regulators were asleep at the controls. In a series of talks before his appointment as Hurley's successor, Patrick Honohan, then a TCD economist, highlighted the scale of the regulatory failure. He said that 'a very simple warning sign' used by most regulators is rapid balance-sheet growth. An annual growth rate of 20 per cent is often taken as the trigger for regulatory action to keep risk under control. In the nine years from 1998 to 2007, Honohan told a UCD economic workshop in January 2009, Anglo crossed the 20 per cent threshold eight times and 'its average annual rate of growth 1998–2007 was 36 per cent'. Irish Nationwide, Honohan said, crossed the line in six out of the nine years. Its average loan growth over the same period was just above 20 per cent.

This sort of growth was a 'very obvious and public danger', Honohan said, not only for these banks – whose failure will end up costing the Irish taxpayer an estimated €40 billion – but because of the 'potentially destabilizing effect of reckless competition on the entire sector'.

Honohan said that 'it was not just one bank that went bad (although one bank's egregiously rapid growth certainly accelerated the infection of others). Instead, the error of judgement that led to the banks lending so much with so little solid security into an unprecedented property bubble reflects a system-wide failure to appreciate the scale of the risk assumed.'

On the relatively few occasions when informed observers with no axe to grind attempted to call attention to the dangers brewing in the Irish property market and the banks, their views were attacked by everyone with an interest in prolonging the boom – including the government. In 2007, in two separate papers, University College Dublin economist Morgan Kelly rubbished the idea of a soft landing for the Irish property market and warned of the implications for Irish banking of a crash.

FitzPatrick's view of the impact of Kelly's interventions gives a fascinating insight into the mindset of the people at the controls of the Irish economy. 'In some ways, actually, the Morgan Kellys who were predicting [the bust] actually prolonged [the bubble] because people were, you know, really determined to prove him wrong – [to] say, Ah no, that is a whole load of shit, that is not going to happen.'

From early 2008 there was a procession of professional accountants, investment bankers and consultants through the doors of Anglo, sizing up its operations. They all failed to flag up the scale of the looming loan losses on the bank's books. Ernst & Young did the 2008 audit, in which it was predicted that only about €700 million would be lost. Non-executive directors Donal O'Connor and Lar Bradshaw did the look-back exercise prior to the publication of the accounts, in which it was predicted that the loss would be only €1 billion. PwC went back into Anglo on behalf of the government in late 2009, and projected loan losses only marginally in excess of what Anglo management had forecast. In May 2009, long after FitzPatrick had left the bank, PwC concluded that a 'not unreasonable' estimate of the bank's bad debts was €4 billion – still dramatically short of the reality.

Aynsley reckons that there was one fault at the centre of the bank's problems: hubris. There was a collective belief inside the bank that it was indestructible. This belief permeated the board, the shareholders, even, probably, the regulator and the government. Nobody wanted to believe it could possibly end so badly.

Sean FitzPatrick has an office in the Dublin docklands. From his office window, he can see the sparkling new Grand Canal Theatre. Anglo funded the development of the theatre by Joe O'Reilly, a member of the Maple Ten.

FitzPatrick drives to the office daily in a second-hand Volkswagen Passat, having sold his €300,000 Mercedes. He is completely engrossed in bankruptcy affairs and in legal preparations relating to the ongoing investigations into his activities as chief executive and chairman of Anglo. (David Drumm, for his part, filed for bankruptcy on 14 October 2010, in Boston, where he moved shortly after leaving Anglo. The bank had rejected all efforts by Drumm to settle his €8.5 million debt.)

During the boom it was quite an effort to arrange a lunch date with FitzPatrick. His life was organized daily by his faithful personal assistant Monica Kearney. She neatly slotted the great, the good and the not so good into his daily diary of board meetings, lunches, dinners and golf. Now, work is a solitary pursuit, in a spartan office, the silence interrupted only by occasional calls to his mobile phone.

On 12 July, the day FitzPatrick was declared bankrupt in the High Court, he went into the office as usual. 'I have lived with the realization that it [going bankrupt] was going to happen for some time,' FitzPatrick says. 'My life is going to change dramatically from what it was maybe a year and a half ago or maybe even nine months ago. But it won't change dramatically from what it has been like the last six months or what it is going to be like for the next seven or eight years.'

FitzPatrick feels he was 'an obvious scapegoat for the media and politicians' because of 'the break in trust over my loans, which I admit was wrong in hindsight. I am not trying to ever excuse it. What I did was wrong and it was a mistake. But it does not deserve the odour or the punishment that has been inflicted on me over the last two years.

'I have done everything that I can do to make sure that the stress does not get on top of me. By and large it hasn't but that doesn't mean that there aren't dark days or there aren't dark nights or dark mornings or dark weeks. But it was never so dark that there wasn't a light somewhere around the place. Friends have been very good to me, ex-colleagues have been very good to me, people I don't know have been very good to me. My family have been incredible. All of that has helped me get through it.'

He speaks of 'the humiliation' of what has happened to him, and says 'my whole social circle has diminished' as a result of the events of the past few years. 'I can't repay all of the liabilities that I owe,' he says of his bankruptcy. 'I didn't run and steal the money. I made a mistake and for that I am very happy to put my hands up. I am very happy to apologize to all my creditors.

'I don't feel ashamed, but I do feel regret, very serious regret, and I am sorry that it is going to cause people losses. Anyone who has suffered on that, I really am sorry. But that is it. I have got to get on and live my life.'

The last interview between Sean FitzPatrick and Tom Lyons took place on 30 November 2010, two days after Ireland agreed a deal with the International Monetary Fund, the European Union and the European Central Bank on an €82.5 billion bailout. The country's banks and its government had lost the confidence of their lenders. A crisis that originated in the banks had ended in the humiliation of a nation.

Was Ireland brought down by just one bank? Hardly. But Anglo will forever be synonymous Ireland's economic collapse.

FitzPatrick says he accepts his share of responsibility, but only his share. 'Of course I have to accept it. I am not accepting it reluctantly. I think that I have been blamed for too much, but that is a side issue. So do other bankers as well. Were we the only ones? No. We were part of a group of people. If you are looking back at who is to blame, you could argue that the regulators contributed to it. The government contributed to it, the punters contributed to it as well, the investors contributed to it. I had a duty. To whom? Investors. What was it? It was to make more money. How do we make more money? We made it doing what we did. We were admired for doing that and doing it well.

'It was a reasonable-sized bank when I left as chief executive and it kept growing. I can't abdicate responsibility up until then, nor can I after it, because I was still chairman of the bank. In a way I was still in a pivotal position to stop it. Cries from me that I wasn't really responsible diminish when you take that stance. I accept that.'

As snow drifted across the South Dublin docklands, FitzPatrick returned to his preparations for the battles ahead of him.

Acknowledgements

The authors would like to thank Brendan Barrington, our editor at Penguin Ireland. He has been a tough taskmaster and has contributed immensely to the final result. Thanks also to the eagle-eyed copy-editor, Donna Poppy.

We would also like to thank Michael McLoughlin, the managing director of Penguin Ireland, and his team for taking the risk of pursuing the project in the first place.

Thanks to Frank Fitzgibbon, editor of the Irish *Sunday Times*, for his support and understanding.

We are grateful to all the people who have provided source material and answered our questions regarding the Anglo story. Many of the people who contributed most to this book must remain anonymous, but we would like to offer them our heartfelt thanks.

In putting together a project of this kind, we also had to draw upon newspaper and broadcast reports on Anglo Irish Bank over the last thirty years. The publications used are acknowledged in the text, but we would like to acknowledge by name some of the many great journalists whose work helped us complete this book. In no particular order, they include Simon Carswell, Ian Kehoe, Pat Leahy, Alan Ruddock, Cyril Hardiman, Michael Murray, Emmet Oliver, Joe Brennan, Paul Murphy, David Clerkin, David Murphy, Kathleen Barrington, Cliff Taylor and John Mooney.

We would both like to thank all our colleagues at the *Sunday Times*, including John Burns, Richard Oakley, Áine Coffey, Mark Paul, Niall Brady, Rose Costelloe and Bryan Meade.

Brian Carey would like to thank Tom Lyons for generously giving him the chance to work on putting this story together. He would also like to recognize the patience, support and forgiveness of dearest Deirdre and lovely Eva, and apologize for the countless lost weekends and broken promises, and to thank all the Carey clan. Respect and gratitude to the guiding lights along the way: Aileen O'Toole, James Morrissey, Damien Kiberd, the Fitzgibbon fellow again, Helen Rogers, Nick Mulcahy, John Doherty, Ted Harding, Matt Cooper, Paul O'Kane and Nick Webb.

Tom Lyons would like to thank Brian Carey above all others for agreeing to co-author this book. He has been at all times a fantastic partner to work with. Tom would also like to thank his parents, Lorcan and Frances; his three brothers; and the late Julia Foley, Peggy Lyons, Tommy Lyons and Kevin Lyons. Tom is particularly happy to be able to tell Lynne that the book is finally finished. He would also like to thank his friends, who probably wondered where he had disappeared to over the last six months.

Tom would also like to acknowledge other colleagues in journalism for their support and friendship, including Richard Curran (an inspiring first business editor), Brendan Keenan, Chris Donoghue, Conor Brophy, Dearbhail McDonald, Juno McEnroe, Scott Millar, Nicola Cooke, Declan Power, Paul Dunne, Tom McEnaney, Charlie Weston, Bairbre Power, Michael Denieffe, Samantha McCaughren, Ailish O'Hora, Pat Boyle, Jim Aughney, Niamh Lyons, Eamon Keane, Paddy McDonnell and all in Newstalk radio.

Tom would also like to acknowledge the late Vinnie Doyle, a great editor of the *Irish Independent*.